Each Hour Redeem

Each Hour Redeem

Time and Justice in African American Literature

Daylanne K. English

University of Minnesota Press
Minneapolis
London

An earlier version of chapter 5 was published as "The Modern in the Postmodern: Walter Mosley, Barbara Neely, and the Politics of Contemporary African American Detective Fiction," *American Literary History* 18 (Winter 2006): 772–96. Another version of chapter 5 also appeared as "Being Black There: Racial Subjectivity and Temporality in Walter Mosley's Detective Novels," *NOVEL* 42, no. 3 (Fall 2009): 361–65.

Published by the University of Minnesota Press
111 Third Avenue South, Suite 290
Minneapolis, MN 55401-2520
http://www.upress.umn.edu

Cataloging-in-Publication Data is available from the Library of Congress
ISBN 978-0-8166-7989-8 (hc : acid-free paper)
ISBN 978-0-8166-7990-4 (pb : acid-free paper)

Printed in the United States of America on acid-free paper

The University of Minnesota is an equal-opportunity educator and employer.

20 19 18 17 16 15 14 13   10 9 8 7 6 5 4 3 2 1

Contents

Acknowledgments

I am deeply grateful to colleagues and friends who made this book possible. First, I thank Michelle Wright and Rod Ferguson; their delightful friendship and steadfast intellectual companionship have made not just this project, but the last decade so much better than it ever could have been without them. I also thank Richard Morrison for being, simply, the ideal editor: supportive, rigorous, and utterly committed to this project. I am grateful, as well, to other editorial staff at the University of Minnesota Press, including Erin Warholm, and to the anonymous readers for the Press, whose careful reading and incisive critique improved this book significantly.

I thank, too, the following colleagues for their long-standing interest in and support of my work and for their extraordinary scholarship, which inspired and shaped this project throughout: Nancy Armstrong, Sara Blair, Madhu Dubey, Guy Mark Foster, Jonathan Freedman, Sharon Patricia Holland, Meta DuEwa Jones, Deborah E. McDowell, Joycelyn Moody, Aldon Nielsen, and Xiomara Santamarina.

I owe a great deal to friends and colleagues at Macalester College, including Lynn Hudson, Sung Kyu Kim, Jane Rhodes, and the tremendously fun and brilliant members of the English Department. Thanks as well go to my wonderful students, whose deep commitment to intellection is both joyful and inspiring; thanks especially go to Jeesun Choi and Nathan Wilson-Traisman for their invaluable research assistance. I also wish to express my appreciation to librarians Angi Faiks, Terri Fishel, and Aaron Albertson for their dedication and their support of my scholarship and my field.

Finally, thank you, Eugene, for always being there and for being such a fine reader-critic, listener, and friend.

Political Fictions

Standard Time Line and Standard Plot Line are in cahoots!

—Suzan-Lori Parks, *Elements of Style*

This book demonstrates that, across genre and era, African American writers have disclosed and explored the complex and high philosophical and material stakes inherent in time and its measure. They have long understood that time, justice, and the written word are deeply intertwined—so much so that this triad lies at the heart of the African American literary tradition, and from its very beginning. The publisher's preface to Phillis Wheatley's 1773 book *Poems on Various Subjects, Religious and Moral,* the first published book by an African American author, states that "the following POEMS were written originally for the Amusement of the Author, as they were the Products of her leisure Moments."[1] To ascribe "leisure moments" to a *slave,* who owns neither her body nor her time, is simply astounding. Time was necessarily experienced differently by U.S. slaves and masters, if only because masters owned time itself. The clock will not readily benefit those denied not only the power to control their time but also the means to measure it. Wheatley observes that fact in her well-known poem "To the University of Cambridge, in New England," wherein she notes the privileges of the men who are attending Harvard: "Students, to you 'tis giv'n to scan the heights / Above, to traverse the ethereal space, / And mark the systems of revolving worlds."[2] Because they have the power to "mark" celestial "systems," the students therefore have the power to measure time. She, "an *Ethiop,*" advises them to use that power wisely: "Improve your privileges while they stay, / Ye pupils, and each hour redeem," with the poetic speaker understanding and underscoring time's status in 1773 as an unevenly distributed commodity ("redeem").[3]

Wheatley's poem, along with a great deal of the African American literature that follows it, complicates contemporary, and influential, understandings of modern time as increasingly uniform and collective. For instance, Benedict Anderson has argued that, in contradistinction to a religious "medieaval conception of simultaneity-along-time," the simultaneity of modern nationalism is "transverse, cross-time, marked not by prefiguring and ful-filment, but by temporal coincidence, and measured by clock and calen-dar."[4] In other words, modern identities such as nationality or citizenship are forged on the grounds of shared, secular temporality in physical space. But, as Lloyd Pratt has shown, modernity and its identities, particularly nationality, cannot be so easily understood as unfolding across one di-mension in time, given the "temporal heterogeneity" and "nonsynchronic-ity" documented in the antebellum African American narratives of Fred-erick Douglass and others.[5] Likewise countering Anderson's views, Wai Chee Dimock has recently made a case for "deep time," arguing persua-sively that "the uneven pace of modernity suggests that standardization is not everywhere the rule."[6] Dimock offers deep time as an alternative model that, in her view, overcomes "the glaring inadequacy of a nation-based model" in literary studies by "binding" American literature together with "other geographies, other languages and cultures" and by "threading the long durations of those cultures into the short chronology of the United States."[7] Yet the contingencies of nation-based citizenship, either allocated or withheld, shape our experiences and our literary texts, including (and perhaps especially) our experiences and representations of time, both in the here and now *and* in the long term. As E. L. McCallum has observed, although "citizenship has conventionally been conceived in terms of space," it "is inalienably conceived through time as well, since it is granted through government, and government is inherently contingent upon time."[8] For ex-ample, raced slavery in the United States across centuries was predicated on the alleged premodernity of African Americans and on their federally codified noncitizenship status, a combination that matches neither Ander-son's model of shared time among citizens of a nation nor Dimock's model of transnational time across periods. Moreover, as Dimock herself has ar-gued elsewhere, "we might think of literature, then, as the textualization of justice, the transposition of its clean abstractions into the messiness of representation."[9] Just so, prolonged, racialized injustice produced by and experienced within the nation has been registered and resisted in not-tidy ways by African American literature from 1773 to the present. As a result, neither "simultaneity" nor "deep time" explains the work of African Ameri-can writers, who regularly represent the complex, multivalent nature of time as experienced within the United States by its citizens and by those it renders partial citizens or noncitizens.

This book will be the first to explore how time, in both philosophical and material senses, has been treated throughout the African American

literary tradition as a fundamental aspect of literary form, of daily experience, and of U.S. citizenship. From Phillis Wheatley to Suzan-Lori Parks,
African American writers have represented a profound connection between
differential temporalities and differential justices in the United States; in
the process, they have revealed how racialized injustice discloses the
shortcomings within dominant period philosophies, particularly philosophies of time. Deploying the various literary strategies available in their
chosen genres, these writers have developed their own philosophical analyses of the ways time and justice work together as interdependent "political fictions," to adapt a useful phrase from Pauline Hopkins's 1900 novel
Contending Forces, wherein her African American hero declares that
"Constitutional equity is a *political fiction.*"[10] I conclude that African
American writers, along with their characters and their poetic speakers,
are fully *of* their time—or "coeval," to use Johannes Fabian's anthropologi-
cal term.[11] This coeval status underlies my argument that many African
American writers have been full, if generally unacknowledged, partici-
pants in their period's major cultural developments and philosophical debates. Yet I argue, too, that the same writers have advanced as well the only
apparently paradoxical notion that black people in the United States live
within a distinct temporality produced by both race and injustice. Such
an inclusive approach to local, literary-philosophical representations of
time within African American texts corresponds to the broad model of
African American literary history that this book constructs: African
American literature belongs fully to American literature even as it also
constitutes its own separate tradition in much the same way that African
American writers belong fully to their period even as they repeatedly
represent African American people as inhabiting a distinct temporality
produced by the contingencies of their experiences and the social relations of that period.

This book will show that the African American literary tradition, from
its earliest texts and on into the present, has documented not only that
unevenness of time but also time's integral relationship to federal and state
law. African American writers regularly represent how citizenship, along
with its abrogation, functions as an abstraction across time and as a material, quotidian reality. This rich combination of abstract and material understandings of time drives African American writers' profound, even if
often implicit, interventions in contemporary—for the writers, that is—
philosophers' understandings of time. From the eighteenth through the
twenty-first centuries, African American writers have challenged an

abstractly universalized time, never losing sight of what differential time really means, experientially, in a nation built on hierarchical social and political status—and, quite literally, on slave labor. In the African American literary tradition, temporality functions as a component of citizenship every bit as powerful as geography, with black characters often restricted on all three counts: justice, time, and space. Just so, the ex-slave narrators who followed Phillis Wheatley in the tradition returned again and again to the theme of time, like justice, as being allocated and experienced unequally. This interconnection of time and justice is nowhere more evident than in the process of assigning citizenship and its attendant rights.

As African American writers have repeatedly demonstrated, the law can place, indeed trap, individuals and groups in time and outside citizenship. For example, *Plessy v. Ferguson*, the notorious U.S. Supreme Court decision of 1896 that established black–white racial segregation as the law of the land, effectively pulled African Americans back in time to the equally notorious *Dred Scott* decision of 1857, in which the majority ruled that Dred Scott, the plaintiff, "is not a citizen . . . because he is a negro."[12] The *Dred Scott* decision, in turn, pulled African Americans back to the nation's founding documents and therefore to a perpetual state of inferiority and noncitizenship. Chief Justice Roger Taney wrote in the majority opinion in *Dred Scott* that the situation of "negroes" is "altogether unlike that of the Indian race," because Indians "may, without doubt, like the subjects of any other foreign Government, be naturalized by the authority of Congress, and become citizens of a State, and of the United States; and if an individual should leave his nation or tribe, and take up his abode among the white population, he would be entitled to all the rights and privileges which would belong to an emigrant from any other foreign people." African Americans, by contrast, are not entitled to those rights and privileges, including "the privilege of suing in a court of the United States," because

they are not included, and were not intended to be included, under the word "citizens" in the Constitution, and can therefore claim none of the rights and privileges which that instrument provides for and secures to citizens of the United States. On the contrary, they were at that time considered as a subordinate and inferior class of beings, who had been subjugated by the dominant race, and, whether emancipated or not, yet remained subject to their authority, and had no rights or privileges but such as those who held the power and the Government might choose to grant them. . . .

In the opinion of the court, the legislation and histories of the times, and the language used in the Declaration of Independence, show, that neither the class of persons who had been imported as slaves, nor their descendants, whether they had become free or not, were then acknowledged as a part of the people, nor intended to be included in the general words used in that memorable instrument.[13]

In 1857, the Supreme Court essentially imports the "legislation and histories" of the past into the present, and it does so for African Americans alone.

As I will discuss at length in chapter 1, slave narratives offer the earliest extended analyses of the legal, philosophical, and material implications of such multiple American temporalities—that is, the absence of Anderson's simultaneity. The chapter establishes early African American writers' keen awareness of the inconsistencies among the gradual development of commercial standardized time, prominent eighteenth- and nineteenth-century philosophical understandings of time, and the psychic and material experiences of U.S. slaves whose lives testified to the distinctly nonuniform nature of both time and the law during the period. For the purposes of this Introduction, I offer just one especially striking case study of this layered temporal-political dynamic in the nineteenth century, taken from the 1850 *Narrative of Sojourner Truth*. There is an extraordinary passage in Truth's narrative wherein location, time, and the law do not simply intersect but collide. Having escaped from slavery, Truth hears that her son, whom she had to leave behind, has been illegally sold "down South":

A little previous to Isabel's leaving her old master, he had sold her child, a boy of five years, to a Dr. Gedney, who took him with him as far as New York city, on his way to England; but finding the boy too small for his service, he sent him back to his brother, Solomon Gedney. This man disposed of him to his sister's husband, a wealthy planter, by the name of Fowler, who took him to his own home in Alabama.

This illegal and fraudulent transaction had been perpetrated some months before Isabella knew of it, as she was now living at Mr. Van Wagener's. The law expressly prohibited the sale of any slave out of the State,—and all minors were to be free at twenty-one years of age; and Mr. Dumont had sold Peter with the express understanding, that he was soon to return to the State of New York, and be emancipated at the specified time.

When Isabel heard that her son had been sold South, she immediately started on foot and alone, to find the man who had thus dared, in the face of all law, human and divine, to sell her child out of the State; and if possible, to bring him to account for the deed.[14]

After being repeatedly rebuffed by whites of her acquaintance to whom she turns for help, Truth, with the aid of local Quakers, eventually takes her son's case to the local court in New Paltz, New York. There, she is told that the New York court's judicial process would probably decide the case in her favor, but that the process would take "some months" (68). Truth refuses to accept this temporal verdict: "The lawyer used his every argument to convince her, that she ought to be very thankful for what they had done for her; that it was a great deal, and it was but reasonable that she should now wait patiently the time of the court. Yet she never felt, for a moment, like being influenced by these suggestions" (68). Instead, Truth seeks the assistance of another attorney, who promises to help retrieve her son from slavery. He tells her to return to his home in twenty-four hours. But Truth,

having no idea of this space of time, went several times in a day, to ascertain if her son had come. Once, when the servant opened the door and saw her, she said, in a tone expressive of much surprise, "Why, this woman's come again!" She then wondered if she went too often. When the lawyer appeared, he told her the twenty-four hours would not expire till the next morning; if she would call then, she would see her son. The next morning saw Isabel at the lawyer's door, while he was yet in his bed. He now assured her it was morning till noon. (69)

Such representation of black people as existing outside modern temporality was not at all unusual for the period. A little over a decade before the publication of Truth's *Narrative*, Georg Wilhelm Friedrich Hegel, perhaps the most influential philosopher of his day, had declared (in a posthumously published 1837 volume of lectures delivered in 1830 and 1831) that

Africa "is no historical part of the World; it has no movement or development to exhibit. . . . What we properly understand by Africa is the Unhistorical, Undeveloped spirit, still involved in conditions of mere nature, and which had to be presented here only as on the threshold of the World's History."[15] This representation of Sojourner Truth as at once utterly ignorant of linear clock time and at the mercy of lawyers does smack disconcertingly of Hegel's notion, to be discussed at length in chapter 1, that black people reside in a space of nature rather than a time of history. But just as important, while waiting on the doorstep, Truth is positioned, figuratively and literally, at the intersection of time *and the law,* with lawyers in charge of meting out both; seemingly *they* are the gatekeepers at Hegel's "threshold of the World's History."

Of course, we know that Truth did not actually write her narrative. Never having learned to read or write, she is said to have dictated her story to an amanuensis, the white abolitionist Olive Gilbert. Perhaps, then, Truth's utter ignorance of linear time is simply Gilbert's invention, a means of reinforcing the narrative's often rather racist and Hegelian representation of Truth as, in Gilbert's words, a "child of nature" (110). And it does seem unlikely that Truth would be ignorant of a twenty-four-hour day. On the other hand, it is not entirely implausible that as a former slave, she may never have learned to read a clock. The historian Mark Smith observes that slaves generally "were denied access to the mechanical time piece," with their masters "guard[ing] both the secret of time telling and the instruments themselves, reserving the use of a clock or watch for the few slaves whose plantation duties necessitated reading and understanding mechanically defined time."[16] Smith cites one "Alabama planter" who in 1852 shared his time and labor management practices with readers of *De Bow's Review* (subtitled *Agricultural, Commercial, and Industrial Progress and Resources*), a popular monthly in the United States at the time, particularly in the South:

I have them rise in time to be at their labor by light. Their breakfast hour is eight o'clock. At this meal they have bread, a small portion of meat, a cup of coffee, and butter-milk, which requires fifteen minutes. At dinner, at twelve o'clock, I repeat the meat and bread, and as many wholesome vegetables as they wish. Vegetables I find to be very wholesome, and they then require less meat and bread. In the winter they have one hour, and summer three to rest, in the heat of day. I don't know what I lose by this, as they work much faster while they are at it. . . . I never permit them to work after night, as I feel fully compensated with their day's labor. I require them to retire at nine o'clock precisely. The foreman calls the roll at that hour, and two or three times during the night, to see that all are at their places.[17]

Such regulation by plantation owners and overseers of the slaves' day was fairly typical, even if it was not always quite so elaborate and so thoroughly intrusive. Slave narrators, too, often note the "bells" and "horns" that punctuated their daily labors, although in far less cheery terms than does the Alabama slaveholder. Frederick Douglass writes of exhausted slaves who sleep through the "driver's horn":

Woe betides them who hear not this morning summons to the field; for if they are not awakened by the sense of hearing, they are by the sense of feeling: no age nor sex finds any favor. Mr. Severe, the overseer, used to stand by the door of the quarter, armed with a large hickory stick and heavy cowskin, ready to whip any one who was so unfortunate as not to hear, or, from any other cause, was prevented from being ready to start for the field at the sound of the horn.[18]

Harriet Jacobs, too, writes of slaves on a neighboring plantation who "when finished with their daily toil . . . must hurry to eat their little morsels, and be ready to extinguish their pine knots before nine o'clock, when the overseer went his patrol rounds."[19] Surely, then, with her past experiences of manual slave labor, Sojourner Truth, even if she were unable to read a clock, would have understood that morning lasts until midday. Yet more important than whether or not Truth actually experienced or related the incident as written is the fact that she is *represented* as residing so thoroughly outside the tempo of the law and the rhythms of U.S. citizenship. In E. L. McCallum's words, it's worth considering "whether citizenship were even possible without a common citizen's watch."[20] Patently without watch, and soon to be subject to the Dred Scott decision that was only a few years away as of the publication of her *Narrative,* Truth doesn't have much time left to be a citizen permitted to bring any suit at all in a U.S. court; in short, she's running out of time for justice.

Although Gilbert's representation of Sojourner Truth as ignorant of clock time likely strikes most contemporary readers as outlandish and racist, the *Narrative of Sojourner Truth* is not wholly unlike even long-postbellum writings by African Americans in representing black people as alienated from the timekeeping practices of the majority. Pauline Hopkins begins her novel *Hagar's Daughter* with one slave character saying, "Ef I live to see the next corn plantin' I'll be twenty-seven, or thirty, or thirty-five, I dunno which," and another saying, "I was born at sweet pertater time."[21] Hopkins's focus on the slave past, and on slave time, in her 1901–2 text functions as a political statement about the retrograde state of black civil rights in the post-Reconstruction era. As Hopkins's narrator puts it in her 1902 novel *Winona*, "reversion is the only god worshipped by the south."[22] As I discuss in chapter 2, many late nineteenth- and early twentieth-century African American texts trace the same pattern: racially differential time mirroring a "reversion" in the citizenship status of African Americans during the period that the historian Rayford Logan has influentially termed the "nadir" of postbellum race relations in the United States.[23] This persistent linkage of race, (in)justice, and time in so many African American novels of this period, particularly those published after *Plessy v. Ferguson,* immediately puts their authors in conversation with Charles Peirce, Oliver Wendell Holmes, and William James, the founders of pragmatism, the most influential American philosophical movement of the late nineteenth century. Indeed, it was perhaps inevitable that Hopkins and Chesnutt, along with other African American authors in the period, who were preoccupied by the law's shaping of debates over race and citizenship, would offer a challenge to pragmatism, which was from the start a legal as well as a philosophical school of thought.

Among Holmes's most famous pragmatist legal sayings was that "the life of the law has not been logic: it has been experience."[24] African American novels published during the time of pragmatism's origins and its rise frequently represented racially specific experiences of both the law and time, experiences that invariably led to tragedy and injustice. The plot of Charles Chesnutt's 1900 novel *The House behind the Cedars,* for example, turns on a white male judge relying on a black child's sense of urgency in delivering a letter that, if received in time, will prevent the novel's mulatta heroine, Rena, from being discovered as passing for white and therefore losing her white fiancé. "Make haste," says the judge to Billy, who promptly joins his friends for a game of marbles and only much later delivers the letter, too late to prevent the novel's tragic outcome: Rena's death from "brain fever."[25] Similarly, Paul Laurence Dunbar begins his 1902 novel *The Sport of the Gods* (set in about the same year as its publication) with the intertwined themes of nostalgia in relationship to progress, and race in relationship to fiction: "Fiction has said so much in regret of the old days when there were plantations and overseers and masters and slaves, that it was good to come upon such a household as Berry Hamilton's, if for no other reason than that it afforded some relief from the monotony of tiresome iteration."[26] The novel sustains this motif of time, race, and fiction and does so within the context of the failure of Reconstruction and the period's deeply racialized forms of justice; thus, it provides an ideal second case study for this Introduction.

Dunbar's Hamilton is the African American butler for the wealthy white Oakley family in a "fine old Southern town"; his wife, Fannie, is their housekeeper, and the Hamilton cottage is located just "some hundred paces from" the Oakley "mansion" (6, 1). The narrator assures us that although this arrangement might seem "somewhat in the manner of the old cabin in the [slave] quarters," the Hamilton cottage was "unlike the cabin of the elder day" because "it was a neatly furnished, modern house, the home of a typical, good-living negro" (1). Yet despite their apparently being forerunners of the "New Negro," Berry and Fannie Hamilton are ultimately doomed, victimized by the plot's central miscarriage of race-based justice. Berry is wrongly accused of stealing money from the Oakley home, and the Hamiltons quickly become aware that their cottage home on their employer's land and their livelihood as his servants closely resemble the "old plantation quarters system" and that they live in a world wherein "no servant is beyond suspicion" (37, 14). As the narrator observes in the chapter "The Justice of Men," given Berry Hamilton's longstanding reputation for honesty, "it seems a strange irony" that there were "so few who even at the first telling doubted the story of his guilt" (27). Hamilton is arrested, tried, found guilty, and sentenced to "ten years at hard labor," and the Oakleys force Fannie to leave their land (34). But five years into Berry's sentence, it is discovered that the real criminal was one of the Oakley's own sons. Charles Chesnutt's 1901 novel *The Marrow of Tradition* likewise includes a subplot in which a decadent white grandson in a distinguished southern family actually dresses and makes himself up in blackface so as to appear to be one of the family's servants, Sandy Campbell, in order to commit murder. Sandy is promptly arrested and jailed and is immediately at risk of lynching. As the novel's narrator puts it, "the mere suggestion that the crime had been committed by a negro was equivalent to proof."[27] Indeed, it appears that despite the passage of five decades, little had changed since Douglass's 1853 novella *The Heroic Slave*, wherein the title character was "guilty of no crime but the color of his skin."[28]

Even the advent of the New Negro did not seem to bring much in the way of progress toward full citizenship and justice, at least according to many of the African American writers who followed Hopkins, Chesnutt, and Dunbar. A number of Harlem Renaissance writers seemed to believe that (at least some) black people weren't truly modern even in the modernist era, however involuntarily. In 1911, W. E. B. Du Bois argued that "Negroes" must slip "the bonds of medievalism" in order to join the modern body politic.[29] In 1925, Alain Locke declared that in order to be truly "New," black Americans must "shed the old chrysalis of the Negro problem."[30] Du Bois and Locke were urging African Americans to push themselves ever more quickly along a developmental pathway they believed to have been already trod by others. As I argue in chapter 4, writers of the Harlem Renaissance—rather like the Black Arts Movement writers who would follow (and yet deny) them nearly forty years later—endorsed and aimed for, and sometimes even achieved, a sort of "simultaneity" in the first decades of the twentieth century. With their sense of the New Negro Movement as one among a number of cultural nationalisms of the period, along with their attempt to forge a specifically modern black identity, Locke, Du Bois, and James Weldon Johnson contributed to an unprecedented sense of presentism and possibility within the African American literary and cultural tradition.

But while Locke was declaring the birth of the "New Negro" and sounding the death knell of the "old Negro," other African American writers of the period remained concerned with literal enactments of black mortality in conjunction with black people *still* being held back in time.[31] The paradigmatic African American literary genre that represented racially differential time in the modern period—over and against the presentism of Locke or Du Bois—has to be antilynching drama of the 1910s and 1920s, for these plays threw into relief just how costly Pauline Hopkins's turn-of-the-century "reversion" remained for black families in later decades. Lynching, as a repeated act of brutality, seemed designed to exclude African Americans from modern temporalities and economies. Angelina Weld

Grimké, Mary Burrill, Georgia Douglas Johnson, and other authors of antilynching plays were well aware of that intention. In these plays, as I have
argued elsewhere, black characters experience lynching as a "predictable,
often-repeated form of violent trauma that, in certain ways, was not only
fully known but fully expected."[32] Again and again, the plays represent
lateness of black male characters as a sure sign—particularly if they are
strong, successful, or resistant—that they have been murdered in acts of
terrorism by enraged whites. Thus, the men's deaths are preordained; their
futures closed. Yet it is an "open" future, according to the influential modern philosopher Henri Bergson, a contemporary of these writers, that inheres in modern human experience and secures the subject's free will.[33]
According to Bergson, modern humans exist in a "state of pure possibility,"
wherein "only the present [is bound] to the present."[34]

Suggestively, both the peak years of lynching in the United States and
the birth of the antilynching genre coincide with Bergson's development
of a theory of an open future for a free human subject who exists in and
across time—a person's "durée," or duration.[35] As Michael Vaughan explains, "Henri Bergson was the philosopher who, in an intellectual career
stretching from the 1880s to the 1930s, provided a rigorous account of the
real efficacy of time (which he called *duration*). This allowed him to conceive of creativity as the source of both psychological freedom and of life
as an open system."[36] Bergson's most prominent recent champion, Gilles
Deleuze, understands Bergson's notion of creative vitality, or "élan vital,"
as signifying the vibrancy and possibilities in organic life that proceed
from its duration and variation; or, in Deleuze's words (in translation),
"the élan vital is duration that differentiates itself."[37] Elizabeth Grosz
points out the optimism embedded in this combination of élan vital and
duration: "Bergson, Minkowski and others have accepted, as few others
have, the (perpetually impending) precedence of the future over the past
and present; they have acknowledged and delighted in the uncaptured
playing out of the forces of duration, temporal continuity and eruption or
emergence, and the coincidence of this movement with the surprise and
openness of life itself."[38] Bergsonian notions of time and "openness" obviously resonated with, and in some cases directly influenced, a great deal of
modernist literary and visual art. Surrealist and Italian futurist artists offered perhaps the clearest celebratory representations of human motion
via the dynamic visual forms in iconic works, for example Marcel Duchamp's *Nude Descending a Staircase* (1912) and Umberto Boccioni's *Unique*

Umberto Boccioni (1882–1916), Unique Forms of Continuity in Space. *1913. Bronze, H. 48, W. 15¹/₂, D. 36 inches (121.9 x 39.4 x 91.4cm). Bequest of Lydia Winston Malbin, 1989 (1990.38.3). Image source: Art Resource, New York. Courtesy of the Metropolitan Museum of Art, New York, N.Y., U.S.A.*

Forms of Continuity in Space (1913). Modern theatre, too, was interested in new ways of representing space and time. Radical experimentation characterized avant-garde European staging from the late 1800s, when the "fourth wall," the separation of actors/stage from audience/theater, was first being breached by dramatists and directors, including Adolphe Appia and Max Reinhardt. Futurist playwrights took things even farther in the 1910s as they attempted to do away with the fourth wall altogether.[39] The content of modern experimental drama was just as revisionary, exemplified by August Strindberg's psychoanalytically inspired *Dream Play* (1902), with its near-constant transformations of props and sets mirroring the play's fluid, dream-like content. As Strindberg himself explained, he "sought to reproduce the disconnected but apparently logical form of a dream. Anything can happen; everything is possible and probable. Time and space do not exist."[40]

Given the antilynching plays' traditional staging and unchanging sets, their melodramatic content, and their repetitiveness of theme, it is hard to believe that they were written and performed in the same decade as the Strindberg plays and other avant-garde modernist dramatic works. They in fact resemble Victorian melodrama far more than they resemble even the non-experimental or popular theatre of their day. The best known of the antilynching plays, Grimké's *Rachel,* will be my third case study in this Introduction, as it perfectly represents the racially differential temporal-formal literary politics that developed in the African American literary tradition during the first decades of the twentieth century. Grimké offers the following stage directions for act 1:

The scene is a room scrupulously neat and clean and plainly furnished. The walls are painted green, the woodwork, white. In the rear and at the left [left and right are from the spectator's point of view], an open doorway leads into a hall. Its bare, green wall and white baseboard are all that can be seen of it. It leads into the other rooms of the flat. In the center of the rear wall of the room is a window. It is shut.[41]

Act 2 begins:

Time: October 16, four years later; seven o'clock in the morning.
Scene: The same room. (43)

Act 3 begins:

> Time: Seven o'clock in the evening, one week later.
> Place: The same room. (61)

Rachel is not unusual here; nearly every scene in every antilynching play in the 1910s takes place in a flat, a cabin, a kitchen, or a bedroom. Yet *Rachel* was first performed in 1916, exactly when modernist experimental theatre was flourishing. For example, in striking contrast, it was also in 1916 that Gertrude Stein wrote her relatively accessible yet still distinctly Steinian play *Mexico*. *Mexico* lacks stage directions and a cast of characters and consists of lines such as these:

> Now let us understand each other. We have more
> time than we had. Let us begin now.
> A cab stand.
> Who is restless.
> We all are not we are not willing to go.
> Very well do not go.[42]

Published six years later in 1922, the play depends on movement—not only of its "restless" characters (who "have more time," it seems, than they know what to do with) but of ideas and language. "Mexico" in the play comes to signify not just a literal travel destination for peregrinating expatriates, but a metaphorical escape from World War I and its material and emotional toll on and in Europe. The antilynching plays, by contrast, offer no escape from the violence of the period, nor any hope of escape. So there appears to be little common ground between Stein and Grimké. Gertrude Stein was a celebrity in the U.S. who, in Annalisa Zox-Weaver's words, even "enjoyed a degree of iconicity in America twenty years before" her appearance on the cover of *Time* magazine and the publication of *The Autobiography of Alice B. Toklas* in 1933 "and the grand 1934 tour that followed."[43] Stein was a key patron and collector for the 1913 New York Armory Show of modernist visual art, the most pivotal modernist event certainly in the U.S. and perhaps anywhere during the period. The show even included Stein's portrait of well-known arts partron Mabel Dodge as well as Duchamp's *Nude Descending a Staircase*. Grimké, by contrast, never achieved anything like national celebrity or broad influence or diverse audience.

As I have argued elsewhere, she might have intended, as she once stated, for *Rachel* to be addressed primarily to whites, "but the play was in fact performed by and for predominantly African Americans," as in its March 1916 production at a normal school for African American young women in Washington, D.C.[44] Of course, Jim Crow segregation of theaters helps explain part of the playwrights' contrasting receptions and their plays' performance histories. But it would seem, as well, that the works of the antilynching dramatists simply did not belong on either the avant-garde or the popular stage (for example, Ziegfeld Follies, Vaudeville, and minstrel shows) of the 1910s. Neither did their plays find a place alongside other, non-avant-garde drama of the day; their representations of racial injustice and its damage to black families found no counterpart in the works of Shaw or Wilde, for example.

Even in a slightly broader and longer genealogy of modern drama, one that would include the plays of Chekhov or Ibsen, the antilynching plays are hard to place. A character like Rachel, who possesses a "spirit of abounding life, health, joy, youth," and believes that "the loveliest thing of all the lovely things in this world is just being a mother" just would not fit into *A Doll's House* (28, 33). Indeed, *nothing* about the antilynching plays seems to fit their time and place; even the playbill for that 1916 Washington, D.C., performance of *Rachel* seems wrong for the era. It represents the play's heroine in an utterly static, desperate state; on her knees clutching a piece of parlor furniture, Rachel and her body conform to the unchanging angles of a Victorian occasional table. How unlike the art nouveau curves of the day's popular art, how unlike the emergent modern art photography of an Alfred Stieglitz. How utterly unlike the iconic European and American modernist and futurist visual art of the 1910s, including virtually all cubist paintings and sculptures, which depend on and represent the dynamism not only of human experience and human bodies but even of solid objects, as in George Braque's 1910 *Violin and Candlestick*.

Rather than conclude that the plays of Grimké, Burrill, and Douglas Johnson were simply hopelessly behind the times and old-fashioned, I argue, rather, that they were challenging the notion of the existence of the dynamism in modern human experience that Bergson, Stein, Duchamp, James Joyce, and other iconic white modernist philosophers, writers, and artists posited. Indeed, given the antilynching playwrights' profound and sustained concerns with racially different experiences of temporality, they must be understood in relationship to their modernist contemporaries

"RACHEL"

The Drama Committee
of the District of Columbia Branch
of the N. A. A. C. P.

—PRESENTS—

"RACHEL"

A Race Play in Three Acts by
Angelina Grimke

under direction of

NATHANIEL GUY

AT

Myrtilla Miner Normal School

Friday Eve., March 3rd and
Sat. Eve., March 4th, 8 P. M.

Tickets   -   75 and 50 Cts.

Tickets on Sale at Gray and Grays Drug Store 12th & U
Sts. N. W. after February 1st from 6 to 8 o'clock P. M.
All Seats Reserved.

PRINTED BY MURRAY BROS.

Playbill from a performance of Angelina Weld Grimké's Rachel *in 1916. Angelina Weld Grimké Papers, Box 38-13, Folder 223; Manuscript Division. Courtesy: Moorland-Spingarn Research Center, Howard University.*

who were likewise in the business of theorizing and dramatizing time. In the context of such a relationship, antilynching drama's anachronistic literary form and staging must be viewed as strategic and political. When seen in this way, the plays' continuing insistence on static settings and the "fourth wall," even as modern experimental theatre was in the business of doing away with both, makes perfect sense. For instance, European psychoanalytic "dream plays" cannot convey the United States-specific content of white racial terrorism. Their form does not enable the exposure and exploration of a real-life, material, and recurring nightmarish reality. The family damage in antilynching plays never results from African American culture; it does not arise spontaneously from within individual psyches nor is it induced by other family members. Rather, individual psychological or familial damage in the plays is always provoked by external action. In other words, if psyches are fractured in the plays, they are fractured as the result of racism and its paradigmatic act of lynching.

Similarly, the fluid setting and dialogue of *Mexico* suit Stein's content about the white expatriate artistic set—not Grimké's content about a black middle class family like the Lovings in *Rachel*. The Lovings need to keep the outside world outside simply in order to survive; staying put is their safest choice. Whenever the characters, especially the male characters, venture outside, they will certainly encounter racism, and they always run the risk of being lynched, particularly if they challenge that racism. In sum, the antilynching plays locate crossgenerational misery as coming from without, not within; therefore, the black family remains trapped in a flat throughout the play, and so, too, do all African Americans, who then remain, symbolically, trapped in premodern times. Rachel's brother, Tom, points out that despite his training as an "electrical engineer," a necessarily modern profession, he cannot "practice" it because of racial discrimination in the workplace. He concludes that this is "God's justice, I suppose" (49). Tom ends up, like his friend John Strong, as a "waiter" (51). In other words, as late as the 1910s, though black people may try and try, they will still be kept waiting—much like Sojourner Truth was kept waiting—for justice, as modernity and its emergent professions pass so many of them by, regardless of their talent or training. There is no "élan vital" expressed in the antilynching plays, but instead a devitalized domestic sphere in which black families can enjoy neither secure economic well-being nor a free and open future. Grimké, Burrill, and Johnson understand there to be no variation in narratives or performances of lynching, and only tragically limited duration for its victims and their families. In a sense, they are coping with a continuous past over and against Stein's well-known "continuous present," as she termed her sustained use of repetition, though with variations, as a means to represent an ongoing, dynamic reality always taking place in the present, rather like a movie camera with its series of frames.[45] And the antilynching dramatists, with their challenge to such modernist representations of fluid, dynamic time and subjectivity, are clearly, if implicitly, participating in and contributing to their period's philosophical debates over the nature of time. This preoccupation of African American writers with racially differential understandings and experiences of time and its measure did not end with the modernist era of 1890–1940.

After the brief respite of an imagined presentism offered by Du Bois, Locke, and other Harlem Renaissance writers in the 1920s, midcentury African American writers returned resoundingly to the strategic anachronism launched by Grimké and Douglas Johnson in the 1910s. As I argue in chapter 3, Richard Wright's naturalism, characteristic of Theodore Dreiser, Frank Norris, and Upton Sinclair at the turn of the twentieth century, suits the grim content of *Native Son*, a midcentury novel that registers just how thoroughly the Progressive Era had bypassed neighborhoods like Chicago's South Side. Neither Wright nor his era is alone in this literary-political strategy; nearly all twentieth-century African American literature that deals centrally with a black man's death by lynching or capital punishment also represents time and injustice together as bringing about his fate. Therefore, in chapter 3 I focus on different periods, genres, and styles so as to demonstrate how a thematic of time intertwined with justice works not only within but also across time and form. Alongside *Native Son*, the chapter considers Ernest Gaines's elegiac novel *A Lesson before Dying* (1994) and Suzan-Lori Parks's postmodern play *The Death of the Last Black Man in the Whole Entire World* (1990), arguing that these apparently disparate texts share black male mortality as their content and repetition as their form, signaling the persistence of justice coded by race and gender throughout the century. Indeed, the repetition in these texts mirrors the transhistorical reality of black men's deaths in settings both legal and extralegal. Chapter 3's combination of genres and eras thus serves to acknowledge a particular kind of repetitive injustice and to explore African American writers' repetitive aesthetic forms as an expression of that injustice. This is not to argue that all genres signify identically. Just as Grimké used repetitiveness of performance and setting to deliver her verdict on modern justice, Suzan-Lori Parks deploys the formal possibilities inherent in drama to explore the ongoing, repeated nature of black male mortality enacted by state violence. And Wright and Gaines, much like Chesnutt at the end of the nineteenth century, use formal possibilities inherent in long narrative fiction to explore the sustained nature of racial inequities in the United States. Still, Wright, Gaines, and Parks share a fundamental literary-political and philosophical strategy; as I detail in the chapter, their aesthetic-formal expressions of grimly repeating, lived reality stand in direct contrast to broadly influential—and distinctly more optimistic—twentieth-century philosophical understandings of time like those of Bergson and Deleuze.

As I show in chapter 4, it was only during the era of Black Arts and Black Power that a significant number of African American thinkers found a relatively comfortable fit between their own aesthetic-political agenda and received philosophical understandings of time. Likewise, only in this period did so many African American writers, performers, and activists begin to imagine and represent black people as living fully in their times, and with the possibility of full citizenship. Many believed that the "revolution" was truly at hand. I contend that the strategic presentism founded on black identity and simultaneity that emerged, however briefly, during the Harlem Renaissance flourished, if again only briefly, during the Black Arts Movement. That a number of Howard University–based poets, active between 1958 and 1973, called themselves the "Dasein group" underscores the Black Arts era's sense of presentism and even optimism. Named after Heidegger's notion of human subjectivity as unfolding in time and in the present, the group set the stage for Black Arts writers' and Black Power figures' agenda to seize justice by "seizing the time," a popular Black Panther slogan.[46] This strategic presentism, this sense of *being there,* was expressed perhaps most clearly and notably via "conversations" between African American writers and musicians. Unlike early African American literature, which had been invested in black sameness and U.S. citizenship articulated via long-established Western literary and rhetorical forms, much 1960s and early 1970s African American writing consciously partook of, and let itself be in conversation with, contemporary African American vernacular and musical forms in order to articulate black difference and black nationalism that were, nonetheless, very much in and of their day. Yet once again, this cautiously optimistic strategic presentism of the 1960s and 1970s did not last.

African American writers in our contemporary moment—when space seems to have been almost fully bridged by time via technologies that permit us to speak to and see others in the present and across vast distances—remain aware that neither time nor justice is "created equal," that the revolution was not only not televised but that it never took place. As I discuss at length in chapter 5, no works in the African American literary tradition investigate the persistence of racially differential experiences of law, time, and space more thoroughly and explicitly than do recent detective novels by authors such as Walter Mosley and Barbara Neely. Their return in this "postmodern" era to a hard-boiled form, one seemingly more characteristic of the 1930s than the early 2000s, suggests that they are commenting on the intractable nature of racialized justice in the United States. Returning to strategic anachronism, they deploy a form born of post-Depression misery and cynicism, hard-boiled detective fiction, to comment on stasis in South Central Los Angeles, Roxbury, and other majority-nonwhite urban neighborhoods. Moreover, just as Grimké and other antilynching dramatists implicitly challenged Bergson, contemporary African American detective fiction writers are offering a challenge to twentieth- and twenty-first-century European and U.S. philosophers who have expended—and continue to expend—a great deal of energy debating the nature of time and human subjectivity. Some philosophers have engaged and challenged the assertion delivered by Aristotle that time cannot exist without change; others have upheld the notion that time *is* the dimension of change.[47] Not unlike Wright's *Native Son*, Mosley's Easy Rawlins novels of the 1990s and early 2000s intervene in the abstractions of this debate by grounding their analysis of time in terms of day-to-day, physical, violent experiences in Watts, another neighborhood bypassed by reform in the 1920s and 1930s and then again by urban renewal in the postwar decades. As Easy says in *Little Scarlet,* the 2004 installment in the series, "no matter how far back you remember, there's a beatin' there waiting for you."[48] There is no Heideggerian "being there" for him, because he is always being *black* and therefore being *back* there. Yet Easy Rawlins and the Easy Rawlins series, over and against a model of temporal suspension, of a temporal alterity that pulls the present back toward the past—and, I will conclude, African American literature as a whole—must also be seen as "coeval": that is, as fully inhabiting, shaping, and being shaped by present-day temporalities, legal systems, economies, philosophical debates, and literary canons.

I take one of Walter Mosley's recent nonfiction books, the 2006 *Life out of Context*, as my final case study for this Introduction because it insists on the "being there" that Easy Rawlins conspicuously lacks. The first sentence of Mosley's book reads: "This monograph was written over a very short period of time. It was a feverish episode in which I felt it necessary to uncover and articulate methods we could employ to make the world safer for the millions who are needlessly suffering."[49] Here, Mosley is very much in the present tense; he is outlining a plan for *now*, for overcoming the past's apparently relentless pull. As part of that plan, he advocates science fiction as a valuable "tool . . . in the realm of literature" because it can "move your consciousness fifty years into the future or a hundred years back. From that point of view, we can look back (or forward) at ourselves. . . . The science fiction story is almost always a criticism of the lives we are living today . . . [through it] we are able to question the contexts of our lives that have hitherto seemed absolute" (91, 93). In the same breath that he argues for science fiction, Mosley advises the "Black and Brown" citizens of South Central Los Angeles that they must demand to be included on "city boards and town councils, federal and congressional fact-finding groups and police reviews" (84, 83). He concludes that "our place at the table is always a possibility, but if we never go there, we will never *be there*" (84; emphasis added). This book explores the long-standing African American literary and political project of working toward *being there*, showing that time, understood both ontologically and materially, has always been a fundamental theme in African American literature, one that has worked to explore and expose the lived experience of race-bound justice in the United States.

We are left, then, with an understanding of time and justice as intertwined and represented through literature, the central premise of this book. But the contemporary African American playwright Suzan-Lori Parks perhaps best captures the spirit, even the method, of this book with her declaration "Standard Time Line and Standard Plot Line are in cahoots!"[50] I aim to show that African American writers, although all too often unacknowledged, have intervened, historically and consistently, in philosophies of time and constructions of citizenship. Or, as Parks expresses her method: "Through each line of text I'm rewriting the Time Line—creating history where it is and always was but had not yet been divined."[51] My goal in this combination of historical, literary, philosophical, and legal studies is to offer a new understanding of the African American literary tradition as a whole. Tropes of timekeeping, because of their power and pervasiveness across that tradition, reveal commonalities among African American texts from 1773 to the present and so permit us to construct a new version of that tradition, one based on shared aesthetic, philosophical, and material grounds. This book concludes that African American writers have always shown how black people live at once fully within modernity, as well as postmodernity, *and* along a distinct timeline—one that effectively traces racially differential justice in the United States from the late eighteenth century to the present.

Some scholars have raised concerns about such positing of black people's temporal or social alterity. Madhu Dubey, for one, rightly cautions us against "situat[ing]" African Americans in "residual zones" outside the socioeconomic structures of postmodernism, because "to perceive African-American culture in residual terms is to exempt it from the contingencies of the postmodern condition."[52] Dubey's point is well taken; still, I argue that we must nonetheless attend to temporal and justice differentials that, however contingent and nonessential they may be, persist in our postmodern era. Just as important, it may be impossible to extricate Dubey's spatial metaphor of "zones" from the temporal dimensions of postmodernity. Indeed, postmodern culture has perhaps too often been analyzed as relying on spatial rather than temporal categories, as Ursula Heise has argued.[53] By contrast, it is a commonplace to understand that modern time is distinct from premodern time. Charlie Chaplin movies, Heidegger's philosophies of time, current academic studies of modernism in relation to time—a wide range of cultural texts across disciplines have seemingly agreed with Hegel that modernity *means* modern time. In literary studies, no one disputes the fact that modernist artists and writers believed in and imagined their era's temporal dimensions—its consciousnesses, histories, and narratives—as nonlinear and fluid. Yet, as Chaplin's *Modern Times* shows us, aesthetic form, whether filmic or literary, cannot alone establish and certainly cannot control an era's temporalities. Economic *and* spatial formations, in concert with aesthetics, contribute to, perhaps even create, time.

In other words, we should not, indeed cannot, separate the temporality of lived experience—particularly labor taking place in specific times and places—from aesthetic, philosophical, and scientific representations of normative modernity, or of normative postmodernity. As Gerhard Dohrn-van

Rossum has shown, the technology of time measurement emerged out of a need to regulate nonagricultural labor during the rise of postfeudal urbanization.[54] When we identify a shift from time to space as coterminous with the shift from modern to postmodern, we risk missing the ways that social and economic formations continue to shape time in different ways for different individuals, different groups, different regions, and different aesthetic traditions. Therefore, in this book I argue for a "both/and" approach: African American people and African American literature can be seen as occupying at once temporal-aesthetic dimensions of alterity *and* dominant or "mainstream" temporalities and canons. I am not speaking here of what Mark Smith terms the "stereotype of Colored People's Time," a sort of everyday, vernacular notion of black difference or resistance.[55] I am speaking instead of the awareness, the deep understanding, on the part of African American writers of what Stephen Kern terms "the ontological primacy of time."[56] As represented within the African American literary tradition, time and justice—although often imagined to be standard and uniform—are actually contingent and unevenly available: in other words, they are *political fictions.*

1

Ticking, Not Talking: Timekeeping in Early African American Literature

Lina says from the state of my teeth I am maybe seven or eight when I am brought here. We boil wild plums for jam and cake eight times since then, so I must be sixteen.

—Toni Morrison, *A Mercy*

With little controversy, African American literature has conventionally been understood as following a distinct timeline, as possessing its own literary genealogy and history. The towering *Norton Anthology of African American Literature,* with its explicit aims "to make available in one representative anthology the major texts in the tradition and to construct a canon inductively,"[1] dates that tradition from 1746 to the present, identifying Lucy Terry's 1746 poem "Bars Fight" as the "earliest known work of literature by an African American."[2] Even when they dispute the *Norton's* selection process or its point of origin for the tradition, competing anthologies concur that African American literature forms a separate tradition both literarily and temporally. The editors of *Call and Response,* the Riverside anthology of African American literature, "believe that African American literature is a distinct tradition, one originating in the African and African American cultural heritages and in the experience of enslavement in the United States," while the editors of the *Prentice Hall Anthology* "employ an approach that places African American aesthetic contributions within historical context," arguing that literature and history "define" one another.[3]

On the other hand, ascribing a distinct temporality to black *people* has been far more controversial—and rightly so. For to the degree that black people have been described and perceived as being in or of another time, they have also generally been excluded, and in distinctly racist ways, from dominant definitions of Western modernity. For instance, many eighteenth- and nineteenth-century white European and U.S. philosophers believed that black people represented an earlier, less evolved form of human and asserted that they were neither fit nor ready for modern times. In a posthumously published volume of his collected lectures, *The Philosophy of History* (1837), Georg F. W. Hegel (1770–1831), claimed that "in Negro life the characteristic point is the fact that consciousness has not yet attained to the realization of any substantial objective existence—as for example God, or Law—in which the interest of man's volition is involved and in which he realizes his own being."[4] In Hegel's developmental model of culture, the only hope for "Negroes" to come into modernity, including its culture and law, lay in their contact with the white West:

> From these various traits it is manifest that want of self-control distinguishes the character of the Negroes. This condition is capable of no development or culture, and as we see them at this day, such have they always been. The only essential connection that has existed and continued between the Negroes and the Europeans is that of slavery. . . . Slavery is itself a phase of advance from the merely isolated sensual existence—a phase of education—a mode of becoming participant in a higher morality and the culture connected with it. Slavery is in and for itself *injustice,* for the essence of humanity is *Freedom*; but for this man must be matured. The gradual abolition of slavery is therefore wiser and more equitable than its sudden removal. (98–99; emphasis in original)

Slavery becomes, in his view, the necessary condition for "Negroes" to gain maturity and "the essence of humanity," or, as Paul Gilroy succinctly explains, for Hegel "slavery is itself a modernising force."[5] Having thus dispatched black people as presently unworthy of justice, as residing outside modern consciousness and below a "higher" plane occupied by white Europeans, Hegel proceeds to dismiss an entire continent: "At this point we leave Africa, not to mention it again. For it is no historical part of the world; it has no movement or development to exhibit. . . . What we properly understand by Africa is the Unhistorical, Undeveloped spirit, still involved in conditions of mere nature, and which had to be presented here only as on the threshold of the World's History" (99). As Michelle Wright observes, Hegel "located the Black outside analytical history, mired in a developmental stasis from which only Western civilization can rescue him."[6] But note that Hegel's framework for human development is not solely or strictly teleological but is also broadly and fundamentally temporal. For

him, *time* is the essential dimension of the full consciousness he associates
with modern Europe. In his words, "history in general is therefore the development of Spirit in *Time*, as Nature is the development of the Idea in
Space" (72; emphasis in original). He, along with other eighteenth-century
philosophers of race, including Thomas Jefferson and Arthur de Gobineau,
imagined full modern subjectivity as being contingent implicitly on whiteness and maleness, and explicitly on contemporaneity; being modern
means being in modern time.

Perhaps surprisingly, the idea that black people inhabit a distinct temporality, albeit an imposed one, was also advanced by black U.S. intellectuals, at least as early as 1845 with the publication of Frederick Douglass's
Narrative of the Life. In the very first paragraph of this work, Douglass
declares that slaves "seldom come nearer" their birthdays than "planting-
time, harvest-time, cherry-time, spring-time, or fall-time."[7] Here Douglass countermands Hegel's notion, published just eight years before, that
slavery functions as the only potential means to bring black people to history, to progress, to modernity. For Douglass, slavery suspends black
people in a perpetual laboring season and in a premodern condition of
crossgenerational serfdom; his representation of time thus provides at
once a material analysis of profound injustice and a philosophical intervention regarding understandings of time at mid-nineteenth century.

Paul Gilroy makes a similar observation about the *Narrative*'s well-
known description of the fight between Douglass and the notorious slave-
breaker Covey, arguing that in that famous scene, Douglass "inverts"
Hegel's master-slave dialectic (60). Gilroy then assigns Douglass a "compound outlook—an uneasy hybrid of the sacred and secular, the African
and the American" (61). Gilroy therefore reads the *Narrative* as exhibiting
an "Africentric" quality, at the same time asserting that violence and death
function for Douglass as a means of escaping feudal plantation slavery and
attaining modernity (62–63). I do not think Gilroy is wrong here, but he
focuses on the *Narrative*'s "compound outlook" and its "masculinist resolution of slavery's oppositions" to such a degree that he overlooks Douglass's more gender-neutral, more material, and less dialectical analyses of
U.S. slavery and of time. For Douglass, modernity cannot be understood
solely according to what Gilroy terms "the antinomies of modernity" in
which such oppositions as master–slave, white–black, man–woman, oral/
vernacular–written/rhetorical underlie all "social relations" (115). That
is, Douglass's theory of time and print culture confines itself neither to

Hegelian dialectics nor to polarities wherein diasporic black texts are African (rather than American or European) and vernacular and oral (rather than rhetorical and literary). In other words, Douglass is not simply remedying Hegel's analysis of modernity but is offering another, deeper way to understand time.

To that end, Douglass continues to spin out the material and epistemological implications of slaves' living in premodern time in that very first paragraph of the *Narrative*:

> I have no accurate knowledge of my age, never having seen any authentic record containing it. By far the larger part of the slaves know as little of their ages as horses know of theirs, and it is the wish of most masters within my knowledge to keep their slaves thus ignorant. I do not remember to have ever met a slave who could tell of his birthday. They seldom come nearer to it than planting-time, harvest-time, cherry-time, spring-time, or fall-time. A want of information concerning my own [birthday] was a source of unhappiness to me even during childhood. The white children could tell their ages. I could not tell why I ought to be deprived of the same privilege. (*NL* 21)

According to Douglass, in the absence of written legal documentation of his birth date, his knowledge and his psyche, along with those of all slaves, are shaped by the "peculiar institution" and its rhythms just as surely as are his body and labor.[8] As Henry Louis Gates Jr. eloquently writes in *Figures in Black* (1987), "the knowledge the slave has of his circumstances he must deduce from the earth; a quantity such as time, our understanding of which is cultural and not natural, derives from a nonmaterial source, let us say the heavens."[9] Likewise, as a slave, Douglass is not represented by, has no presence in, what Benedict Anderson terms the "huge modern accumulation of documentary evidence" that includes "birth certificates, diaries, report cards, letters, medical records, and the like" and serves as the basis of "personhood, *identity*."[10] His autobiography therefore *cannot* begin, as does Benjamin Franklin's, say, with genealogy; Douglass lacks a modern identity in conventional ontological and literary senses, while he is out of step with modern time materially. Douglass suffers not so much from "deprivation" of time, as Gates has argued, as from a surfeit of a particular kind of time that is unfolding alongside other kinds of time (90). In other words, Douglass is not "outside time," as Gates suggests (101). Rather, while residing in modernity, he must also live according to what Lloyd Pratt terms "laboring time," or "the kind of time slave labor produces."[11] More specifically, slaves working in the fields on southern plantations measured their time and their lives according to the seasons of region-specific agricultural production (not all places have "cherry-time")—*not* by the modern modes of timekeeping that were becoming commonplace, at least in white and middle-class households, in the slave South, and in the nation as a whole at the same time that Douglass was laboring as a slave and then writing about that experience.

Yet, even if they did not own or use them, slaves were nonetheless controlled by nonagriculturally based and characteristically modern methods of time measure. As the historian Mark M. Smith notes, U.S. plantation owners "adopt[ed] clock time during and after the 1830s as a legitimate arbiter of work and social organization," with this result: "From cradle to grave, the clock monitored antebellum slave life and labor."[12] Of course, the clock monitored far more than "slave life and labor" in the nineteenth century; Lewis Mumford famously went so far as to argue that "the clock, not the steam engine, is the key machine of the modern industrial age."[13] Certainly, time and time management were central concerns of mid-nineteenth-century American factory and plantation owners, industrialists, and agriculturalists, as well as philosophers, scientists, and inventors. The historian of time Ian Bartky notes that "the fifth message" transmitted over the first American telegraph wire in 1844 was "What is your time?"[14] Time, telegraph, and commerce functioned as interlocking mechanisms of social and economic power from the 1830s until the end of the nineteenth century. Indeed, it turns out that Wheatley was prescient in her 1773 admonishment to Harvard students to "redeem" their hours responsibly, for by the late 1850s, the Harvard Observatory had become one of the first astronomical sites to supply time for railroads, thereby cementing a relationship among astronomical time, the university, and commercial transport, while effectively "establish[ing] the first regional time zone in the United States."[15]

Time became an even more literal commodity in the United States as of 1869, when the university-based astronomers Benjamin A. Gould, Truman Safford, and Samuel P. Langley (both Safford and Langley had held positions as assistant astronomers at the Harvard Observatory) came up with the idea of selling time from observatories to railroads.[16] Langley was particularly successful, and by 1873 "had established a timekeeping system that was generating thirty-five hundred dollars in annual receipts—an amount greater than any other American observatory would ever receive."[17] By the late 1870s, selling time had become a widespread practice in the United States as had "competition among time-sellers," namely university and private observatories in cooperation with regional telegraph companies.[18] By the early 1880s, time was a commodity unregulated on an open temporal market.[19] It was only after U.S. railroads standardized time according to a system of four geographic time zones in 1883, and the U.S. Naval Observatory in Washington started to supply free time to Western Union, that time ceased to be such a literal commodity in the United States.

By the beginning of the twentieth century, uniform time had become readily available to most U.S. citizens in the form of telegraphed Standard Railway time, as Bartky observes (204). So the historian Alexis McCrossen's assertion that "over the course of the nineteenth century, Americans moved from multiple times to a single standard of time" at first seems accurate.[20] Yet the process of standardization was not quite so neat. Bartky shows that the "adoption of Standard Time in the United States" resulted only after a lengthy and uneven period of transition and was presided over by entities as various as the American Metrological Society, university-based and independent astronomers, railroads, observatories small and large, and telegraph companies (103, 141). But even Bartky's painstaking analysis of the complex process of standardizing civic and commercial time fails to take into account the fact that *lived* versions of time across the nineteenth century were equally uneven, and remained so, well after the adoption of uniform time in the United States. Literary scholars have yet to account fully for the ways African American writers have complicated received historical narratives of the nation's steady move toward standardized time. Lloyd Pratt's *Archives of American Time* (2010) stands as a significant recent exception; in it, Pratt argues persuasively for a "temporal variety pervading African American life writing and its criticism" (168).

Why then, when it is clear that African American writers have long been preoccupied by time, have only a handful of scholars, Gilroy and Pratt among them, extensively engaged and analyzed its role in the African American literary tradition? At least regarding early African American literature, we may still be relying too heavily on fundamentally dialectical and discursive interpretive frameworks, such as those of Gilroy and Gates.

For example, in *The Signifying Monkey* (1988), Gates argues for the "talking book" as *the* image connecting New World black literary texts, describing it as "the ur-trope of the Anglo-African tradition."[21] The trope of the Talking Book—that is, ex-slave narrators' reporting that they at one time believed that books literally spoke—underlies Gates's theory of "signifyin(g)," a model he applies to black Atlantic literature from James Gronniosaw's 1770 slave narrative to Alice Walker's 1982 novel *The Color Purple*. According to Gates, the Talking Book works as an overarching theory for the tradition because it expresses the "curious tension between the black vernacular and the literate white text" and "between the spoken and the written word" and therefore expresses "black difference" (131, 46). In *The Signifying Monkey*, Gates returns to Douglass's *Narrative*; this time, however, he focuses not on Douglass as a slave "outside of the linear progression of the calendar," as he did in *Figures in Black* (90), but on Douglass as "a masterful Signifier" who "noted the crucial role of the signifier in the determination of meaning" (66–67). In other words, Douglass has now become a kind of deconstructionist *avant la lettre*, with the relationship between oral and written discourse preeminent as a mode of understanding Douglass's narrative along with all of African American literature. But in the early texts on which Gates founds his theory, we actually find little evidence of African American or African oral cultural practices. Certainly, as Dickson Bruce has argued, oral "slave testimony" functioned as an important precursor to published slave narratives, yet the slaves' stories provided "content" for the abolitionist movement's written narratives rather than form.[22] Published slave narratives, from James Gronniosaw's to Harriet Jacobs's, are quite thoroughly literary, with travel and captivity narratives, conversion and confession narratives, and picaresque, gothic, and sentimental novels their most obvious ancestors. Still, critics continue to associate written slave narratives, including Douglass's *Narrative*, with an oral tradition.[23]

Granted, Douglass's is one of the very few slave narratives to consider in any depth oral African American cultural practices—specifically, the sorrow songs or spirituals. But even in the well-known passage in which Douglass describes the songs, he establishes his distance from them: "I did not, when a slave, understand the deep meaning of those rude and apparently incoherent songs" (*NL* 31). He finds that he can "analyze" their "sounds" only after his escape from slavery (*NL* 32). Admittedly, Douglass also tells his readers that he has "often sung to drown my sorrow, but seldom to express my happiness," suggesting that he himself is still participating in the sorrow song tradition (*NL* 32). Yet he includes no quotation or notation of the songs in the *Narrative*; in both form and content, they lie outside his literary and political aims—so much so that even in the midst of the sorrow song passage, he reminds us of his expressly and self-consciously literary project: "The mere recurrence to those songs, even now, afflicts me; and while I am writing these lines, an expression of feeling has already found its way down my cheek" (*NL* 32). He cannily reminds his readers of his writing body, in the present, precisely in the context of his consideration of an oral cultural practice. At the same time, pathos and an awareness of audience verging on apostrophe drive Douglass's writing here. His *Narrative* derives these qualities not from the sorrow songs but, according to Douglass himself, from the prevailing rhetorical practices of his day—in particular from *The Columbian Orator*, the only book (other than the Bible) he cites in the *Narrative*, one that "gave tongue to interesting thoughts of my own soul, which had frequently flashed through my mind, and died away for want of utterance" (*NL* 55). It is, then, a fundamental text of a Western, Euro-American rhetorical tradition that "gives tongue" to Douglass's innermost thoughts, rather than sources from an African or an African American oral tradition. Even Gates asserts that "Douglass's major contribution to the slave's narrative was to make chiasmus the central trope of slave narration" (172), as in the famous line "You have seen how a man was made a slave; you shall see how a slave was made a man" (*NL* 77). But chiasmus is, of course, a classical Western rhetorical term, not an African retention. Despite the profoundly rhetorical and literary nature, as well as the clear Western-ness and mid-nineteenth-century-ness, of Douglass's *Narrative* (and of many slave narratives and other early African American writings), even much recent scholarship on them continues to insist on their orality.[24] In other words, quite a few literary scholars have yet to heed Aldon Nielsen's 1997 caution in *Black Chant* about a tendency toward "the construction of an idealized orality in opposition to a devalued writing."[25]

Of course, connecting oral and print cultures, without idealizing either, in African American literary studies is not a problem in and of itself; indeed, as I will argue in chapter 4, such a connection actually characterizes many Harlem Renaissance and Black Arts Movement writings and contributes to these writings' presentism, their embeddedness in their times. On the other hand, focusing on "oracy" or orality poses problems for our understanding of *early* African American texts. For example, his trope of the Talking Book leads Gates to the arguable conclusion that "the slave wrote not primarily to demonstrate humane letters, but to demonstrate his or her own membership in the human community" (128). Surely, "the slave" wrote for many reasons that could be considered "primary," including what Phillis Wheatley termed "intrinsic ardor," a deeply felt desire simply to create art, as well as what all the pre-Emancipation ex-slave narrators represented as their most immediate and explicit purpose: abolition.[26] Gates's assertion does make perfect sense in that a slave's proving his or her humanity implicitly challenges the morality of slavery. Yet his conclusion about the *primacy* of that proving project stems from an equally debatable syllogism: that because Enlightenment thinkers associated reason with humanity, and reason with writing, therefore "blacks were reasonable, and hence 'men,' if—and only if—they demonstrated mastery of the 'the arts and sciences,' the eighteenth's century's formula for writing" (129).

But dominant Western understandings of full-fledged humanity in the eighteenth century did *not* hold writing—or even reason—as the sole, or perhaps even primary, sign of humanity. It turns out that the eighteenth century's "formula" for "the arts and sciences" called for many ingredients. Thomas Jefferson, among the foremost eighteenth-century philosophers of both race and the arts and sciences, offered this infamous assessment of the ways black people fell short of Enlightenment standards of humanity as embodied by whites and, to a lesser degree, by American Indians:

> They [blacks] seem to require less sleep. A black, after hard labour through the day, will be induced by the slightest amusements to sit up till midnight, or later, though knowing he must be out with the first dawn of the morning. . . . In general, their existence appears to participate more of sensation than reflection. To this must be ascribed their disposition to sleep when abstracted from their diversions, and unemployed in labour. An animal whose body is at rest, and who does not reflect, must be disposed to sleep of course.
>
> Comparing by their faculties of memory, reason, and imagination, it appears to me, that in memory they are equal to the whites; in reason much inferior, as I think one could scarcely be found capable of tracing and comprehending the investigations of Euclid; and that in imagination they are dull, tasteless, and anomalous. . . . Some have been liberally educated, and all have lived in countries

where the arts and sciences are cultivated to a considerable degree, and have had before their eyes samples of the best works from abroad. The Indians, with no advantages of this kind, will often carve figures on their pipes not destitute of design and merit. They will crayon out an animal, a plant, or a country, so as to prove the existence of a germ in their minds which only wants cultivation. They astonish you with strokes of the most sublime oratory; such as prove their reason and sentiment strong, their imagination glowing and elevated. But never yet could I find that a black had uttered a thought above the level of plain narration; never see even an elementary trait of painting or sculpture. . . . Religion indeed has produced a Phyllis Whately [sic]; but it could not produce a poet. The compositions published under her name are below the dignity of criticism. The heroes of the Dunciad are to her, as Hercules to the author of that poem.[27]

Wheatley fails Jefferson's test *not* because she cannot write but because she has insufficient imagination and originality. And Indians pass his test not because they write—they were not literate peoples when European colonists first encountered them—but because they paint and sculpt, and because they speak with reason, sentiment, and imagination. Perhaps most interestingly, blacks as a whole first fall short for Jefferson because he believes they have no sense of the value of time, staying up until "midnight" even when they know they must labor at "dawn." Franklinesque they are not, at least according to Jefferson.

Black Atlantic writers well understood and engaged with these other, powerful standards of humanity, time perhaps foremost among them. Gates began his exploration of the Talking Book with one of the earliest published slave narratives, James Gronniosaw's 1770 *Narrative of the Remarkable Particulars of the Life*, citing Gronniosaw's description of his first impression of a prayer book, which reads as follows:

He used to read prayers in public to the ship's crew every Sabbath day; and when first I saw him read, I was never so surprised in my whole life as when I saw the book talk to my master; for I thought it did, as I observed him to look upon it, and move his lips.—I wished it would do so to me.—As soon as my master had done reading I follow'd him to the place where he put the book, being mightily delighted with it, and when nobody saw me, I open'd it and put my ear down close upon it, in great hope that it wou'd say something to me; but was very sorry and greatly disappointed when I found it would not speak, this thought immediately presented itself to me, that every body and every thing despis'd me because I was black.[28]

Gronniosaw at this point in the narrative is in the business of contrasting his early ignorance with his enlightened, postconversion present, presumably in order to appeal to his Christian English audience. He was once unlike them, and that difference, as Gates suggests, Gronniosaw associates with blackness; however, contra Jefferson, Gronniosaw does not represent his differences from whites as inherent. At the beginning of the narrative, Gronniosaw had been at pains to show his specialness, expressed via his natural difference not from white English readers but from his black African kin:

I had, from my infancy, a curious turn of mind; was more grave and reserved in my disposition than either of my brothers and sisters. I often teazed them with questions they could not answer: for which reason they disliked me, as they supposed that I was either foolish, or insane. 'Twas certain that I was, at times, very unhappy in myself: it being strongly impressed on my mind that there was some GREAT MAN of power which resided above the sun, moon and stars, the objects of our worship. My dear indulgent mother would bear more with me than any of my friends beside.—I often raised my hand to heaven, and asked her who lived there? was much dissatisfied when she told me the sun, moon and stars, being persuaded, in my own mind, that there must be some SUPERIOR POWER. (1)

Gronniosaw here represents himself as somehow naturally monotheistic; he goes on to frame the contrast between the northeastern Nigerian religious practices he finds so worrisome and the English Christian practices he finds so congenial in terms of *time*:

To this moment I grew more and more uneasy every day, in so much that one saturday, (which is the day on which we keep our sabbath) I laboured under anxieties and fears that cannot be expressed; and, what is more extraordinary, I could not give a reason

36 · TICKING, NOT TALKING

for it. —I rose, as our custom is, about three o'clock, (as we are oblig'd to be at our place of worship an hour before the sun rise) we say nothing in our worship, but continue on our knees with our hands held up, observing a strict silence 'till the sun is at a certain height, which I suppose to be about 10 or 11 o'clock in England. (2)

He expresses uneasiness with a Saturday Sabbath and imposes European clock time on his people's nature-based methods of timekeeping (via the sun). As his amanuensis puts it in her preface to the narrative: "*Who can doubt but that the Suggestion so forcibly press'd upon the Mind of* ALBERT (when a Boy) that there was a Being superior to the Sun, Moon, and Stars (the Objects of African Idolatry) came from the Father of Lights, and was, with Respect to him, the First-Fruit of the Display of Gospel-Glory?" (iv; emphasis in original). Before he can take up the literal gospel, the book that speaks, Gronniosaw must first supplant celestial bodies, which are both his people's "objects of worship" and natural instruments of time-keeping, and then translate African time into English time.

Similarly, in another text Gates relies on to establish the "ur-trope" of the Talking Book, *The Interesting Narrative of the Life of Olaudah Equiano*, first published in 1789, a book is *not* the first item to startle Equiano during his introduction to New World slavery. On entering his Virginia master's plantation house for the first time, Equiano notices, with shock, an "iron muzzle" on a black slave woman who is "cruelly loaded with various kinds of iron machines."[29] "Soon after," Equiano reports, he enters his master's bedroom, having been ordered to fan him as he sleeps:

While he was fast asleep I indulged myself a great deal in looking about the room, which to me appeared very fine and curious. The *first object that engaged my attention was a watch* which hung on the chimney, and was going. I was quite surprised at the noise it made and was afraid it would tell the gentleman anything I might do amiss. (63; emphasis added)

In *The Signifying Monkey*, Gates does attend to Equiano's reactions to the watch but ends up subsuming them under a rubric of text and discourse, with the watch an object like the Talking Book that "speak[s]" only to the master and that, like Equiano himself, is owned by the master (156). But I am interested in the ways the watch might *not* signify text, or voice, or narrative, or discourse of any sort. We can instead approach the watch—and, more broadly, timekeeping—not as a text that speaks, in Gates's words, "a language that has no counterpart in [Equiano's] culture" (156), but as an actual means of telling time. Long before he encounters a Talking Book, Equiano encounters an object of timekeeping that helps constitute his abject legal status as black slave as well as his ontology, his personal state of being and becoming. Timekeeping is positioned, then, in both his narrative and his experience of enslavement, *prior* to discourse. As Mark Smith cogently argues, "simultaneously tyrannical, modern, and profit-oriented, the nineteenth-century clock and its attendant ability to rationalize and order the behavior of human beings became the planters' weapon of choice in their ongoing battle with the chattel" (5).[30]

Such analysis of the material conditions of timekeeping and slavery in the antebellum South is both necessary and on target. Yet we should not therefore rush to apply that analysis to antebellum *literature,* and we should be cautious about equating "real" time and timekeeping with their literary representation. As Mario Vargas Llosa has said,

> time is an essential aspect of fiction that gives it a separate identity, a personality that is different from the real reality. For obvious reasons time in a novel is never like time in real life. This is true in even the most realistic novel, in the novel that succeeds in imitating life. In a novel, time always has a beginning and an end. It never flows as it does in real life. . . . The manipulation of time occurs in all novels.[31]

Just so, early African American writers "manipulated" time in complex and often ambivalent ways that do not fit a single, or even double, explanatory model and that only sometimes map clearly onto what Vargas Llosa terms "real reality." For instance, African American writers have not always represented time and its measure as oppressive; modern time and timekeeping often appear as objects of desire in both early and modern African American texts, for example *Native Son,* wherein Bigger Thomas decides after being hired as the Daltons' chauffeur that he ought to buy a new watch, a gold one that better suits his new situation. Such ambivalence is in keeping with the always double-edged nature of timekeeping in relation to labor. Workers have long experienced the clock's "dual character . . . as an instrument of anachronistic lordship and simultaneously a means of overcoming it."[32] Understanding African American literature's tropes of timekeeping either as always-oppressive regulatory instruments or as inevitably tools of modern capitalist exploitation of labor belies their range and power not only in African American literature but in literature in general. Literature's ability to represent time in nonreal ways constitutes much of its power and meaning; in Vargas Llosa's words, literature's "artificial" constructions of time permit us to "better understand how daily experience, living experience, is happening in reality" (98–99).

Once again, no author in the African American literary tradition offers us a deeper understanding of "daily experience, living experience" by means of complex, multivalent representations of time than Douglass does. His multiple autobiographical narratives show us that although Douglass's writing life, from 1845 to 1881, may have matched up well with the historical arc of modern American timekeeping, his writing *content* challenges and complicates any unitary or tidy understanding of the development of American time across the nineteenth century. Despite the nation's gradual, if uneven, move toward standardized time from the 1830s to the 1890s, driven by the imperatives of modern technologies of commerce (factory), communication (telegraph), and transport (railway), there was never a single standard of time in terms of lived experience, especially in the antebellum South. As Mark Smith puts it, "clock time and natural time were never mutually exclusive in the South. Rather, they were complementary" (11). To Smith's clock time and natural time must be added white slave-owner time and black slave time. In his second autobiography, the 1855 *My Bondage and My Freedom*, Douglass distilled the problem: "In regard to the *time* of my birth, I cannot be as definite as I have been respecting the *place*."[33] This passage confirms that U.S. slaves inhabited a distinct temporality, if not geography. In 1860, a popular southern white periodical, the *Southern Cultivator,* offered the following about the passing of time and the significance of New Year's Day: " 'The close of the year is one of those milestones in the journey of life. Each of them naturally suggests a review of the past, a consideration of the present, and an anticipation of the future.' "[34] Slave narrators, too, pointed to the significance of January 1: "Hiring day at the south takes place on the 1st of January," Harriet Jacobs explains. "At the appointed hour the grounds are thronged with men, women, and children, waiting, like criminals, to hear their doom pronounced. . . . O, ye happy free women, contrast your New Year's day with that of the poor bond-woman!"[35] Douglass echoes

Jacobs; his term of servitude with Covey commences "on the 1st of January, 1833," and one year later, "on the first of January, 1834," he leaves Covey "to live with Mr. Freeland" (NL 71, 86). In *Life and Times,* Douglass reports that his New Year's resolution of 1836 had been to escape slavery.[36] In the same spirit in which he challenged Hegel's views, Douglass offers a startlingly direct challenge to Jefferson's notions of slaves, time, and sleep:

> There were no beds given the slaves, unless one coarse blanket be considered such, and none but the men and women [i.e., not the children] had these. This, however, is not considered a very great privation. They find less difficulty from the want of beds than from the want of time to sleep; for when their day's work in the field is done, the most of them have their washing, mending, and cooking to do, and having few or none of the facilities for doing either of these, very many of their sleeping hours are consumed in preparing for the field the coming day; and when this is done, old and young, male and female, married and single, drop down side by side, on one common bed,—the cold, damp floor,—each covering himself or herself with their miserable blankets; and here they sleep till they are summoned to the field by the driver's horn. (*NL* 28–29)

According to Douglass, slaves, men and women alike, are *more* than Franklin-esque; they are exemplars who exceed, even if involuntarily, American hardworking temporality: they are both late to bed *and* early to rise. Douglass hereby undoes received racial, and racist, scientific hierarchies and philosophical analyses, including those of Jefferson and Hegel, on the grounds of his own theory of time, a theory that puts the lie to black inferiority even as it moves beyond dialectic and beyond Gilroy's "antinomies of modernity" (115). For Douglass, slaves' time is regulated at once by owners and by the slaves themselves, by both labor and by what constitutes their domestic space. In fact, Douglass's formulation anticipates C. L. R. James's well-known argument in *The Black Jacobins* that West Indian slaves on sugar plantations were the first to enter modernity and "from the very start lived a life that was in its essence a modern life."[37] They performed quintessentially alienated labor within a system of global commodity-trade. But, as Simon Gikandi has recently argued, slaves' collectively experienced and imposed version of modernity does not match Hegel's version, in which the individual modern subject embraces the future, with its "new forms of social identity."[38] "On the contrary," Gikandi says, the "enslaved spirit was dominated by fear of the future."[39]

Douglass understands that it is through time and its measure—first, through an embrace of the future—that he will eventually achieve freedom as well as a documented, self-conscious modernity of the Hegelian sort. On the eve of his escape from slavery, he sees clearly the perpetual state of bondage inherent in his master's advice "to lay out no plans for the future" and to embrace "complete thoughtlessness of the future" (*NL* 107). As he says in *Life and Times*, the "thought of being only a creature of the *present* and the *past* troubled me, and I longed to have a *future*" (604; emphasis in original). Partly in reaction to his master's advice, Douglass found himself "ready to work at night as well as day" in order to make his escape (*NL* 108). In *My Bondage and My Freedom*, Douglass details his plans: "Once master of my own time, I felt sure that I could make, over and above my obligation to him, a dollar or two every week. Some slaves have made enough, in this way, to purchase their freedom. It is a sharp spur to industry; and some of the most enterprising colored men in Baltimore hire themselves in this way" (343).

But Douglass's process of becoming master of his own time was just as uneven as the nation's. When he fails to return on time one day, his master refuses to allow Douglass to work for wages any longer; as Douglass puts it, "Thus ended my partial freedom. I could hire my time no longer; and I obeyed my master's orders at once" (*MBMF* 344). Fortunately, Douglass's master relents as a result of Douglass's passive resistance—Douglass refuses to work at all and thus can no longer deliver to his master a portion of his wages. His master swiftly changes course, and Douglass is once again permitted to "hire his time" (*MBMF* 345). Just as soon as Douglass has saved enough money to escape, he promptly does so and ends up in the shipping town of New Bedford, Massachusetts. Although New Bedford turns out not to be the site of utter freedom and opportunity Douglass has hoped for, he does see its advantages over the South. For instance, he immediately notices the town's "Northern efficiency" (to misquote John F. Kennedy[40]):

How different was all this from the noisily fierce and clumsily absurd manner of labor-life in Baltimore and St. Michael's! One of the first incidents which illustrated the superior mental character of northern labor over that of the south, was the manner of unloading a ship's cargo of oil. In a southern port, twenty or thirty hands would have been employed to do what five or six did here, with the aid of a single ox attached to the end of a fall. Main strength, unassisted by skill, is slavery's method of labor. An old ox, worth eighty dollars, was doing, in New Bedford, what would have required fifteen thousand dollars worth of human bones and muscles to have performed in a southern port. I found that everything was done here with a scrupulous regard to economy, both in regard to men and things, time and strength. (*MBMF* 356)

Douglass understands that economy of time means modernity, and he represents his own movement to a modern state of being as very much temporal. In his third autobiography, he describes his escape from slavery, remarking: "Though I was not a murderer fleeing from justice, I felt, perhaps, quite as miserable as such a criminal. The train was moving at a very high rate of speed for that time of railroad travel, but to my anxious mind, it was moving far too slowly. Minutes were hours, and hours were days during this part of my flight" (*LT* 645). Here he articulates both his alienation from U.S. legal citizenship and his gradual incorporation into that citizenship in terms of time, including the standardized time established by the railways. Literally in transit, Douglass is also positioned figuratively between slave time and free time. On a train, not coincidentally the "engine" of the establishment of uniform U.S. time, Douglass occupies fugitive time, a temporal state of disorientation and dislocation preceding full citizenship and full, Hegelian modernity. Eventually, however, he will, it would appear, occupy standard U.S. time as a fully modern subject and citizen of the nation.

After his escape and his subsequent emergence as a powerful abolitionist on the national scene, Douglass grew ever more prominent as a racial and even a national representative. In 1871, he was appointed by President Ulysses S. Grant to the Santo Domingo Commission, charged with exploring the possibility of the United States' "annexing," to use Douglass's term, the island of Santo Domingo. Douglass initially supported annexation, and in an undated handwritten speech (likely from around 1870) he describes Santo Domingo as "standing on the verge of civilization," as if he now subscribes to Hegel's developmental model of history—at least in regard to Haiti and the Dominican Republic.[41] Becoming part of the United States would, he says, keep Santo Domingo from falling into "the depths of ignorance, weakness, and barbarism." He describes his own feelings as he first set foot on the island where Columbus arrived in 1492:

> I am only a distant relative of the Caucasian race and have only a *half* interest in the glory of its achievements, but even I must confess that I felt a peculiar thrill when for the first time in my life I stepped upon the soil where Caucasian civilization began its work in the new world. I know not now, and did not stop to consider then, whether there was any feeling of race connected with the sensation or not. Greatness does not ask permission of any race or nation as to what effect it shall produce upon them, it kindles enthusiasm in all who comprehend it and the measure of their comprehension is the measure of their enthusiasm.
>
> Hence, to stand upon that part of the American soil where Columbus first stood to breathe the first American air that Columbus first breathed, to view those grand old mountains covered with the rich verdure of perpetual summer, filling the sense far out over the sea with a delightful fragrance, lifting their soft-grayish blue summits, seven thousand feet between sea and sky and to know that they were the first lands to soothe and gladden the strained and fevered eyes of the great discoverer might kindle emotion in the most stolid American, of whatever color or race![42]

Douglass becomes most American when he becomes a partner in the processes of colonization and empire, and he understands his presence on the Santo Domingo Commission as an expression of his incorporation into the national body.[43] In *Life and Times,* he expressed that belongingness in terms of time:

> My selection to visit Santo Domingo with the commission sent thither, was another point indicating the difference between the OLD TIME and the NEW. It placed me on the deck of an American man-of-war, manned by one hundred marines and five hundred men-of-wars-men, under the national flag, which I could now call mine, in common with other American citizens, and gave me a place not in the fore-castle, among the hands, nor in the caboose with the cooks, but in the captain's saloon and in the society of gentlemen, scientists and statesmen. (847)

As Merline Pitre has suggested, what Douglass means here by "OLD TIME and the NEW" is not entirely clear; as Pitre puts it, the "new" time could simply signify Reconstruction, when "many blacks participated in the function of government, either by voting or through elective or appointive offices," but "it can also be seen as the period during which the pace of American imperialism quickened" and "a time when a comparatively militant black, like Frederick Douglass, would participate in a plan contemplating the extinction of one, if not two, republics controlled by men of color."[44] Douglass, in this reading, late in his career becomes not a representative black man and former slave but a citizen among citizens, one who has finally acquired Hegel's version of modernity as well as Anderson's "personhood." As of his third autobiography, Douglass was even able to speculate about his birth date: "From certain events, however, the dates of which I have since learned, I suppose myself to have been born in February, 1817" (*LT* 476). But there is some evidence that Douglass understands the temporal dimension of free and full citizenship, as he did slave time, as not merely personal but also collective, as his description of the glorious day of emancipation in the West Indies suggests:

> How vast, sudden, and startling was this transformation! In one moment, a mere tick of a watch, the twinkle of an eye, the glance of the morning sun, saw a bondage which had resisted the humanity of ages, defied earth and heaven, instantly ended; saw the slave-whip burnt to ashes; saw the slave's chains melted; saw his fetters broken and the irresponsible power of the slave-master over his victim forever destroyed. (*LT* 926)

Douglass here neatly expresses E. L. McCallum's much later idea that "citizenship has conventionally been conceived of in terms of space," but it "is inalienably conceived through time as well."[45] He likewise anticipates the imagination of an impossibly swift passage from old time to new time, from slavery to freedom, from empire to postcoloniality that is powerfully and sardonically expressed in Derek Walcott's verse line "And then there was no more Empire all of a sudden."[46] It turns out that Douglass's ascent to full citizenship may have been just as imaginative.

The ultimate public expression of that citizenship may well have been Douglass's 1889 appointment as U.S. consul-general to Haiti, a post he held for two years. In a well-known 1890 photographic portrait that Matthew

Photographic portrait of Frederick Douglass by Matthew Brady. 1890. Library of Congress, Rare Book and Special Collections Division, Daniel A. P. Murray Pamphlets Collection.

Brady made of Douglass, taken during his ambassadorship, Douglass's watch chain shows up so prominently as to be the picture's focal point. Here, near the end of his life, Douglass has become not just a citizen but an ambassador of the nation, with the watch signifying his status as a personage to whom time matters and who will matter to time. Counting hours signifies, at this point, not the regulation of Douglass's body and labor, whether in slavery or freedom, but the importance and busyness of a successful and representative American. He is free of what he termed the "method of counting time in slave districts" (*LT* 485); he is free of fugitive time; he occupies modern times and owns modern timekeeping technologies.

An awful irony lies in this written and photographic documentation of Douglass's representative American-ness and modernity—in such contrast to his undocumented birth—coming not only near the end of his life but at a time when African Americans were being systematically disenfranchised and terrorized. Douglass was of course well aware of this state of affairs. He was not so naïve as to believe that his citizenship, or that of any African American person, was unfettered or unmarked, regardless of how, or how fashionably, he kept time. On his return from his imperial mission to Santo Domingo in 1871, he alone among the commissioners was excluded from invitations to White House dinners. Two decades later, he was apparently pressured to resign his ambassadorship as a result of his growing and expressed dissatisfaction with U.S. policies toward Haiti.[47] When he married the white Helen Pitts in 1884, her father did not permit Douglass to enter his house. Douglass might have, for a couple of years at least, been an official representative of the nation outside its borders, but within its borders he was an African American living in an era that historian Rayford Logan famously identified as the "nadir" of race relations in the United States, a time when lynching was entering its peak years. Douglass spent much of the last stage of his career fighting the abrogation of African American civil rights that was taking place in the 1880s and 1890s. The year of his death, 1895, witnessed 113 documented lynchings of black Americans, along with the rise of the Ku Klux Klan, the passage and enforcement of state "black codes" restricting black franchise and other civil rights, and federal jurisprudence limiting African American citizenship.

The late nineteenth- and early twentieth-century African American authors who came after Douglass regularly and explicitly positioned their works within and against this context of injustice in the post-Reconstruction era. They, too, were quite aware of the ways African American people were being dragged back in time by the nation's failure to uphold the Civil Rights Acts of 1866 and 1875 and, especially, the Fourteenth Amendment, which ostensibly guaranteed full citizenship rights and due process for "all those born or naturalized in the United States." As Will Smith, the black hero of Pauline Hopkins's 1900 novel *Contending Forces*, declares, for African Americans at the end of the nineteenth century, "constitutional amendments are dead letters; the ballot-box is nil."[48] In the next chapter, I will explore how Hopkins and Charles Chesnutt, along with Frances Harper, Paul Laurence Dunbar, and Sutton Griggs, understood and used the novel as a simultaneously aesthetic, temporal, and philosophical vehicle through which to protest and attempt to remedy the injustices of their times—and to imagine a better future.

2

"Temporal Damage": Pragmatism and *Plessy* in African American Novels, 1896–1902

Invisibility, let me explain, gives one a slightly different sense of time, you're never quite on the beat. Sometimes you're ahead and sometimes you're behind.

—Ralph Ellison, *Invisible Man*

In 1853 when William Wells Brown's *Clotel; or, The President's Daughter*, believed to be the first African American–authored novel, was published, black people in the United States—regardless of region, class, free or slave status, or skin tone—could be fully African *American* only in fiction. That this first sustained African American fiction was about Thomas Jefferson's slave mistress and their daughters and granddaughters highlights the instrumentalism of the first published African American novel and of the four, known to date, that followed it in the mid-nineteenth century. As William Andrews has suggested, the authors of these novels turned to fiction, to "novelization" (following Bakhtin), to represent "the insufficiency, if not the collapse, of recognized authority in the world experienced by" African Americans of the period.[1] Indeed, it is no coincidence that *Clotel*, along with Frank Webb's novel *The Garies and Their Friends* (1857), Harriet Wilson's *Our Nig* (1859),[2] and Martin Delany's *Blake* (serially, 1861–62), were written and published in the era of the 1850 Fugitive Slave Act and the 1857 Dred Scott decision. Even Frederick Douglass's novella *The Heroic Slave* (1853) and Julia Collins's recently rediscovered novel *The Curse of Caste* (serialized in 1865) date from the years from 1853 to 1865. African American novels thus arose at a time when Congress and the Supreme Court appeared almost to be conspiring to deny citizenship to black people.

At just this time, when recognized *legal* authority, specifically, most actively sought to punish blackness and curtail black citizenship in what Eric Sundquist has termed "living reality," or what philosophical pragmatists at the time might have termed "experience," the first African American

novels asserted varied and sustained forms of individual black subjectivity.[3] As a sympathetic white "gentleman" in Webb's *The Garies and Their
Friends* remarks, for "Negroes," "there is no such thing as justice to be ob-
tained in any of the State courts."[4] Apparently this gentleman perceived,
four decades beforehand, that Oliver Wendell Holmes's pragmatic 1897
notion that a long-sitting judge will reach "the proper conclusion" as a result of his "fund of experience which enables him represent the common
sense of the community" would apply strictly to the *white* community.[5]
Note that this scene from *The Garies* takes place on a train, as the youngest
black hero of the novel, Charlie Ellis, and his older white woman companion and patron, Mrs. Bird, are being forced by the conductor and "one or
two of the Irish brake-men" to move "into the negro car" (111). The white
gentleman urges Mrs. Bird to comply, warning her that he "saw a coloured
man ejected from here last week, and severely injured" (111). Via this
representation of the Jim Crow car and an immigrant presence, along with
the omnipresent and *predictable* threat of violence and lynching, Webb at
midcentury efficiently presages both the many train scenes to come in
later African American novels and, inextricably, how those novels would
respond to the failures of the post-Reconstruction era, especially the landmark Supreme Court decisions of the late nineteenth century regarding
the allocation of U.S. citizenship.

By the end of the nineteenth century, African Americans could "obtain
justice" neither in "State courts" nor in federal courts. With his majority
opinion in the *Plessy v. Ferguson* (1896) Supreme Court decision uphold-
ing the constitutionality of Jim Crow streetcars in Louisiana, Justice Henry
Billings Brown rendered segregation the law of the land: "We think that
the enforced separation of the races, as applied to the internal commerce
of the State, neither abridges the privileges or immunities of the colored
man, deprives him of his property without due process of law, nor denies
him the equal protection of the laws, within the meaning of the Fourteenth Amendment."[6] The genealogy of African American novels in the
second half of the century bears out a reading of the form as a literary
intervention being conducted in response to such increasingly hostile
federal constructions of blackness. After the appearance of the first five
published African American–authored novels known to date, only a few
more appeared during the 1860s, the 1870s, and the better part of the 1880s:
Frances Harper's serialized works *Minnie's Sacrifice* (1869), *Sowing and
Reaping* (1876–77), and *Trial and Triumph* (1888–89), along with Thomas

Detter's *Nellie Brown; or, The Jealous Wife* (1871). Granted, as Frances Smith Foster has argued, "some of our received knowledge about African American literary heritage is misinformed and incomplete," so it is quite possible that more long works of African American fiction will be recovered from those years.[7] Nonetheless, it seems clear that there was a surge in the publication of African American novels in the post-Reconstruction era, with the prominent writers Frances Harper, Sutton Griggs, Pauline Hopkins, Charles Chesnutt, and Paul Laurence Dunbar all producing at least one novel between 1891 and 1903. Indeed, the period offered more than enough content.

The 1880s and 1890s witnessed the failure of Reconstruction, the rise of the Ku Klux Klan, the passage of state Black Codes, the peak years of lynching, and, of course, *Plessy v. Ferguson*. Virtually every late nineteenth-century African American novel explicitly addresses the period's state and federal laws enforcing black subjection: clear evidence that their authors were acutely aware of, and were just as clearly protesting and representing alternatives to, the regression in juridical constructions of blackness that characterized the era. As Gregg D. Crane concisely puts it, "race provided the most intense and challenging spur to higher law debate in the nineteenth century."[8] In response, African American writers of the period, particularly Chesnutt and Hopkins, used the novel to write against the post-Emancipation legal "constitution of blackness as an abject and degraded condition," to use Saidiya Hartman's words.[9] As a character in Sutton Griggs's novel 1899 novel *Imperium in Imperio* remarks, "the Supreme Court of the United States, it seems, may be relied upon to sustain any law born of prejudice against the Negro, and to demolish any law constructed in his interest. Witness the Dred Scott decision, and in keeping with this, the decision on the Civil Rights Bill and Separate Coach Law."[10] Ironically, Griggs and other African American novelists of the time were also struggling to find narrative forms, including the speculative fiction of *Imperium in Imperio* itself, to suit a "new" kind of African American, one who could pave the way for what Griggs's novel terms "the New Negro" (163). These writers repeatedly confronted conflicts between their own desire to "move forward," to use William James's apposite formulation, into a (possibly postracial, and certainly more just) future and the nation's steady refusal to permit them to do so.[11] In this literary-political struggle, the novel became an instrument of choice—but not the only one.

Other forms of African American writing were likewise thriving at the end of the nineteenth century, particularly nonfiction prose in newspapers and magazines. Dozens of local African American newspapers began publication between 1890 and 1900, among them the *St. Paul Broad Axe* in 1891, the *Baltimore Afro-American* in 1893, the *Kansas City American Citizen* in 1897, the *Washington (D.C.) Colored American* (the newspaper rather than the magazine) in 1898, the relatively long-lived *Topeka Plaindealer* in 1899 (it ceased publication in 1931), and the *Portland (Ore.) New Age* in 1900. Influential national African American periodicals began publication in these years as well. *The Woman's Era*, the official organ of the black women's club movement, was first published in 1894; the *Colored American Magazine* was founded in 1900, according to Hazel Carby, "as a direct response to the political climate at the turn of the century—that is, to black disenfranchisement, Jim Crow laws, the widespread murder of black people in the South, and political apathy in the North."[12] Still, nearly all prominent late nineteenth-century African American writers eventually turned to the novel, including those who had already written and published widely in periodicals. Hopkins, a frequent contributor to and briefly editor of *Colored American*, wrote four novels, three of which were serialized in it.[13] Chesnutt, although his *Atlantic Monthly* "conjure stories" garnered him far more popularity and success, began writing novels at the turn of the century (his first, *The House behind the Cedars*, was published in 1900), reserving his starkest and most impassioned political content for that form. Likewise, Dunbar, who was best known and appreciated for his dialect poems, turned to the novel with *Sport of the Gods* (1902), an utterly bleak exploration of a deeply racialized and racist miscarriage of justice. Harper, too, had achieved success with poetry and speeches long before she published her first novel, *Iola Leroy*, in 1892, when she was sixty-seven. The questions naturally arise: Why novels? Why then? And why for these particular authors?

It is a commonplace, at least since Ian Watt's *The Rise of the Novel*, that the genealogy of the English novel coincides with the rise of the bourgeois individual. As Watt put it, "the society must value every individual highly enough to consider him the proper subject of its serious literature."[14] In Nancy Armstrong's more recent, and bolder, formulation, novels, regardless of their location in a national tradition or particular period, "think like individuals about the difficulties of fulfilling oneself as an individual under specific cultural historical conditions," to such an extent that, in her view, "the history of the novel and the history of the modern subject are, quite literally, one and the same."[15] Even if one balks at the notion of a novel "thinking," or at such a blunt equation of novel and human subject, it is probably easy to agree with a slightly revised formulation: that novels written in English during the past three centuries quite often center on an individual's negotiation of period-specific material and social conditions. African American novels around the turn of the twentieth century, or at the very least their authors, had to "think" about the "historical condition" of a nation that was not just devaluing "Negroes" but refusing to consider them as individuals at all. African American novels between 1896 and 1902 were therefore "thinking" about what to do about the nation's aggressive reassertion of white supremacy. African American writers turned particularly and pragmatically to the novel, a form in the business of "reproducing modern individuals," as a literary-political strategy in a national time when neither modernity nor individuality was allocated equally.[16]

Granted, there are many other material, social, literary-historical, and economic reasons—in addition to the urgency of legal protest and the assertion of black subjectivity at the "nadir"—for this surge in the writing and publishing of African American novels. At the very least, it must also be seen as part of a generally expansive American literary picture in and immediately following the Gilded Age. Chesnutt's fiction, for example, easily can be and has been read in the context of the rise and predominance of American realism, regionalism, and local color, placing him in the company of Mark Twain, Sarah Orne Jewett, and Hamlin Garland. Yet we can equally easily and legitimately draw a connection between the state of black citizenship and the state of black U.S. literary production from the late 1860s to the end of the century, while also drawing a distinction between white U.S. fiction and African American fiction of the period. Whereas Twain and Jewett were engaged, at least in part, in epistemological nostalgia in their best known works, Chesnutt and Hopkins were writing of the dangers of prior ways of knowing that threatened to bind African Americans perpetually to the past and to noncitizen status. *Huckleberry Finn,* for instance, registers with some sadness the passing away of seemingly universal, especially (but not only) rural boyhood knowledge and ways of life: how to build a raft; how to catch, clean, and cook fish; how to determine gender definitively in a crossdresser, and so on. Likewise, Sarah Orne Jewett registers and mourns the passing of traditional rural ways of life in Maine. At the same time, Thomas Nelson Page and

Thomas Dixon (perhaps not coincidentally, both were lawyers as well as writers) were promulgating a far more retrograde and damaging form of nostalgia in plantation tradition novels that imagined glorious days of slavery gone by, contributing substantially to what Sundquist terms the period's (white) "Confederate nostalgia" (233). Pauline Hopkins, by contrast, sounds the alarm about any possible return to the social and economic practices or epistemologies of the past, filtering them through the legal reality of the contemporary (for her) disenfranchisement of African Americans. In her 1902 novel *Winona*, set entirely before the Civil War, Hopkins's narrator says the following about postbellum "Black Codes" in Southern states restricting African American civil rights, particularly voting rights:

> With the memory of recent happenings in the beautiful Southland, against the Negro voter, engraved upon our hearts, these words [a violently proslavery speech delivered in 1854] have a too familiar sound. No, there is very little advancement in that section since 1854, viewed in the light of Gov. Davis' recent action. The South would be as great as were her fathers "if like a crab she could go backward." Reversion is the only god worshipped by the South.[17]

In this passage, the narrator brings the novel's narration, if not its action, into the present, asserting the not simply anachronistic but devolved nature of the period's racial injustice and violence.

The "recent action" Hopkins's narrator mentions may well refer to an actual incident in 1902. "Gov. Davis" is likely Jefferson "Jeff" Davis (named after, but no relation to, the former president of the Confederacy), who was governor of Arkansas from 1901 to 1907. Davis, well known both as a racist and as a colorful speaker, was fond of "wearing the garb common to politicians half a century before," and, in historian Richard L. Niswonger's words, believed that "enfranchisement was despicable" and black voters were, as Davis himself once put it, an "'ever present eating, cankerous sore.'"[18] Among the most notorious of his actions while in office was his 1902 pardon of Andrew Johnson, an African American man convicted of a crime (that newspapers variously reported as assault or burglary), an incident that made national news in both white and black venues. As the (African American) *Topeka Plaindealer* reported, Davis had granted the pardon "on the condition that the liberated man go at once to Massachusetts to become a citizen," because, quoting Davis, of "the many expressions of sympathy by the citizens of Massachusetts for what they were pleased to call the 'the poor, oppressed Negro of the South.'"[19] The *Plaindealer* assessed this pardon as part of Davis's attempt to carry forward the agenda of the *other* Jefferson Davis, "his departed chieftain," "by the nullification of the 13th and 14th amendments" and "by enacting black laws."[20] The *New York Times* called the incident an "outrage" without specifying the nature of that outrage.[21] The (white) *Telegraph* of Macon, Georgia, had a rather different take, reporting that Davis "seems to like the results of his first experiment. He writes to a friend in Texas that he is going to send as many negroes to New England as he can, and 'hopes the other Southern states will join him in this enterprise.' The Telegraph hopes so too, having long believed that this is the next best way to solve the negro problem."[22]

Niswonger notes that the pardon was first covered in the *Little Rock Arkansas Gazette* on May 9 and 10, 1902; *Winona* was serialized in the May–October 1902 issues of the *Colored American*.[23] By serializing her novel, Hopkins capitalized at once on the capacity of journalism to cover contemporary events as they were happening and on the capacity of the novel to represent crossgenerational racial oppression that, in her time, seemed to be rendering the present nearly indistinguishable from the past.

Such "reversion" concerned not just Hopkins but all African American writers in the post-Reconstruction era, and the Jim Crow car often provided them with the ideal setting in which to explore the regression they associated with the South. In Hopkins's *Contending Forces* (1900), her distraught and beautiful light-skinned heroine, Sappho, is traveling from Boston to New Orleans by train: "She did not mind anything now. As she moved farther south the brutality of the conductor who ordered her out of the comfortable day-coach into the dirt and discomfort of the 'Jim crow' car, with the remark that 'white niggers couldn't impose on him; he reckoned he knew 'em,' failed to arouse her."[24] Here, as in *The Garies and Their Friends*, a black character, regardless of racial mixture or gender or class, is forced to ride Jim Crow cars down south (by a conductor imbued with the power to determine race) but is also, quite reasonably, too exhausted or afraid to resist this very public form of segregation and discrimination. These scenes recur so often in the African American literary tradition as to constitute *stock scenes* that encapsulate the always-potentially-violent intersection of blackness, law, and time. Indeed, in nearly all nineteenth-century African American novels, modern modes of conveyance serve, painfully and paradoxically, to reinforce the noncitizenship status of African Americans, with the threat of lynching ever-present as a consequence for challenging that status (presumably that is the Macon *Telegraph*'s imagined *first* "best way to solve the negro problem").

These stock scenes also connect African American novels of the late nineteenth century to—or, more precisely, disconnect them from—both the period's white-authored fiction and philosophical pragmatism's origins during the same years. And it makes sense that such moments of legally shaped, even determined, experience would put African American novelists in conversation with pragmatism, which was, uniquely among major philosophical movements, from the first a legal as well as a philosophical school of thought. Oliver Wendell Holmes, was, after all, a Massachusetts Supreme Court justice from 1882 to 1902 and a U.S. Supreme Court justice from 1902 to 1932. He, along with Charles Sanders Peirce and William James, helped establish pragmatism as one of the most influential of all American philosophical movements.

In 1878, Peirce published in *Popular Science Monthly* what would come to be considered the founding text of pragmatism, "How to Make Our Ideas Clear." Although he did not use the term "pragmatism," Peirce presented in the essay what were to become some of the movement's basic tenets, including a rejection of Cartesian infallibilism and an embrace of philosophy undertaken rationally, like science, guided by what William James later termed Peirce's "principle of pragmatism" or what is often termed the "pragmatist maxim":[25] "Consider what effects, which might conceivably have practical bearings, we conceive the object of our conception to have. Then, our conception of those effects is the whole of our conception of the object."[26] In other words, practical effects produce belief; what we believe to be true is founded on what we experience. Or, as Louis Menand concisely explains, "if behaving as though we had free will or God exists gets us the results we want, we will not only come to believe those things; they will be, pragmatically, true."[27] The 1870s–1880s pragmatism of Peirce, Holmes, and James, particularly its anti-ideological and antiabsolutist bent, must be understood as offering solace and some possibility of resolution and progress, a way into the future in the aftermath of the Civil War and what Edward Purcell sums up as the nation's "deep sectional conflict and moral crisis."[28] That strong appeal helps explain, at least in part, why pragmatism became the predominant philosophical movement in the United States around the turn of the twentieth century.[29]

This is not to say that pragmatism was uncontroversial at the time of its origin (or since, for that matter). A number of philosophers in the late nineteenth century registered alarm about the movement's apparent moral relativism. Bertrand Russell, for one, famously decried the dangers of pragmatist philosophy, declaring in 1909: "In the absence of any standard of truth other than success, it seems evident that the familiar methods of the struggle for existence must be applied to the elucidation of difficult questions, and that ironclads and Maxim guns must be the ultimate arbiters of metaphysical truth."[30] Russell had a point. Because experience was, quite clearly, not universal in the post-Reconstruction era when pragmatism arose—nor is it in any era—then, "pragmatically" speaking, there will always be competing beliefs and therefore competing truths. And this is the case even if one defines experience not as individual in nature but as collective or cultural, as the pragmatists did. Such a state of affairs would not likely bother them, for, as pragmatists, they comfortably accepted beliefs and truths as contingent and experience-based, as in William James's well-known formulation "*The true is the name of whatever proves itself to be good in the way of belief, and good, too, for definite assignable reasons.*"[31] Russell worried above all about this central premise, arguing that pragmatism is a "power-philosophy" that "gives to those in power a metaphysical omnipotence which a more pedestrian philosophy would deny to them."[32] In Russell's view, some truths will inevitably prevail over others, with the result that "practical bearings" might result in harm to some and benefit to others. That ethical differential—what is "good in the way of belief" for some is not necessarily good for all—was starkly apparent in the United States when pragmatism emerged. As Sundquist observes, "the problem of segregation—the theory, fact, and the living reality of segregation—was the defining legal and social experience of the late nineteenth century for many Americans" (11). Of course, it is not news that the founders of pragmatism, Peirce, James, and Holmes, did not reside at the progressive, cutting edge of racial thought in the late 1800s. Menand, for one, has made a strong case for their being very much (white) men of their times on this score as on others, reminding us that they were "not in radical opposition" to "the conditions of modern life" in America.[33] In other words, while the pragmatists might have been able to avoid past metaphysical philosophy's "penalty of anachronism," paid for aiming at transcendental truth, they were not able to escape the penalty of their own situated beliefs—that is, the contingency of all ideas (including their own) that they themselves posited (362). "If we are looking for alternative visions of American life in the decades following the Civil War," Menand concludes, "Holmes, James, Peirce, and Dewey are not the figures we should turn to" (xi).

Some figures we *can* productively turn to in the period for "alternative visions" of national life, visions that also offer strong challenges to pragmatism's myopia regarding race, are African American writers at the turn of the twentieth century. Just as Frederick Douglass implicitly engaged and challenged Hegel, Frances Harper, Sutton Griggs, Pauline Hopkins, Charles Chesnutt, and Paul Laurence Dunbar engaged and challenged Charles Peirce, William James, and Oliver Wendell Holmes. However, unlike Douglass, who issued his implicit challenge to Hegel fourteen years after Hegel's death, these novelists contended with the pragmatists on their own terms and *at the same time* that they were advancing those terms. In 1896, of all years, James wrote: "Our errors are surely not such awfully solemn things," calling for "a certain lightness of heart" about them.[34] As a group, African American novelists around 1896 implicitly critiqued the limitations, one might say the errors, of philosophical pragmatism on the grounds of race, law, and time (and their intersection), errors thrown into relief by the individual and the collective experiences of African Americans. In the process, the novelists revealed themselves and their characters to be at once contemporaneous—like the pragmatists, situated in their own times, for better and for worse—*and* doubly anachronistic, being pulled back toward the past by the period's jurisprudence even as they were imaginatively inhabiting a more just future.

In 1899, Charles Chesnutt delivered a speech, "Literature in Its Relation to Life (The Relation of Literature to Life)," to the Bethel Literary and Historical Association, a major African American political and literary forum founded in 1881 in Washington, D.C. In his speech, Chesnutt offered the following by way of explanation of his title and topic:

> Literature may be viewed in two aspects—as an expression of life, past and present, and as a force directly affecting the conduct of life, present and future. I might call these the subjective and objective sides of literature—or, more lucidly, the historical; and the dynamic, the forceful, impelling. History is instructive, and may warn or admonish; but to this quality literature adds the faculty of persuasion, by which men's hearts are reached, the springs of action touched, and the currents of life directed.[35]

Chesnutt here builds a literary-historical framework into which nearly all late nineteenth-century and early twentieth-century African American novels can fit—certainly all those published between 1896 and 1902. If Peirce famously posited a "laboratory-philosophy"[36] wherein men "animated by the true scientific Eros"[37] would test philosophical hypotheses, then African American authors in the same period were "forced to some experiment" to quote from Harriet Wilson's preface to her novel *Our Nig*. These authors were testing political hypotheses via their literary representations of a truly free individual black subject even under the "historical conditions" of Jim Crow.[38]

In their "laboratory-literature," African American writers were producing novels in order to "warn" and "admonish" and to "reach men's hearts, touch the springs of action, and direct the currents of life" toward establishing African American citizenship and securing justice for all. That interested nature of their literary experiments in and of itself challenged pragmatist philosophy. Peirce had explicitly and ardently aimed to distinguish "Philosophy" from "Practice," arguing that in philosophy, as "in physiology and in chemistry," the "true scientific investigator completely loses sight of the utility of what he is about."[39] Peirce was also famously dismissive of any connection between a scientific, uninterested philosophy and the "moral influence" of literature: "There is no philosopher of any age who mixes poetry with philosophy with such effrontery as Plato."[40] Yet other pragmatist tenets could readily be adapted for the purposes of the novelists. If for William James *"theories thus become instruments,"* means by "which existing realities may be *changed*," then African American novels in the post-Reconstruction era became instruments in the struggle to "make" not "nature," as James says, but the *nation* "over again by their aid," allowing their authors to imagine how to "move forward" toward justice.[41] This is not to argue that their novelistic enterprise was strictly utilitarian; Chesnutt himself prefaced his definition of "literature" with a kind of Arnoldian aesthetics: "Literature should include all that body of writings of which form constitutes an important element, and which, by virtue of their form . . . are likely to be preserved for some length of time. . . . Only when our best thoughts have passed laboriously, and painfully for the most part, through the loom of language . . . —then and only then do they rise to the dignity of literature."[42] Yet Chesnutt's thesis remains, essentially, that literature serves a purpose and that it reflects a national reality; in his words, "would you know a nation, read its books."[43]

Just so, from the very beginning, African American novels fulfilled an instrumentalist role through their conscious interweaving of past and present, history and activism, so as to permit their authors to create a vision of a deeply flawed present, flawed inasmuch as it was mired in race, indeed in racism, *and* in the past—and pragmatism was as mired in them as was *Plessy*.

In "How to Make Our Ideas Clear," Peirce explains pragmatism by drawing several examples from experiences of travel. When explaining the relationship between "Doubt and Belief" (for Peirce, the tension between the two often provides the initial spark for philosophical thought), he offers the example of deciding what sort of coins to use to pay his fare "in a horse-car" (128). Despite its apparently trivial nature, Peirce explains, this moment of "such small mental activity" effectively demonstrates that "most frequently doubts arise from some indecision, however momentary, in our action" (128). He elaborates by means of another transportation example: "I have, for example, to wait in a railway-station, and to pass the time I read the advertisements on the walls, I compare the advantages of different trains and different routes which I never expect to take, merely fancying myself to be in a state of hesitancy, because I am bored with having nothing to trouble me" (128). Peirce argues that this "feigned hesitancy," like the actual hesitancy in the earlier horsecar fare example, functions to spur decision and then, in turn, belief (128). Yet it is difficult to imagine a less trivial, less untroubled site for African Americans at that time than any public conveyance; in 1878, as Peirce is writing, no African American person could possibly view imagining "different trains and different routes" as an experience linked to, or emerging out of, low-stakes boredom. If, as Holmes famously declared in 1881, "the life of the law has not been logic; it has been experience,"[44] then African American writers at the time were quick to point out the ways both the law *and* experience—on a broad social as well as on an individual scale—were racially distinct in the United States in the late nineteenth century. And that intersection of law and (racialized) experience was, if anything, *especially* evident on the railway. As Sundquist remarks, "the train car was easily one of the most charged symbols of racial politics in American culture, a field of ritual drama" (439).

The often not merely dramatic but traumatic experience of railway travel was repeatedly examined and analyzed in African American novels well into the twentieth century, from Frank Webb's *Garies* to Hopkins's

Contending Forces and to James Weldon Johnson's *Autobiography of an Ex-Colored Man* (1912), in which the narrator explains:

> The effort is sometimes made to convey the impression that the better class of colored people fight against riding in "Jim Crow" cars because they want to ride with white people or object to riding with humbler members of their own race. The truth is they object to the humiliation of being forced to ride in a *particular* car, aside from the fact that the car is distinctly inferior, and that they are required to pay full first-class fare. To say that whites are forced to ride in the superior car is less than a joke. And, too, odd as it may sound, refined colored people get no more pleasure out of riding with offensive Negroes than anybody else would get.[45]

Such recurring, deeply troubled representations of conveyance in the African American literary tradition, in stark contrast to Peirce's own untroubled state, reveal that at least some of pragmatism's origins were tied up with, perhaps even dependent on, racially distinct "ways of thinking," as well as racially distinct material experiences.

Indeed, in Peirce's writings, we can locate other examples and demonstrations clearly intended to be experientially neutral or universal but that just as clearly testify to racial, class, or national specificity. In explaining his terminology for philosophical logic or reasoning, what Nathan Houser and Christian Kloesel term Peirce's "best-known semiotic triad (icon, index, symbol)," Peirce offers the following: "The pole star is an *index*, or pointing finger, to show us which way is north."[46] On determining probability through mathematical calculation, Peirce offers the examples of "the number of inhabitants to a dwelling in New York" and "the average number of children in families living in New York."[47] And perhaps most notoriously, one of his favorite examples of what Peirce termed "abduction," or the human ability to make decisions based on subliminal cues, involved his loss of an overcoat and a watch while on a steamship trip to New York in 1879. The watch, as Kenneth Ketner puts it, "was no ordinary timepiece, but a prize chronometer in a gold hunting case, designed for Tiffany's by Charles Frodsham. The watch was bought for Peirce by the United States Coast and Geodetic Survey for use in his pendulum research."[48] According to Peirce, on discovering his loss, he

then made all the colored waiters, no matter on what deck they belonged, come up and stand in a row. . . . I went from one end of the
row to the other, and talked a little to each one, in as *dégagé* a manner as I could, about whatever he could talk about with interest, but
would least expect me to bring forward, hoping that I might seem
such a fool that I should be able to detect some symptom of his being
the thief. When I had gone through the row I turned and walked
from them, though not away and said to myself, "Not the least scin-
tilla of light have I got to go upon." But thereupon my other self (for
our communings are always in dialogues) said to me, "But you simply *must* put your finger on the man. No matter if you have no reason, you must say whom you will think to be the thief." I made a little
loop in my walk, which had not taken a minute, and as I turned toward them, all shadow of doubt had vanished. There was no self-
criticism. All that was out of place.[49]

The watch was soon recovered from a New York pawnshop, and the pawn-
broker, in Peirce's words, "described the person who pawned the watch so
graphically that no doubt was possible that it had been 'my man'" (20). He
immediately wrote to an official of the Survey, which had given Peirce the
watch, to boast of his success: "The two negroes who stole the watch were
today committed for trial. Everything is recovered. The thief is the very
man I suspected throughout contrary to the judgment of the detective"
(22). Peirce also wrote to William James that this incident demonstrated
his "theory of why it is that people so often guess right" (22).

It is hard to imagine a more thoroughgoing demonstration than this
watch incident, if not of abduction, then certainly of how some pragmatist
thought and writing emerged right at the intersection of race, time, and
the law. Peirce's anecdote depends first on his possession of a fine timepiece
that is both like and unlike Douglass's watch in the 1890 Brady photograph
and Bigger Thomas's new watch in *Native Son*. For all three men, the timepiece signifies social and professional ascent, but Peirce's Tiffany-designed
"prize chronometer" places him unreachably beyond the station of an African American man in 1879 and at the cutting edge of mathematical and
technological inquiry. And while Peirce's Geodetic Survey research centered on gravity and hydrodynamics, nonetheless the pendulum is, fundamentally, a chronometer. Time and its measure thus underlie Peirce's
work and the recognition of that work; "waiters" must not take either. So

Peirce summons all of them, "no matter on what deck they belonged," enacting a belief in the potential criminality of all black men. Indeed, there was no "light," no conscious rational process, Peirce could access in the face of such undifferentiated, impenetrable (for him) blackness. The theft thus provides Peirce with an occasion to reinforce the period's deindividuation of African Americans that was, in turn, keeping them back in time; Chesnutt and Hopkins would soon respond to such injustices via a literary technology of the individual.

Although their role in the philosophical debates of their day has generally been overlooked, Chesnutt, Hopkins, and other writers of late nineteenth-century African American novels developed a politically invested form of the novel that served to disclose the racial specificity embedded in philosophical pragmatism as encapsulated in Peirce's abduction demonstration, one that took place, not coincidentally, on yet another mode of conveyance. These novels offer scene after scene taking place at the same intersection of race, law, time, and travel. For example, the narrator of Charles Chesnutt's 1901 novel *The Marrow of Tradition*, describes an encounter aboard a train between "two acquaintances," the black hero of the novel, Dr. Miller, and his white colleague, Dr. Burns, who are both traveling via train from Philadelphia to Wellington, North Carolina:

> A celebrated traveler, after many years spent in barbarous or savage lands, has said that among all varieties of mankind the similarities are vastly more important than the differences. Looking at these two men with the American eye, the differences would perhaps be the more striking, or at least the more immediately apparent, for the first was white and the second black, or, more correctly speaking, brown; it was even a light brown, but both his swarthy complexion and his curly hair revealed what has been described in the laws of some our states as a "visible admixture" of African blood.[50]

Here Chesnutt offers one of those "alternative visions of American life" Menand mentions, and ironically enough, that vision describes in turn a colonial vision broader and more egalitarian than a national one. The vision of "the American eye" is narrowed by a racialization that in turn is (variously and inconsistently) codified by state law. Indeed, in Chesnutt's first novel, *The House behind the Cedars*, a sympathetic white judge counseling a mixed race young man on where best to pass for white "took down a volume bound in legal calf" to study varying states' legal definitions of blackness:

> "The color line is drawn in North Carolina at four generations removed from the Negro. . . . But let us see what South Carolina may say about it," he continued, taking another book. . . . "'The term mulatto,'" he read, "'is not invariably applicable to every admixture of African blood. . . . Juries would probably be justified in holding a person to be white in whom the admixture of blood did not exceed one eighth.'"[51]

These two passages juxtapose transnational ideas of human sameness with nation- and state-based ideas of human racial difference. The first actually sounds rather like Holmes's admonition in *The Common Law* (1881) that we neither assume our current laws are based on transcendental, ahistorical truth nor ask "too much of history" by assuming that we have, in teleological fashion, finally arrived at the most fully evolved form of law: "It may be assumed that the earliest barbarian whose practices are to be considered, had a good many of the same feelings and passions as ourselves" (2). What Holmes leaves out but Chesnutt's novels carefully include is the fact that the law works to create, determine, and reinforce race itself and therefore racial experience and knowledge, complicating Holmes's notion of experience as the natural basis of law, what he terms the "fair teaching of experience" (123). And from that fact, Chesnutt, himself trained in the law, delivers his fundamental challenge to pragmatism, one that continues to unfold, in *The Marrow of Tradition*, on the Jim Crow car.

When Dr. Miller and Dr. Burns are asked in Richmond to transfer from their sleeper car to day coaches, "Miller stood a moment hesitatingly, but finally took the seat indicated [next to Dr. Burns in the white car]" (76). Miller's "indecision, however momentary" stems from his and other African Americans' experiences of what it means for a visibly "Negro" person to sit in the white car.[52] Unlike the white Dr. Burns, Dr. Miller can readily predict the likely outcome of his decision, the resolution of his "hesitancy," because of the "fair teaching" of *racial* experience. This particular application is probably not what Holmes meant when he defined the law as "systematized prediction," but it is certainly what Chesnutt means: the law is systematically racial and predictably discriminatory and threatening for black people.[53] In fact, the train conductor promptly insists that

Miller relocate to the Jim Crow car. Over the objections of Dr. Burns, Miller complies, explaining: "It is the law, and we are powerless to resist it. If we made any trouble, it would merely delay our journey and imperil a life at the other end. I'll go into the other car" (78). Although Miller is apparently referring to a very ill Wellington patient whom the two physicians plan to treat together, we can readily infer that Miller's life, too, would be, predictably, imperiled (by lynching) should he challenge segregation in the train cars. The narrator of the novel refers to this implicit possible fate as the "judicial strangulation" of "black, or yellow, or poor-white," "a not uncommon form of taking off, usually resultant upon the infraction of certain laws, or, in these swift modern days, upon too violent a departure from established social customs" (50). Of course, even in the absence of such a clear pragmatist context, it should not be surprising that a Jim Crow car scene takes place in so many African American texts after 1896, the year the U.S. Supreme Court in *Plessy* upheld the "constitutionality of an act of the General Assembly of the State of Louisiana, passed in 1890, providing for separate railway carriages for the white and colored races."

It is hard to overstate the influence on African American literature, in the period immediately after *Plessy,* of the Court's rendering "equal, but separate, accommodations for the white and colored races" the law of the land. Yet many scholars of the literature have focused in recent years on late nineteenth-century African American authors' participation in, or challenge to, notions of race as biology, aiming to determine to what degree Hopkins, Chesnutt, and other late nineteenth-century African American novelists were racial essentialists. But these writers far more directly and obviously challenged *legal* constructions of race, which had a greater and more immediate—one might say pragmatic—impact on the daily lives of those the state determined to be "Negro" than did abstract ideas about race as either biological reality or social construction.[54] And, as the foregoing scenes from *The Garies and Their Friends, Contending Forces, The Autobiography of an Ex-Colored Man,* and *The Marrow of Tradition* suggest, both quotidian and legal constructions of race and citizenship played out dramatically and substantially on board the train.[55] As Edlie L. Wong has recently argued, the assertion of the "right of locomotion as the bodily practice of national citizenship" is a, if not *the,* fundamental expression of full citizenship, and as such constituted a central line of argument for Justice John Marshall Harlan in his dissenting opinion in *Plessy.*[56] In Harlan's words in the dissent,

"Personal liberty," it has been well said, "consists in the power of locomotion, of changing situation, or removing one's person to whatsoever places one's own inclination may direct, without imprisonment or restraint, unless by due course of law." If a white man and a black man choose to occupy the same public conveyance on a public highway, it is their right to do so, and no government, proceeding alone on grounds of race, can prevent it without infringing the personal liberty of each.[57]

Wong concludes that "racial regulations" regarding travel in the nineteenth century, including *Plessy*, "redefined the individual right to travel as normatively *white* and infringed on the civil rights" of "all citizens regardless of race."[58] Although Wong is certainly right about freedom of travel as requisite for full citizenship, her analysis of nineteenth-century travel "as normatively white" does not quite match the complexities of the period's representations of travel by train either in *Plessy* or in African American novels. The period's "American eye"—whether the beholder was Justice Henry Billings Brown, Justice Harlan, Charles Peirce, Charles Chesnutt, or Pauline Hopkins (or their characters and narrators)—perceived more than simply "a white man and a black man."

Just so, the Jim Crow car scene in The *Marrow of Tradition* is further elaborated, as Dr. Miller, who "was something of a philosopher," observes and contemplates the comings and goings once he is on board (81).[59] One might say Miller engages not in "small" but in expansive, detailed, and intense "mental activity" as considers his experience on the train. While waiting on board between stops, he is joined by "quite a party of farm laborers, fresh from their daily toil, [who] swarmed out from the conspicuously labeled colored waiting-room . . . [and] were noisy, loquacious, happy, dirty, and malodorous" (82). At first, Miller "was amused and pleased" by the black workers (82). But after a while, he seeks relief on the platform because "the air became too close"; for Miller in 1901, as for the ex-colored man in 1912, "personally, and apart from the mere matter of racial sympathy, these people were just as offensive to him as to the whites on the other end of the train" (82). Miller dilates further still on the social picture of the Jim Crow car, observing at the first stop "a huge negro," a stowaway on one of the rear cars, drinking from a bucket and "plunging his head into the water," and who then "shook himself like a wet dog" and returned to his hiding place (81). An actual dog later boards the train from the rear car; Miller finds him a "handsome dog" and thinks to himself that he "would not have objected to the company of a dog, as a dog. . . . Miller was not entirely sure he would not have liked the porter to leave the dog there; he was a friendly dog, and seemed inclined to socialize" (81–82). At yet another station stop, he observes that "a Chinaman, of the ordinary laundry type, boarded the train and took his seat in the white car without objection" (81). This remarkable, complexly unfolding scene discloses some of the corrections but perhaps also some of the errors made in late nineteenth-century African American novelists' "laboratory-literature." Chesnutt, too, was a man of his time, after all. So while Dr. Miller's philosophizing discloses the partiality and contingency of Peirce's and Holmes's versions of pragmatist thought, it also constructs a troubling social hierarchy wherein "an educated man of his race" ranks above swarming black "farm laborers," while a handsome, friendly dog ranks above "offensive Negroes."[60] At the same time, Miller's stereotypical description of a Chinese man demonstrates nativism even as it underscores the apparent injustice, illogic, and arbitrariness of Miller being forced to ride the "colored" car when other nonwhites may ride in the white car.

This last element of the scene, Miller's observation of the Chinese man, also serves to connect the novel decisively to *Plessy* as well as other, related late nineteenth-century Supreme Court decisions regarding race, ethnicity, and citizenship. Two sentences from Justice Harlan's famous dissent in *Plessy* are often quoted: "Our Constitution is color-blind, and neither knows nor tolerates classes among citizens. In respect of civil rights, all citizens are equal before the law." But in an equally often overlooked passage from the same dissent, Harlan displays nativism, even xenophobia, in support of black Americans' unfettered access to public conveyance:

There is a race so different from our own that we do not permit those belonging to it to become citizens of the United States. Persons belonging to it are, with few exceptions, absolutely excluded from our country. I allude to the Chinese race. But by the statute in question, a Chinaman can ride in the same passenger coach with white citizens of the United States, while citizens of the black race in Louisiana, many of whom, perhaps, risked their lives for the preservation of the Union, who are entitled, by law, to participate in the political control of the State and nation, who are not excluded, by law or by reason of their race, from public stations of any kind, and who have all the legal rights that belong to white citizens, are yet declared to be criminals, liable to imprisonment, if they ride in a public coach occupied by citizens of the white race. It is scarcely just to say that a colored citizen should not object to occupying a public coach assigned to his own race. He does not object, nor, perhaps, would he object to separate coaches for his race, if his rights under the law were recognized. But he objects, and ought never to cease objecting to the proposition, that citizens of the white and black races can be adjudged criminals because they sit, or claim the right to sit, in the same public coach on a public highway.

Not just Charles Chesnutt, but a number of African American novelists followed Harlan's line of reasoning. In the wake of *Plessy*, they were attempting to imagine a successful, middle-class, black subject not simply within a state-enforced black–white racial binary but also intraracially *and* in relationship to white ethnic and nonwhite immigrants whose citizenship status was being debated and codified in federal jurisprudence during the same period.

Like Chesnutt, Hopkins understood that citizenship was not simply a matter of black and white and that African American writers did not have the luxury of writing novels primarily as vehicles of aesthetic pleasure. In her preface to *Contending Forces*, she explicitly framed the project of fiction as being "of great value" in the face of real, though largely ineffective, political alternatives in a larger late nineteenth-century project of achieving justice for all (13). She argues: "The colored race has historians, lecturers, ministers, poets, judges and lawyers,—men of brilliant intellects who have arrested the favorable attention of this busy, energetic nation. But, after all, it is the simple, homely tale, unassumingly told, which cements the bond of brotherhood among all classes and complexions" (13). Her categorical list of "colored" professionals culminates in her tacit admission that juridical activism and thought have failed to secure full citizenship for African Americans—and in that, of course, she was correct. Hopkins knew that federal jurisprudence had not only codified segregation but had determined that states have the power—and the ability—to determine racial identity, as represented in Sappho's experience on board the southbound train and as written into national law by Justice Brown in *Plessy*: "these are questions [of racial identity] to be determined under the laws of each State and are not properly put in issue in this case." Given the context of that opinion, Hopkins's novels of passing and interracial romance, all published between 1900 and 1903, necessarily function, at least in part, as political-legal commentary.[61] As if offering a direct rebuke to Justice Brown, the narrator in Hopkins's novel *Of One Blood,* serially published 1902–3, asks rhetorically: "Who is clear enough in vision to decide who hath black blood and who hath it not?"[62]

Indeed, although in recent years scholars of Hopkins's fiction have focused almost exclusively on biological discourses of the body, race, and sexuality in her four turn-of-the-twentieth century novels, perhaps no African American novelist at the time was more preoccupied with racial identity as constructed by the law than she was.[63] Three of the four novels culminate in trials, with their plots turning so regularly on legal decisions that the processes of law, detection, and punishment actually threaten to submerge the discourses of blood, race, and genealogy. *Hagar's Daughter,* for example, begins as an apparently conventional tragic mulatto romance, only to become, near the book's end, a crime novel complete with a trial in which one of the book's heroes stands wrongly accused of murder. Not only that, but the hero-defendant, the white Cuthbert Sumner, and his beloved, the mixed-race (black and white) Jewel Bowen, marry—in the space of a couple of sentences—*while* he is incarcerated. As Sumner himself explains, "she consented to *marry me in this very cell.*"[64] Here the marriage plot is almost literally contained by a narrative about law and punishment.

Yet, again like Chesnutt, Hopkins does not frame her political concerns solely within the black–white racial binary seemingly being reinforced by *Hagar's Daughter*'s initial "tragic mulatto" marriage plot.[65] At one point in *Contending Forces,* the book's two African American heroines, Dora and Sappho, are discussing black people's limited opportunities for work, even in the relatively enlightened city of Boston. Dora exclaims, "I cannot understand people. Here in the North we are allowed every privilege. There seems to be no prejudice until we seek employment; then every door is closed against us. Can you explain this?" (128–29). The older and wiser Sappho replies, "No, I cannot; to my way of thinking the whole thing is a Chinese puzzle" (129). Offering no direct answer, Dora abruptly ends the conversation: "Bless my soul! Just look at that clock!" as she rushes to prepare tea for the family and the lodgers (129). This striking textual moment, much like Chesnutt's train scene in *The Marrow of Tradition* and Webb's in *The Garies and Their Friends,* filters a crisis of African American citizenship through a subtle immigrant presence—and quite explicitly through the measure of time. Sappho, rather than facing that crisis directly, hews instead to the temporal rhythms of a bourgeois late-nineteenth-century Boston household; however, she will soon face displacement from that household, once her hidden racial and sexual southern past threatens to reemerge in the North. She, and all the African American characters in Hopkins's novels, cannot rely on modernity, or region, or urbanity, or class, or light skin color to secure their citizenship, even as they witness the extension of U.S. citizenship to others at the end of the century. Indeed, as of the 1900 publication date of *Contending Forces*, Hopkins's character Sappho was, in a way, correct that the state of "Negro" citizenship and civil rights was a "Chinese puzzle."

The late nineteenth century, unlike the mid-nineteenth century, witnessed debates over U.S. citizenship spurred not so much by black–white relations as by Chinese immigration. Beginning in the mid-nineteenth century, Chinese laborers began arriving in the United States to join the Gold Rush and to supply much-needed labor for the growing railroad and fishing industries, especially in California. In 1868, the U.S. Senate ratified the United States–China Burlingame Treaty, permitting unlimited immigration from China and thereby issuing an open invitation to Chinese workers. Because a significant number accepted that invitation (nearly 140,000 Chinese people entered the United States between 1870 and 1880),[66] the "Chinese question" began to be posed alongside the "Negro question" in U.S. legislation and jurisprudence throughout the post-Reconstruction era. As early as 1870, the Massachusetts senator Charles Sumner (whom Peirce famously loathed)[67] referred to "the great Chinese question" during congressional debate.[68] And beginning in the 1870s, Supreme Court justices regularly referred to both African Americans and nonwhite immigrants in their opinions—majority and minority—regarding the nature of citizenship. The famous *Slaughterhouse Cases* of 1873, for example, turned on the justices' interpretation of the Thirteenth and Fourteenth amendments, and their decision included an extension of the amendments to Chinese and Mexican laborers, despite the fact that the original complainants in the case were a group of white butchers.[69] Justice Samuel Freeman Miller wrote in the majority opinion in the *Slaughterhouse Cases*: "Undoubtedly while negro [*sic*] slavery alone was in the mind of the Congress which proposed the thirteenth article, it forbids any other kind of slavery, now or hereafter. If Mexican peonage or the Chinese coolie labor system shall develop slavery of the Mexican or Chinese race within our territory, this amendment may safely be trusted to make it void."[70]

Ironically, African Americans thus became a vehicle for the process of defining and expanding citizenship rights even as they were being excluded from that status and subjected to lynch mob "justice." Just as important, Miller went on to prioritize state over federal citizenship, arguing that "the privileges and immunities of citizens of the States . . . embrace generally those fundamental civil rights for the security and establishment of which organized society is instituted, and they remain, with certain exceptions mentioned in the Federal Constitution, under the care of the State governments." With this opinion, Miller set three significant precedents: first, the intertwining of African American with nonwhite immigrant civil rights; second, the establishing of a "dualistic [state and federal] conception of citizenship";[71] and third, the privileging of state over federal citizenship. In the post-Reconstruction era, just as in the mid-twentieth century, such advocacy of states' rights served as a proxy for a segregationist platform.[72] Thus, despite the *Slaughterhouse Cases* decision's apparently progressive extension of the Thirteenth Amendment to Chinese and Mexican laborers, these cases at the same time narrowed the Fourteenth Amendment's scope and, in doing so, provided the fundamental precedent for *Plessy's* "separate but equal" doctrine.[73] As Barbara Jean Fields puts it in her classic essay "Ideology and Race in American History," "the Supreme Court soon interpreted the Fourteenth Amendment out of existence, at least insofar as the rights of black people were concerned."[74]

Indeed, the Thirteenth and Fourteenth amendments were interpreted and reinterpreted not only in the *Slaughterhouse Cases*, but in a series of late nineteenth-century Supreme Court cases that seemingly pertained to everyone *but* African Americans. Several landmark decisions in the 1880s and 1890s indicate that a majority of Supreme Court justices were, at certain times and in certain contexts, at least somewhat receptive to the idea of Chinese Americans and to the extension of civil rights to all persons within U.S. borders. For example, in 1886 the Court decided *Yick Wo v. Hopkins* (Hopkins was the surname of the sheriff named in the suit), a case brought as a result of San Francisco's differential enforcement of statutes prohibiting laundries within city limits from being operated in wooden buildings, because of fire hazard. The city had granted an exemption from the statute for every white petitioner while denying one to every

Chinese petitioner. The Court decided in favor of the plaintiff and in the process extended civil rights to Chinese immigrants, including noncitizens, on the basis of the Fourteenth Amendment. Justice Stanley Matthews wrote for the majority in the case: "The rights of the petitioners . . . are not less, because they are aliens and subjects of the Emperor of China. . . . The Fourteenth Amendment to the Constitution is not confined to the protection of citizens. . . . [Its] provisions are universal in their application, to all persons within the territorial jurisdiction, without regard to any differences of race, of color, or of nationality."[75]

A second landmark case, *United States v. Wong Kim Ark,* decided in 1898, centered on a California-born son of Chinese immigrants, a laborer, who left the United States to visit China. On his return, he was denied reentry into the country on the basis of the 1882 Chinese Exclusion Act. As in *Yick Wo v. Hopkins,* an apparently progressive decision turned on interpretation of the Fourteenth Amendment. Justice Stephen J. Field wrote in the majority opinion: "The Fourteenth Amendment affirms the ancient and fundamental rule of citizenship by birth within the territory . . . including all children here born of resident aliens."[76] *U.S. v. Wong Kim Ark* signaled national acceptance of the concept of citizenship as birthright for all—with the significant exception of its exclusion of some Indians.[77]

This is *not* to say that all of the period's Supreme Court decisions regarding Chinese immigrants were progressive. And certainly the climate in the nation was generally neither warm nor welcoming toward Chinese immigrants, despite the Burlingame Treaty. In fact, in a draconian retraction of that 1868 "invitation," in 1882 the U.S. Congress passed its very first immigration exclusion act in order to stop all immigration to the United States by Chinese laborers, and it was not until 1943 that this act was repealed, and even then only partially.[78] As a number of historians have noted, the Chinese Exclusion Act was the country's first federal law restricting immigration "solely on the basis of race or nationality."[79] The 1880s and 1890s also witnessed Supreme Court cases such as *Fong Yue Ting v. the United States* and *United States v. Ju Toy,* in which the Chinese Exclusion Act was upheld.[80] And Chinese Americans were, like African Americans, subject to virulent discrimination and racism, including violence, in daily life.[81] Moreover, as Erika Lee has convincingly argued, a "narrow focus on legal statutes or judicial decisions obscures our understanding of how government officials, immigrants, and citizens interpreted, enforced, and challenged the law" (11). Lee continues: "the ways in which immigration laws were interpreted and enforced were just as important—if not more important—than the laws themselves" (78). Or, as Holmes put it in 1881 in *The Common Law*, "the felt necessities of the time, the prevalent moral and political theories, intuitions of public policy, avowed or unconscious, even the prejudices which judges share with their fellow-men" constitute the "life of the law" and shape legal outcomes more than does the logical "consistency of the system" itself (1). Just so, no matter how progressive a Supreme Court decision may have been in intent or appearance, it could not dictate local material conditions, including instances of judicial, legal, or extralegal "activism." Likewise, any judicial inclusiveness regarding U.S. citizenship could always be undermined by legislative exclusion at either state or federal levels, not to mention by local practices. Nonetheless, at least some Supreme Court decisions near the century's end appeared to be more progressive regarding Chinese civil rights than *Plessy* was regarding African American civil rights.

These Supreme Court decisions constituted a grim and sustained political-legal theme in Hopkins's novels, which offer a steady accounting of the consequences of a pragmatic acceptance of "the life of the law" as being inevitably influenced by the "prejudices" of its time, to use Holmes's words (1). In *Contending Forces*, Hopkins clearly challenges a pragmatist approach to the law in a scene describing the annual meeting of the white "Canterbury Club of Boston," which was "composed of the flower of Boston's literary savans [*sic*]" (287):

At the rooms of the club men deep in scientific research touched elbows with the advanced theological scholar and the political economist. Side by side with the vital questions of the hour in the world of progress—wireless telegraphy, the philosophy of trusts, the rise and fall of monarchies, the restoration of Greek art, the philosophy of lynching was beginning to engage the attention of two hemispheres, and information was eagerly sought from every source. (287)

In order to gather information about lynching (which the narrator strangely terms a "philosophy"), the Club invites Doctor Lewis, a kind of Booker T. Washington figure, and Will Smith, the black hero of the novel, to speak to its members. During dinner, two members—one, "a noted

theologian of the Episcopalian faith," and the other a "free-thinker"—
begin to debate the existence of God (291, 293). Will Smith soon "plunged
into the conversation, impelled thereto by a certain philosophical reference with which he was familiar and had studied with great interest" (293).
The freethinker asks him, "Are you one with the rest of your race in believ-
ing all this talk of spirituality?" (293). Will replies, "I believe that reason
and religion must act together to discover the perfect power and glory of
God.... There is perfect harmony between them; and it is our own short-
sightedness which causes us to doubt" (293). Smith sounds here a great
deal like a pragmatist. Peirce, for example, had no trouble reconciling his
Christianity with his "laboratory-philosophy," especially late in his career
as he developed his notion of evolutionary cosmology, a kind of Christian-
Darwinist-pragmatist blend. And in his 1896 essay "The Will to Believe,"
William James defended belief in God as a "living option" that provided a
"certain vital good," arguing that faith can supplement the scientific and
the logical: "the freedom to believe can only cover living options which
the intellect of the individual cannot by itself resolve."[82]

But Will Smith most certainly does not remain a pragmatist once the
conversation turns from religion to lynching and the law. A white English
visitor, Mr. Withington, asks Lewis and Smith about racial division in the
United States. Lewis replies, "Over ten thousand graves made since the
war by mob violence, are dotting the South, and of these ninety percent
are the graves of black men" (296). A sympathetic white member of the
club adds: "You do not get these facts abroad because newspaper reports
are doctored by local Southern writers who participate in the lynchings.
Free speech and public discussions are not allowed. In the South you must
think and speak as the mob dictates" (296). Appalled, Withington says,
"But surely you have constitutional equity before the law? You can gain
redress from the Federal government?" (296–97). Will Smith replies:
"Constitutional equity is a political fiction.... The lines are drawn more
sharply than before the emancipation. Constitutional amendments are
dead letters; the ballot-box is nil" (297). Just so, *the Slaughterhouse Cases*
and *Plessy* marked the end of what legal scholar Robert Kaczorowski
terms "a heroic effort by federal judges and legal officers in the South to
protect the civil rights of American citizens" during the Civil War and Reconstruction.[83] At a more abstract level, the two decisions registered the
potential dangers of a judicial system based to any significant degree on
precedent.[84]

Hopkins, like her character Will Smith, was keenly aware of the regression in African American civil rights that was being solidified in the Supreme Court and enacted by the lynch mob from the 1870s to the end of the century, and in turn her novels disclose the shortcomings of American pragmatism. In her preface to *Contending Forces,* she presses home the point that the rise of the Klan and lynching point backward to an antebellum era:

> Mob-law is nothing new. Southern sentiment has not been changed; the old ideas . . . still prevail, and break forth clothed in new forms to force the whole republic to an acceptance of its principles. . . . Let us compare the happenings of one hundred–two hundred years ago, with those of today. The difference between then and now, if any there be, is so slight as to be scarcely worth mentioning. The atrocity of the acts committed one hundred years ago [is] duplicated today, when slavery is supposed no longer to exist. (14–15)

As with her observation about the South's worship of "reversion,"[85] Hopkins here connects repetition, regression, and oppression to state power. Indeed, the elevation of states' rights, as in the *Slaughterhouse Cases* and *Plessy,* effectively proved her thesis that the South had successfully "forced the whole republic to an acceptance of its principles." Hopkins's astute legal-temporal analysis puts her in direct conflict with Holmes. In 1897, he offered a definition of the law as "systematized prediction," arguing that the work of lawyers is "prediction, the prediction of the incidence of the public force through the instrumentality of the courts."[86] For Hopkins and her characters, the fundamental force of the law is not to predict but to punish, not to prophesy but to force African Americans into an anachronistic state of noncitizenship.

In a well-known 1894 *Harvard Law Review* article on tort law, "Privilege, Malice, and Intent," Holmes explained that "actions of tort are brought for temporal damage. The law recognizes temporal damage as an evil which its object is to prevent or to redress, so far as is consistent with paramount considerations to be mentioned."[87] As multiple legal scholars have observed, Holmes never explained what he meant by "temporal damage," but he may have meant harm or loss inflicted on another that, while it must unfold in time, may be either temporally remote or proximate.[88] In the end, Holmes seems to have been more interested in categorizing torts as having been committed either unintentionally or intentionally, with "malice, intent, and negligence," rather than in describing their duration or time of occurrence.[89] But for Hopkins, Chesnutt, Dunbar, and Griggs, "temporal damage" signifies far more literally. The nation has damaged time itself for African Americans across centuries and on into their present; indeed, the phrase perfectly describes the civil and criminal damage done to black people—as individuals and as a group—by the period's federal jurisprudence and its state "black laws." In *Contending Forces*, the narrator asserts that there is a "large class of colored citizens who embody within themselves the highest development of American citizenship" but worries: "Will the Republic learn the value of the black children of her adoption when it is too late?" (289, 290). Sappho, the heroine of the novel, is likewise worried about black citizenship: "If we lose the franchise, at the same time we shall lose the respect of all other citizens. Temporizing will not benefit us; rather, it will leave us branded as cowards, not worthy a freeman's respect—an alien people, without a country and without a home" (125). For Hopkins, a seemingly insoluble puzzle inheres in African Americans' being representative Americans who are nonetheless disenfranchised, segregated, and subjected to terrorist assaults in a process that seeks to relegate them always to the past, a process Saidiya Hartman describes as "the resubordination of the emancipated."[90] That is the actual *temporal damage* being wrought at the turn of the century; or, as the narrator of *Contending Forces* puts it, both echoing and upending Arkansas governor Jeff Davis, it is "the cankering sore which is eating into the heart of republican principles and stamping the lie upon the Constitution" (202). Yet there seems to be no possibility in the real world of the late nineteenth century (or perhaps even in the present) for the corrective justice that such a long-standing constitutional, mass tort would call for.[91]

So Hopkins imagines new and alternative forms of justice. Among her four novels, *Winona* perhaps best expresses her ideal of natural justice over and against the temporal damage being enacted by federal law and jurisprudence. The novel takes place in upstate New York, Missouri, and Kansas in the 1850s. It centers on the lives of two children, the "Negro" Judah and the "quadroon" Winona, whose father, White Eagle, a white man whose mulatto wife, a fugitive slave, has died, and who is living among Indians in rural New York outside Buffalo. As such, White Eagle has become a kind of noncitizen, an undocumented person: "There was not even a scrap of paper found to tell who White Eagle might have been in earlier, happier days" (309). After only a few pages as a story of happy, mixed-race youth, the novel quickly becomes at once a tragic mulatto romance and a murder mystery when White Eagle is shot and killed by party or parties unknown. A visiting white English lawyer, Warren Maxwell, becomes tangled in the affair because he comes to the family's aid after White Eagle's death and, finding the now-orphaned children so sympathetic and appealing, offers to have them educated in England. But when he returns a month later to claim them, he discovers that they have been kidnapped and sold into slavery. Mr. Maybee, the local innkeeper and a friend to White Eagle and the children explains, "in all my life I never befo' felt ashamed of bein' an American citizen . . . the owners of White Eagle's wife an' Judah's mother . . . nigger traders from Missouri . . . puts in a claim fer the two children under the new act for the rendition of fugitive slaves jes' passed by Congress" (314). At once, Maxwell, despite being an attorney himself, finds himself at odds with U.S. law: " 'But how could they take the children? They were both born free. It was an illegal proceeding,' cried Warren in amazement" (315). Mr. Maybee quickly corrects him: "The child follows the condition of the mother. That's the law" (315).

The novel repeatedly juxtaposes true justice and "the law," showing that when, in the words of one of the novel's villains, we "let all things be done in decency and order and according to the process of the law," the outcome is often perversely contrary to Hopkins's own sense of natural and religious, if not civil, law (372). In fact, contra Holmes, in this novel, the law does not *predict* justice but rather *causes* grave errors and injustices to unfold in the future. When Maxwell is arrested and jailed for helping Winona to escape slavery, he witnesses terrible atrocities in the prison, including the scene of "a Negro undergoing the shameful outrage, so denounced in the Scriptures, and which must not be described in the interests of decency and humanity" (385). "Unhappily," the narrator informs us, "we tell no tale of fiction" (385). For Hopkins, the violation of natural and moral law, figured as sexual violation of a black man, constitutes the true nature of race-based law and punishment. Consequently, the novel's happy ending, with justice restored, must be seen as the real fiction in the tale. In *Winona,* as in *Contending Forces,* the ending turns on genealogical discovery—this time by means of what the innkeeper Mr. Maybee describes as "three legal dockymen's [documents] and a few pieces of jewelry" (433). It turns out that there were, after all, some "scraps of paper" to establish Winona's identity and secure her birthright, and they include birth and marriage certificates stored by Mr. Maybee for White Eagle, her father, who was, as it turns out, the heir to an English fortune. "Nothing was missing," the narrator says, "the chain of evidence was complete, even to the trained eye of the legal critic" (433). Fantasy inheres in "the legal critic" reading the chain of evidence rightly so as to establish both the true genealogy of a "quadroon" heroine and the rightful inheritance of an escaped slave. Hopkins thereby creates a kind of fantastical legal allegory in which African Americans ultimately receive their rightful and lawful inheritance as true, original members of the American republic-family.

But as much as Hopkins's novels may argue for progress, for a better future regarding African American civil rights, her characters are perhaps even more susceptible to nativism than is Chesnutt's Dr. Miller. Like Justice Harlan's dissent in *Plessy*, Hopkins's novels resist any analogy or equation of African American and immigrant groups. For instance, her characters are not above ethnic humor at the expense of recent arrivals. In *Contending Forces*, Will Smith actually mimics a Chinese accent while he flirts with Sappho Clark. Suggesting that she consider him like a son so that he can continue, with propriety, to build the fire in her room, he says: "No likee me for sonny?" In response, Sappho laughs "in spite of herself" (174). Later on in the book, during his rousing speech at the American Colored League meeting, Will tells an Irish joke—not coincidentally, a political one: "I remember a story I heard once of an Irishman just landed at Castle Garden. A friend met him, and as they walked up the street said to him: 'Well, Pat, you are just in time to vote for the city government election.' 'Begorra,' replied Pat, "an' is it a guvimint they have here? Sure, thin, I'll vote agin' it'" (265). Will then remarks that the Irish have amassed power via bloc voting; "To the Negro alone," he concludes, "politics shall bring no fruit" (265). Hopkins, via Will, is suggesting that the Irish are in the process of becoming not so much "white," as much contemporary scholarship would have it,[92] as *not black*.[93] Hopkins's novels at once assert and resist notions of African American exceptionalism: native-born African Americans and white Americans, as well as Indians and mixed black-white Americans, are altogether truly American; on the other hand, African Americans alone among ethnic or racial groups, immigrant or not, are being systematically excluded from full citizenship.

Hopkins's representation of that exclusion as an anachronistic, nation-bound process recurs in many late nineteenth-century African American novels. Hopkins, along with Chesnutt, Dunbar, and Griggs, had to look to other times and places in order to represent experiences of authentic justice and full citizenship for black people. For example, Hopkins's novel *Of One Blood,* a fantastic, even bizarre, transcontinental tale of love, passing, and reincarnation, describes a dark-skinned African American man's "anecdotes of Southern life," told during the passing-for-white hero's mystical and imperial ventures in Egypt, as "a portion of the United States . . . transported to Africa" (581). At the end of a convoluted plot, justice is finally meted out "according to the ancient laws of the inhabitants of Telassar," the mystical African land that turns out to have been the origin of the novel's mixed-race hero Reuel (620). Moving beyond the nineteenth-century racial and sexual pattern of U.S. crime and punishment experienced in *Winona, Of One Blood* invents a law that is both true and truly color-blind. Similarly, Sutton Griggs's 1899 novel *Imperium in Imperio* must become speculative fiction in order to imagine full black subjectivity at a time in the United States when "governors would announce publicly that they favored lynching" and the Supreme Court "is the chief bulwark of caste prejudice in democratic America" (131, 144). The plot involves a secret black state within the nation. A black man who was part of the state narrates the novel; he risks death by telling of its existence and of its plans for the violent seizure of Texas and Louisiana in order to establish a black nation within the United States: "Thus will the Negro have an empire of his own," a near-perfect expression of empire founded on and within empire, just as the novel's title implies (168).

Again and again, African American authors at the turn of the twentieth century explore and try to construct alternatives to the traumatic temporal and legal suspension of black people between eras. —"They were not citizens, yet they were not slaves," as Chesnutt's narrator puts it in *The House behind the Cedars* (104). In fact, almost every African American novel published in the late nineteenth century begins with or flashes back to a slave past. Yet, somewhat paradoxically, the authors are attempting to imagine and to invent a new black future out of aesthetic, national, and racial forms they have inherited. At the literary level, their novels revisit and rework the sentimental novel, the seduction novel, the slave narrative, and the narrative of the tragic mulatto; at the level of politics and philosophy, the writers experiment with pragmatism, nativism and imperialism, and futurism. When he was awarded the NAACP's Spingarn Medal in 1928 for his "pioneer work as a literary artist depicting the life and struggles of Americans of Negro descent," Chesnutt remarked, "My books were written, from one point of view, a generation too soon."[94] He may have been right, not only about his books, but about Hopkins's, Dunbar's, and Griggs's as well. On the one hand, African American novelists of the late nineteenth century were very much of their time in that they were "contending" with contemporary legal and social "forces" that were aiming to keep all African Americans mired in the past. On the other hand, they were also, philosophically speaking, ahead of their time—one might say strategically anachronistic. In similarly paradoxical fashion, they sought justice for all African Americans, yet the characters their novels generally identify as having attained the "highest development" are standard English-speaking, often light-skinned uplifters—those who ostensibly will end up being or producing the "New Negroes" of the twentieth century. They are like Harper's Iola Leroy, one of "those upon whose brows God has poured the chrism of that new era,"[95] or they are, like Chesnutt's men "of imagination" in *The House behind the Cedars,* one of the "new people" (97, 57). Just as Frederick Douglass associated his accession to modern subjectivity and temporality with his representation of the United States in an imperial project as a member of the Santo Domingo Commission, these novels idealize individuals who embody the authors' contingent versions of an ideal, often mixed-race and masculine, subjectivity to come: what Chesnutt termed a "future American" and what Sutton Griggs's narrator in his 1905 novel *The Hindered Hand* termed "the coming composite Americanism."[96]

Ultimately, African American writers from 1896 to 1902, while they successfully produced a rich body of fiction, failed to prove that in "the pen" "there is a weapon mightier than" either the "sword or ballot," as *Imperium in Imperio* asserted.[97] The authors' literary-political project foundered partly because of their own period-bound "prejudices," to use Holmes's term, but primarily because of the nation's continued legal and material oppression of all African Americans, despite an adept wielding of what the writers hoped would be the ultimate weapon in the fight for justice. The bleakness of Chesnutt's and Dunbar's novels, along with the fantastical solutions in Griggs's and Hopkins's, suggest that these authors may have already known that pragmatic legal and utilitarian aesthetic approaches would likely fail to produce racially blind justice in their lifetimes, just as Emancipation, the Thirteenth and Fourteenth amendments, the Civil Rights Acts of 1866 and 1875, and Reconstruction had failed: "dead letters." The despair that marks a number of their novels finds its closest parallel not in the literature of the Harlem Renaissance that immediately followed but in the mid-twentieth-century novels of Richard Wright and Ann Petry, whose major works explored Langston Hughes's "deferred dream" as it exploded in neighborhoods that the Progressive Era of the 1920s and 1930s had failed to assist. Just as lynching was the ever-present and predictable threat in turn-of-the-century African American writing, the often predictable violent deaths of black men take center stage in *Native Son* and *The Street*. Thematically and formally, repetitive black male mortality is woven deeply into the fabric of twentieth-century African American literature, a thread the next chapter will take up.

3

"The Death of the Last Black Man"

Repetition, Lynching, and Capital Punishment in Twentieth-Century African American Literature

> *Not your time! My time! High noon my time my time!*
>
> —Suzan-Lori Parks, *Devotees in the Garden of Love*

W. E. B. Du Bois's *The Souls of Black Folk* (1903) bridges the gap between the despair of many late nineteenth-century African American novels and the relative optimism of the Harlem Renaissance. Looking to the past in order to understand—and to the future in order to exceed—a dire present, Hopkins, Dunbar, Chesnutt, and Griggs prepared the ground for *Souls*, which in turn writes an epitaph for their revisionary and visionary projects. Du Bois's rich blend of genres and disciplines—political and social history, personal narrative, philosophy, music history, and so on—thus resolves perhaps most readily into elegy. "Surely," laments Du Bois, "there shall yet dawn some mighty morning to lift the Veil and set the prisoned free."[1] Just as he is mourning here "the passing of the first born,"[2] his son, he is mourning what might have been had Reconstruction not failed, and had legal solutions for racial injustice not become "dead letters."[3] In the two decades after the publication of *Souls,* writers of the Harlem Renaissance all but abandoned the past as content. Rather astonishingly, slavery nearly vanishes as an explicit concern of African American writers in the 1920s. Zora Neale Hurston writes in 1928:

> Someone is always at my elbow reminding me that I am the granddaughter of slaves. It fails to register depression with me. Slavery is sixty years in the past. The operation was successful and the patient is doing well, thank you. The terrible struggle that made me an American out of a potential slave said "On the line!" The Reconstruction said "Get set!" and the generation before said "Go!" I am off to a flying start and I must not halt in the stretch to look behind

and weep. Slavery is the price I paid for civilization, and the choice was not with me. It is a bully adventure and worth all that I have paid through my ancestors for it.[4]

Hurston's view of New World slavery here sounds uncomfortably like Hegel's assessment of black access to modernity. Even taking into account her possibly tongue-in-cheek tone in this passage, Hurston represents an extreme in this blithe dismissal of a slave past; yet she is not alone among Harlem Renaissance writers in focusing on the present rather than on the past, even the recent past. As I will argue later in this book, with the significant exception of the period's deep interest in the sorrow songs, the Harlem Renaissance's studied presentism distinguishes it sharply from much of the African American literature that preceded it and much that would follow it. The failure of reform after the first several decades of the twentieth century, like the failure of Reconstruction in the late nineteenth, to deliver reparative or corrective justice to African Americans sets the stage for African American writers' return to despair and to strategic anachronism in the 1940s and beyond. Nowhere does this affective-temporal combination emerge more clearly than in fictional representations of the time-bound experiences of African American men within U.S. judicial and penal systems. What John Edgar Wideman has chillingly termed the "living bodies of dead men" populate African American fiction throughout the century.[5]

In the twentieth-century African American texts that deal centrally with the lynching or the capital punishment of a black man—and there are many—time and justice (or, more often, *in*justice) conspire to bring about his grim fate. Such texts represent two sorts of being "out of time." First, the man faces an inevitable death sentence and has therefore literally run out of time—as in "His Last Day," a 1933 short story by Chester Himes about the final hours and minutes of a black death-row inmate who will soon be "taking the lightning ride."[6] Second, the texts themselves are often out of step with the prevailing literary forms of their day—as in Claude McKay's militant yet formally conventional 1919 sonnet "If We Must Die," written amid the emergence of high modernist poetic forms as well as the "Red Summer" of 1919, when antiblack race riots erupted in a number of cities across the United States, including Atlanta, Tulsa, and Chicago, and resulted in the deaths of hundreds of people, most of them African American.[7] Antilynching drama, a genre invented in the 1910s by African American women authors including Angelina Weld Grimké, Georgia Douglas Johnson, and Alice Dunbar, inaugurated the twentieth-century version of this doubly temporal literary strategy, with mortality their content and anachronism their form. As I argued in the Introduction to this book, formally, antilynching plays most resemble not the naturalist and the modernist drama of their day but Victorian domestic melodrama, yet these plays focus on the present; they hold the distinctively and horrifyingly modern content of lynching at their heart.

Much African American literature since has followed the same pattern. From Grimké's almost bizarrely sentimental 1916 antilynching play *Rachel* to Richard Wright's 1940 grim naturalist novel *Native Son* and to Ernest Gaines's elegiac 1994 novel *A Lesson before Dying*, twentieth-century African American texts have repeatedly used forms from the past to deliver highly charged political content that, by contrast, is firmly grounded in the material conditions of the texts' present, a present wherein differential experiences of time instantiate overdetermined, often adjudicated, black male mortality. Even a recent, clearly postmodern work like Suzan-Lori Parks's 1990 *The Death of the Last Black Man in the Whole Entire World*— an avant-garde play that, unlike *Rachel*, *A Lesson before Dying*, and *Native Son*, is certainly not formally anachronistic—enacts and reenacts the link between distinctively African American experiences of time and a seemingly perpetual, externally enforced black male mortality. As if holding a formal mirror up to that content, all these texts manifest a nearly compulsive repetition in dialogue, image, or structure. Virtually every twentieth-century African American text that centers on black men's punishment by death also engages temporality in the same complex way—affirming the surprisingly poetic opening statement made at trial by Bigger Thomas's defense attorney: "Lodged in the heart of this moment is the question of power which time will unfold!"[8]

Not coincidentally, *Native Son* opens with the sound of a ringing alarm clock, an image most critics have interpreted just as Arnold Rampersad does, as an "urgent call in 1940 to America to awaken from its self-induced slumber about the reality of race relations in the nation."[9] Roger Rosenblatt argues similarly that "the clocks" in both *Native Son* and Chester Himes's *If He Hollers Let Him Go* "serve only as instruments of alarm."[10] But timekeeping works throughout Wright's novel as much more than straightforward allegory—as in "White people, listen!" or "Black people wake up!" Tropes of time are so fully present in *Native Son* that we almost cannot see them; they, and their sustained presence, carry multiple rich meanings, especially for the novel's black characters. Even that initial alarm clock represents not simply an alarm or "wake-up call" to America but an object of both oppression and aspiration for Bigger Thomas and his family. Farah Jasmine Griffin has argued that the clock assesses and quantifies the existence of the urban African American working class; Bigger, for one, invariably comes up short by its standards.[11] Precisely because he alone in the family does not have to be awake at any particular time, Bigger seems in fact to be what his mother calls "the most no-countest man I ever seen in all my life!" (9). She herself has "a big washing on [her] hands" and must quickly get to work (3); Vera, Bigger's sister, worries that she will be "late" for a "sewing class at the Y.W.C.A." (3, 8). "You going to have to learn to get up earlier than this, Bigger," his mother warns, "to hold a job" (11).

Bigger is well aware of "the shame and misery" in his failure to be a breadwinner for his family, and he does want a job—just not one that is available to him in Chicago in the late 1930s and early 1940s (10). Lizabeth Cohen points out that "by 1939, a third of all people employed by the WPA in Chicago were black"; as Bigger says to his buddy Jack, "I'd just as soon go to jail as take that relief job" (31).[12] Farah Jasmine Griffin herself argues, albeit in a somewhat different context, that Bigger "aspires" to have "the chance to participate in civilization with other modern men" (129). He *wants* to be in a post–relief work world, in and on modern time; thus, in *Native Son* the clock is not represented solely as a "detrimental" instrument of oppression to be resisted or countered, as Griffin suggests (107). Bigger has an ambivalent, rather than fully resistant, relationship to the temporality that inheres in the northern urban work world of the 1930s and 1940s. As Robert Felgar notes, "Bigger wants to be part of a world that is dominated by the concept of linear time," by "clock time."[13] That desire comes through clearly in the well-known scene in which Bigger yearns to be a pilot as he and his friends watch a plane skywrite "USE SPEED GASOLINE" (16–17). Here the airplane does not, as Stephen Kern argues, signify a means of "uplifting human consciousness" through its "capacity to unify people and nations"; rather, it serves as a multidimensional symbol of class and racial divisions and hierarchies.[14] For young Chicago working-class black men "with little education," WPA jobs often involved leaving the city for "rural Wisconsin, Oregon, and Washington" to "replant forests and conserve the soil" rather than staying in the city to work in steel mills or meatpacking plants, much less learning to fly planes.[15] Existing in a temporality and a spatiality that are marginal to fast-paced modern urban commerce and transport, Bigger and his peers are "reclining against the wall, smoking," as "cars whizzed past," cars that are presumably running on Speed Gasoline (17). In the friends' ensuing game of "playing white," careful timekeeping and punctuality—"'call me at my club at two this afternoon,'" "'I'm calling a cabinet meeting this afternoon at four o'clock'"—signify white success, wealth, and power (17, 19). Black failure, powerlessness, under- and unemployment, and limitation, by contrast, mean that Bigger "had time on his hands" (20). The narrator explains that the alienated and alienating, out-of-time "rhythms of his life" render Bigger "like a strange plant blooming in the day and wilting at night" (29).

Bigger attempts to take refuge from his social and temporal alienation at the cinema, where he can lose himself in "the rhythm of moving shadows" (31). He seeks comfort in what historian Michael O'Malley identifies as "motion picture's power to compress and expand everyday time."[16] The compression of time O'Malley associates with motion pictures is enacted by planes and cars, as well; indeed, they function as vehicles for the compression of time. The temporalities of modernity seem, then, to work to Bigger's disadvantage in settings of both labor and leisure. As a result, the escapist imagistic and temporal pleasure that Bigger and his friend Jack take in the films they watch is neither simple nor thoroughgoing; it is, the narrator tells us, "tinged with uneasiness" (31). In the original version of *Native Son,* the one prior to the expurgated Book-of-the-Month-Club version, Bigger and Jack masturbate before the picture starts, and they compete to see who can orgasm more quickly, ironically enough measuring their success by minimizing the duration of their pleasure. They then move to other seats and watch a newsreel that precedes the feature film. It portrays rich young white women cavorting on a Florida beach, including, coincidentally, the daughter of Henry Dalton, with whom Bigger has an interview later that evening for a job as chauffeur. The feature film that follows, *Trader Horn,* is of course, an especially provocative choice on Wright's part, and it stands as a kind of fantastic analogue both to the newsreel and to the overdetermined racial narratives that drive the novel's plot. First released in 1931, this MGM film follows the adventures in Africa of a daring white American hunter-explorer and trader, Aloysius Horn, as he helps search for a young white woman long lost in the wilds of Africa and thought to be living with a savage and dangerous black African tribe.

James Smethurst neatly summarizes the racial implications of the film within *Native Son,* arguing that *Trader Horn* is an

> eroticized narrative of a mythic Africa in which Africans, and by extension African Americans, are shown to be "savage" and therefore terrifying as well as "natural" and therefore desirable. . . . What is seen is ultimately a justification of the present social order through narratives of the past which are literally projections of the present.[17]

Although readers might expect Bigger to focus on the representations of blackness on the screen, he actually backgrounds that content as he watches *Trader Horn,* having "replaced" its "pictures of naked black men and women whirling in wild dances" with "images in his own mind of white men and women dressed in black and white clothes, laughing, talking, drinking and dancing" (33). It is unclear whether Bigger is returning imaginatively to the newsreel images of whites or to his own internal stock collection of pictures of white wealth and leisure (or both); regardless, his replacement images, in turn, represent for him his possible future, at least as a bystander, should he get the job as the Daltons' chauffeur: "Was he going to work for people like you saw in the movies? . . . Maybe if he were working for them something would happen and he would get some of it [their money]" (33). Even in the cinema, Bigger is neither comfortable nor stable in time; his pleasure there is contingent and abbreviated. Unlike the African people he sees and hears in *Trader Horn,* who "are at home in their world," Bigger is subject to "fear and hysteria" even in the dark, softly carpeted world of the cinema (34).

Bigger's experience at the movies disrupts and challenges the theories of Gilles Deleuze, among the most influential twentieth-century philosophers of cinema—and of time. Granted, Bigger's mode of film viewing may at first seem to match Deleuze's notion of cinema's "time-image," "where people and things occupy a place in time which is incommensurable with the one they have in space," but Bigger cannot partake of the "emancipation from time" that Deleuze posits as a corollary to the "time-image."[18] Bigger's reverie at the movies is cut short by the urgency of the robbery he and his friends have planned for later that day; it must take place "between three and four in the afternoon" at Doc Blum's poolroom, when "there ain't nobody in the store but the old man" (24). For Bigger and his friends, a robbery that must be timed carefully functions as a parodic version of the white commercial and temporal enterprise they had played at earlier. To interrupt the speedy flow of capital through theft is as much as they can hope for as poor urban black male "players" in modern economic times. But they do not carry out even that plan, because Bigger's fear of carrying out the robbery of a white man leads him to insist that his pal Gus has arrived too late—"It *is* late, Bigger commanded insistently"—even though he knows that "in fact, they still had time" (40–41). Just as antilynching drama punctured Bergson's optimistic understanding of the openness within human experience of modern time, the movie scene and its aftermath in *Native Son* puncture Deleuze's notion that films, at least some of them, can open up our thoughts and imagination, our experiences of time, and even philosophy itself, in new and exciting ways. In Deleuze's words, the "cinematographic image . . . converts into potential what was only possibility" (156). He extends Bergson's sense of dynamism of human experience into the realm of cinematic form, a form that *Native Son* represents, by contrast, as just another avenue of closure.

In sum, Bigger has access neither to Bergsonian openness nor to Deleuzian potential. He not only fails to achieve "emancipation from time," even at the cinema, he actually has little time left. After he and Jack leave the movie theater, the robbery plan goes awry, apparently because of Bigger's anxiety about time ("He had fought Gus because Gus was late"); he then returns home and prepares for his interview with Mr. Dalton, the real estate magnate who owns the rat-infested tenement where the Thomas family lives (42, 43, 256). "Far away a clock boomed five times," the narrator tells us, portending Bigger's entry into a white household, and potentially into white-dominated economy and temporality through a job as chauffeur to the wealthy Daltons (43). At the interview, Bigger grows more and more anxious: he "heard a clock ticking somewhere behind him and he had a foolish impulse to look at it. But he restrained himself" (50). Despite his anxiety, Bigger gets the job and so must begin to follow the rhythms of the white household. He immediately plans his first purchase: "And he would buy himself another watch, too. A dollar watch was not good enough for a job like this; he would buy a gold one" (59). As O'Malley observes of the Horatio Alger stories, "different grades of watch ideally marked a boy's progress through life. The watch in this case served as more than a simple timekeeper—it established the owner's identity, symbolized his or her social status" (174). Bigger believes, at least initially, that he has entered into a contract wherein he will have an opportunity to climb the socioeconomic ladder, buying into a notion commonplace among Americans (including Charles Peirce and Booker T. Washington) in the late nineteenth century and twentieth century: namely, that "a heavy gold watch registered its value, and its owner's success in life," as O'Malley puts it (175). One of Alger's most popular stories, *Struggling Upward or Luke Larkin's Luck* (1890), begins with a chapter titled "The Waterbury Watch," in which several boys engage in an ice-skating contest to win a new Waterbury Watch.[19] Despite being the best skater, Luke Larkin, the plucky and honest hero of the book, unfairly loses the contest and the watch to a snobbish, well-to-do boy, Randolph Duncan. When Randolph taunts Luke with his loss, suggesting that a poor boy has no need of a watch, Luke replies, "Time is likely to be of as much importance to a poor boy as to a rich boy" (150). This sentiment is quite in keeping with the marketing image of the Waterbury Watch Company, the most successful mass-producer of American watches in the late nineteenth century. As one of their 1882 advertisements proclaimed: "It remained for the Waterbury Watch Company to commence within the reach of masses the only luxury they lacked to make them equal in possession to their wealthiest companions—a watch."[20]

But Bigger Thomas is no Luke Larkin or Ragged Dick, two of Alger's best known boy heroes of the Gilded Age. He remains very much outside the rhythms and settings of modern mass production that had brought such watches "within the reach of masses." Bigger isn't even in step with at least some other black men of his period, namely skilled laborers who did benefit from late-1930s unionizing in "mass production factories"; industrial workers in this period in Chicago took on "new kinds of collective action" that sometimes, if not always or perfectly, bridged ethnic and racial divides, at least contingently and if only for a short period.[21] But in Bigger's temporal and spatial neighborhood, *Plessy v. Ferguson* remains the law of the land and post-Depression, New Deal relief his only source of employment. It would seem that in some ways, he fits better into the 1890s than the 1930s and 1940s. Yet Bigger is unlike either Alger's Gilded Age boy heroes or the unionized workers of his own New Deal time in that he understands little about his social and economic setting. Whereas Ragged Dick and Luke Larkin possess a clear vision of how to get ahead, Bigger doesn't know what a "capitalist" is, nor is he sure quite what Communists and unions are (52–53). Because he has little knowledge about, or power over, what happens to him on the job, Bigger cannot inhabit a "rags

Booker T. Washington, three-quarter-length portrait, standing, facing left, with prominent watch chain, by Harry Shepherd. Albumen print, c. 1892. Library of Congress, Prints and Photographs Division, Booker T. Washington Collection. LOT 13164-A, no. 1.

to riches" story. Interestingly, *Ragged Dick* also begins with a wake-up call, as our boy hero has overslept (it's "seven o'clock"), but he quickly gets "ready for the business of the day": the shoeshine business that ultimately leads to his climb up the socioeconomic ladder.[22] The story advances and endorses a narrative of personal advancement through hard work, and Dick, "our hero," mocks a mean-spirited rival bootblack who has a reputation for stealing by saying "Maybe you was an innocent victim of oppression" (65, 66). But for Wright, being "an innocent victim of oppression" is not a matter to be taken so lightly. Unlike Alger's boys, who resolutely and steadily work for their advancement, Bigger cannot even remain chauffeur throughout his very first task of driving for the Daltons. As he is taking their liberal daughter, Mary Dalton, supposedly "to the University," they pick up Mary's Communist boyfriend, Jan, who promptly takes over at the wheel, leaving Bigger enraged and "trapped," sitting between the two of them in the "speeding car" (54, 70, 71). Now just a "miserable" passenger, Bigger is stuck in the middle of the struggles over modern capital represented by the Daltons and the "Reds," looking on with enforced passivity at the major modern social, political, and economic developments and conflicts of his day (70). Once again, he is reduced to watching, just as he had watched planes and cars speeding by earlier in the novel. But in the car, it is not the temporality of modern industrial capital but the temporality of liberalism (and liberal racism) that pins and patronizes him.

As it turns out, Bigger will both take the relief job *and* go to jail. Although he may not understand just how much he stands to lose in the game of "playing white," he fully comprehends the compulsory racialized narrative of crime and punishment that surrounds his killing of Mary Dalton later the same night: "Though he had killed by accident, not once did he feel the need to tell himself that it had been an accident. He was black and he had been alone in a room where a white girl had been killed; therefore he had killed her" (106). Bigger felt that he must silence the white Mary Dalton simply because he, a black man, was in her bedroom when her blind mother entered. As Barbara Johnson put it, "it is because the 'rape' plot is so overdetermined that Bigger becomes a murderer."[23] Johnson goes on to read the murders in the novel—Bigger's conducting and Wright's writing of them—as resulting from an "unavailability of plots," a "deadly" unavailability that means both Bigger Thomas and Richard Wright must "kill" Mary Dalton and Bessie Mears, Bigger's girlfriend (123). Just as important, Bigger murders not simply because of an "unavailability" of plots but because of an overabundance of *particular* plots. Though he might not have been familiar with the *Daily Worker*, as he tells the Daltons' private detective (161), Bigger certainly was aware of the *Chicago Tribune*, Chicago's dominant daily then as now. And in the 1930s and 1940s, the *Tribune*, under the editorship and ownership of the conservative (and colorful) Robert R. McCormick, was very much in the business of attacking communism and the New Deal—and telling stories about black crime.[24]

As several scholars have noted, newspapers and reporters help drive Bigger's actions and therefore the plot, setting the pace and even helping bring about the outcome of his trial and therefore his death.[25] John A. Williams, for one, argues that the "headlines serve to heighten the intensity of the story and to sweep it along toward its pre-ordained conclusion."[26] So Bigger is right to be alarmed by the reporters who show up at the Dalton house in the wake of Mary's disappearance—he "had never seen such men before; he did not know how to act toward them or what to expect of them" (198–99). He finds them possibly even more "dangerous" than the private detective; to him, they "seemed like men out for keen sport" (199). As they repeatedly question him, and one tries to bribe him "to give me the dope," Bigger realizes that "things were happening so fast that he felt he was not doing full justice to them" (199). With the flash of camera bulbs punctuating what little remains of his life (205, 213, 275), Bigger is trapped within the temporal and representational modes of modern media with their urgent pace, like a flashbulb: "Yes; the police would certainly have enough pictures of him" (214). This fast pace is inextricably connected to his fate. Buckley, the prosecutor, shows Bigger the "masses of people" outside below his prison cell: " 'See that boy? Those people would like to lynch you. That's why I'm asking you to trust me and talk to me. The quicker we get this thing over, the better for you. We're going to try to keep 'em from bothering you. But can't you see the longer they stay around here the harder it'll be for us to handle them?' " (303).

As James Smethurst argues, "the posse of the 8,000 racist white police and the racist mob screaming for Bigger's blood outside the courthouse in the third section are clearly inflamed by a narrative of black bestiality retailed by the popular press" (35–36). The press works side by side with the law in the business of delivering swift justice. With the state's attorney fully in charge of Bigger's fate, he is going to die quickly either by lynching or by capital punishment; therefore, he assents to signing a confession. Capital punishment becomes, then, merely a more formal and controlled, and only slightly less swift (at least in the world of this novel), meting out of what the media, court, and white onlookers view as justice. As Buckley's assistant puts it, Bigger "came through like a clock" (310). The rhythms of the justice system are as inevitable and predictable as the popular narrative that incited Bigger to commit murder in the first place. Once he enters prison, "*There was no day for him now, and there was no night; there was but a* long stretch of time, a long stretch of time that was very short; and then—the end" (273; emphasis in original), an end that no less than fifteen newspapermen hasten by means of their testimony at Bigger's trial (378–79). In Bigger's case, the white media, in conjunction with the judicial system, remain fully in charge of the tempo of justice. As the judge curtly reminds Bigger's defense attorney, "the Court reserves the right to determine how much time is needed, Mr. Max" (415). At this point, "Bigger knew he was lost. It was but a matter of time, of formality" (415). Bigger's future is closed, with that determinism finding its literary counterpart in Wright's own "formality": naturalism, a literary form associated with an earlier movement, the Chicago Renaissance and the 1910s–1920s works of Theodore Dreiser and Upton Sinclair.

Such literary anachronism serves a clear political purpose for African American writers in the mid-twentieth century, as it did for earlier writers such as Angelina Weld Grimké. Richard Wright and Ann Petry with their hefty novels argue implicitly that the grim determinism of *An American Tragedy* and *The Jungle* still works in order to represent poor urban black neighborhoods bypassed by the prosperity of the 1940s–1950s. Yet in his infamous dismissal of the Harlem Renaissance—"Negro writing in the past has been confined to humble novels, poems, and plays, prim and decorous ambassadors who went a-begging to white America"[27]—Wright failed to see that earlier African American writers, from Grimké to Hughes, had already deployed his chosen literary political strategy of delivering tough contemporary political content wrapped in older literary forms, all in the service of a vision of a more just United States. Even Wright's Bigger Thomas is capable of imagining a civil rights era to come, a time when the dream would no longer be deferred, a time when black people would unite in protest and action:

> There were rare moments when a feeling and longing for solidarity with other black people would take hold of him. He would dream of making a stand against that white force, but that dream would fade

when he looked at the other black people near him. Even though black like them, he felt there was too much difference between him and them to allow for a common binding and a common life. Only when threatened with death could that happen; only in fear and shame, with their backs against a wall, could that happen. (114)

The content of Bigger's "dream" of black solidarity echoes nothing more clearly than Claude McKay's 1919 sonnet "If We Must Die": "If we must die, let it not be like hogs." McKay's poetic speaker wants "us," even though "pressed to the wall, dying," to fight back.[28] McKay's poem was considered by some later readers, if not by Wright, as quite sufficiently militant; the Black Panther Party included the poem in its entirety in the January 4, 1969, issue of its newspaper, in which they declared 1969 "the year of the Panther."[29] "If We Must Die" offers us a sturdy bridge to yet another, and far more recent, text that likewise offers a story of the overdetermined capital punishment of a poor and ill-educated young black man, a novel that, unlike *Native Son,* was able to benefit from the many progressive political, literary, intellectual and philosophical movements that flourished after Richard Wright's death in 1960, including Black Power and black feminism.

Ernest Gaines's exquisite 1993 novel *A Lesson before Dying,* while it is very much a contemporary work shaped by recent political realities, still owes much to *Native Son.* In form and content, *A Lesson before Dying* emerges out of the predictability and repetition of black male incarceration and death. It takes place in rural Louisiana in 1948 and begins with a description by Grant Wiggins, the college-educated black narrator, of the trial of Jefferson, a local young black man accused of murder: "I was not there, yet I was there. No, I did not go to the trial, I did not hear the verdict, because I knew all the time what it would be."[30] In fact the entire black community knows: "we all knew . . . what the outcome would be. A white man had been killed during a robbery . . . and he, too, would have to die" (4). Perversely, the prosecutor and the defense attorney, both white men, rely on the same horrendous racist stereotype in order to make their cases. According to the prosecution, the crime "proved the kind of animal he really was," while the defense argues that Jefferson is no more than an animal, a "hog" incapable of planning and carrying out such a crime (6, 8). Again, as with Mary Dalton and Jan in *Native Son,* white liberals pin black men to anachronistic racial, and racist, roles. Seemingly patterning his argument on the words of another Jefferson—Thomas Jefferson—the defense attorney argues for his client's lack of the fundamental characteristics of humanity:

> "What you see here is a thing that acts on command. A thing to hold the handle of a plow, a thing to load your bales of cotton. . . . That is what you see here, but you do not see anything capable of planning a robbery or a murder. . . . Ask him to name the months of the year. Ask him does Christmas come before or after the Fourth of July?[31] Mention the names of Keats, Byron, Scott, and see whether the eyes will show one moment of recognition. Ask him to describe a rose, to quote one passage from the Constitution or the Bill of Rights. Gentlemen of the jury, this man planned a robbery? Oh, pardon me, pardon me, I surely did not mean to insult your intelligence by saying 'man'—would you please forgive me for committing such an error? . . .
>
> "What justice would there be to take this life? Justice, gentlemen? Why, I would just as soon put a hog in the electric chair as this." (7–8)

Despite this speech, with its ostensibly universal, nonetheless clearly racialized and classed, standards of knowledge and humanity, the all-white, all-male jury predictably finds Jefferson guilty, and he is sentenced to die in the electric chair: "Death by electrocution. The governor would set the date" (9). The rest of the novel spins out from the shared black project of bringing out and establishing Jefferson's manhood[32]—the fact that he is *not* a "hog"—before he is executed. Gaines seems at once to build from McKay's declaration and to put to rest, once and for all, not only the defense attorney's appalling assessment of Jefferson but also Thomas Jefferson's assessment, in *Notes on the State of Virginia,* of black people as having a "want of forethought" and as living more according to "sensation than reflection." "To this," Thomas Jefferson concluded, "must be ascribed their disposition to sleep when abstracted from their diversions, and unemployed in labour. An animal whose body is at rest, and who does not reflect, must be disposed to sleep of course."[33] The enduring power of such racist ideas to keep black people back in time concerns Gaines more than does anything else in this novel, and it is no coincidence that Jefferson is described in much the same way Wright's narrator described Bigger

Thomas, as an animal, a "cunning beast" (413). Grant Wiggins explains that even in 1948, "there was not a single telephone in the quarter," the black part of town (25). In this premodern setting, "things change very slowly," Grant observes to a white visitor, and he observes the quarter's repeating cycle of black male misery: "They [his young male students] are acting exactly as the old men did earlier. They are fifty years younger, maybe more, doing the same things those old men did who never attended school a day in their lives" (53, 62). With tragic irony, Gaines's black men, like Bigger Thomas, experience a telos that is outside modernity and modern linear time yet is also produced by them. Of course, the ultimate telos for every human subject is death. The ghastly delivery of the electric chair, "around eight," leads to a series of assurances to various characters in different scenes that "nothing would happen" until "between twelve and three" (240–41).

"Things change very slowly"—and sometimes not at all—within the very form of Gaines's novel. Grant is charged by his aunt and Jefferson's godmother, Miss Emma, to help Jefferson become a man. As Miss Emma explains, "The law got him . . . . And they go'n kill him. But let them kill a man" (22). Grant visits Jefferson at the jail many times over the course of the novel, with each visit marked by "the usual routine" (81). Gaines's narrator offers us nearly incantatory descriptions of the food Grant brings, the search he and the food undergo, and the grim grayness he sees in Jefferson's cell; all recur each time: "By now I could probably have done this with my eyes shut," Grant remarks (81). But this repetition of the jailhouse experience only mirrors, for Grant, a bleak stasis on a larger scale:

> She was right; I was not happy. I had heard the same carols all my life, seen the same little play, with the same mistakes in grammar. The minister had offered the same prayer as always, Christmas or Sunday. The same people wore the same old clothes and sat in the same places. Next year it would be the same, and the year after that, the same again. Vivian said things were changing. But where were they changing? (151)

Things do change within the world of the novel, to the degree that Grant succeeds in his mission; Jefferson becomes a man who writes. He produces a moving journal and goes to his death with dignity. However, the process by which he is sentenced to that death is unchanged: "Twelve white men say a black man must die, and another white man sets the date and time without consulting one black person. Justice?" (157). The question of justice thus remains, unchanged and unchanging—and perpetually unanswered. As James Baldwin said in 1970, "no black man has ever been tried by a jury of his peers in America. And if that is so, no black man has ever received a fair trial in this country."[34]

But why, in 1993, does Gaines produce a novel with form and content alike emerging out of a desperate stasis in 1948 Louisiana, a novel that acts and reenacts the unjust imprisonment and eventual execution of a black man? Starting in the 1980s, mainstream media as well as academic presses began publishing scores of articles and books about black men as an "endangered species," among them the 1988 documentary *Black Men: An Endangered Species;* the influential 1988 essay collection *Young, Black, and Male in America: An Endangered Species,* edited by Jewelle Taylor Gibbs; a 1990 *New York Times* article, "Black Men: Are They Imperiled?"; and a 1999 *Time* article on the plight of young urban black men titled "Endangered Species."[35] There have been challenges to this sort of rhetoric. In a 2004 book, bell hooks pointed out the dangers of the "animal analogy," arguing that its users have "embraced racist/sexist iconography that had historically depicted the black male as a beast."[36] Nonetheless, the narrative of black men imperiled persists, with the "endangered species" trope appearing as recently as the February 2009 paperback reissue of Jawanza Kunjufu's *State of Emergency.* Of course, *A Lesson before Dying,* too, objects to likening black men to animals, yet that does not mean that the novel or the novelist would deny the reality of disproportionate rates of black male incarceration and capital punishment at the time either of the book's setting or its publication. Overdetermined narratives of black male crime clearly remain relevant. According to the U.S. Department of Justice, as of mid-2007,

> the custody incarceration rate for black males was 4,618 per 100,000. Hispanic males were incarcerated at a rate of 1,747 per 100,000. Compared to the estimated numbers of black, white, and Hispanic males in the U.S. resident population, black males (6 times) and Hispanic males (a little more than 2 times) were more likely to be held in custody than white males. At midyear 2007 the estimated incarceration rate of white males was 773 per 100,000. Across all age categories, black males were incarcerated at higher rates than

white or Hispanic males. Black males ages 30 to 34 had the highest custody incarceration rate of any race, age, or gender group at mid-year 2007.[37]

As of mid-2007, there were 182,100 black males between the ages of eighteen and twenty-four in prison, and in all there were 2,090,800 people in prison, with black men accounting for 814,700, or about 39 percent of them.[38] Thus, Gaines is only *apparently* writing historical fiction. A *Los Angeles Times* book reviewer observed of Gaines and *A Lesson before Dying*: "The author, a native of south Louisiana, unerringly evokes the place and time about which he writes. Some passages are redolent with the aura of a memoir."[39] The same reviewer is put off by the novel's temporal-formal qualities, its repetitiveness: "The pacing of the novel, however, is a bit too languorous, even for a Southern writer writing about Southern characters. Gaines' use of repetition wears thin over the course of the book."[40] The reviewer overlooks the possibility that repetition constitutes the novel's primary meaning and that Gaines might be writing just as much about the 1990s as the 1940s—and, for that matter, just as much about Los Angeles as about rural and small-town Louisiana. Changelessness surrounding narratives of black male criminality and lack of opportunity is mirrored by Gaines's content and form.

What *has* changed since the 1940s and *Native Son*, however, is the role of black women in such narratives of black men caught in the justice system. In *A Lesson before Dying*, black women are central to the plot and to the lives of black male characters in ways distinctly different from what we saw in *Native Son*, for instance. Likewise, Gaines's best known work, *The Autobiography of Miss Jane Pittman*, represents a black woman at the center of African American and U.S. history; indeed, a number of critics have viewed Miss Jane Pittman as an embodiment of that history.[41] Thus, Gaines, unlike Wright, writes a woman-centered novel, perhaps having benefited from black feminist activism and theory of the 1970s–1990s. However, none of Gaines's books can be said to be formally postmodern; they follow the pattern established by 1910s antilynching drama: a strategic anachronism whereby past literary forms serve to represent and protest the unchanging nature of racially inflected justice. Gaines produced what can only be called an old-fashioned novel at the time, the early 1990s, when Don DeLillo wrote *Mao II* (about which *New York* magazine said: "DeLillo at his most aphoristic; you wonder if he'd been reading too many poststructuralist interpretations of his work and decided to just skip the plot and cut straight to the theorizing");[42] Nicholson Baker wrote *The Mezzanine* and *Vox;* Thomas Pynchon wrote *Vineland;* Ishmael Reed wrote *Japanese Spring;* Toni Morrison wrote *Jazz;* and John Edgar Wideman wrote *Philadelphia Fire.* Simply by featuring a straightforward, chronological story told by a single first-person narrator whose identity remains clear to the reader throughout, Gaines's novel was out of step with the prevailing postmodern forms of much of the literary fiction his contemporaries were writing. Gaines himself, speaking of his writing of *Miss Jane,* says:

> I followed this multiple point of view technique for a year then I discarded it. (I should mention here—I should have mentioned earlier—that the original title was "A Short Biography of Miss Jane Pittman," and that it was changed to "The Autobiography of Miss Jane Pittman" when I decided to tell the story from a single voice— Miss Jane's own. . . .) I decided to change the way of telling the story because I had fallen in love with my little character, and I thought she could tell the story of her life much better than anyone else. The others were making her life too complicated in that they had too many opinions, bringing in too many anecdotes. I thought a single voice, Miss Jane's, would keep the story in a straight line.[43]

Gaines also departs from postmodernist content: "Truth to me is what people like Miss Jane remember."[44] For Gaines, there still is a capital-T Truth, even if that truth is contingent on the memories of our elders.

Suzan-Lori Parks, by contrast, writes unquestionably postmodern drama and prose; her form is seemingly as influenced as DeLillo's is by poststructuralist theory. Still, Parks's content is in some ways familiar and quite compatible with Gaines's and Wright's, and even with that of some much earlier African American texts. Her 1990 play *The Death of the Last Black Man in the Whole Entire World* audibly, if in avant-garde and deeply vernacular fashion, echoes the first page of Frederick Douglass's *Narrative*: "Whensit gonna end. Soon. Huh. Mercy. Thuh tree. Springtime. And harvest. Huh."[45] Just as slaves inhabited a premodern temporality determined by the cycle of regional agricultural labor—Douglass's "planting-time, harvest-time, cherry-time, spring-time, or fall-time"[46]—Parks's characters are trapped in a history defined and delimited by race. They are walking, talking allegories and stereotypes: Black Man With Watermelon; Black Woman With Fried Drumstick; Lots of Grease And Lots of Pork; Yes And Greens And Black-Eyed Peas Cornbread; who date their entrapment from Columbus's arrival in the New World. Indeed, the first words spoken by a character named, aptly enough, Before Columbus, are "Before. Columbus" (102). Queen-Then-Pharaoh Hatshepsut, an ironic invocation of a mythical Afrocentric history, then explains, "Before Columbus thuh worl usta be *roun* they put a /d/ on the end of roun making it round. Thusly they set in motion thus end. Without that /d/ we coulda gone on spinnin forever. Thus /d/ thing ended things ended" (102; emphasis in original).

Queen-Then-Pharaoh Hatshepsut's explanation suggests that Columbus's project, at once colonial and teleological, depended on Western notions of linear time and progress, over and against cyclical, unending ("roun") notions of time. Parks's own ponderings about the nature of time support this reading: "Could Time be tricky like the world once was—looking flat from our place on it—and looking at things beyond the world we found it round?"[47] Before Columbus expands on this intertwining of time and colonization and empire, adding the slave trade to the mix: "Back when they thought the world was flat they were afeared and stayed at home. . . . Them thinking the world was flat kept it roun. Them thinking the sun revolved around the earth kept them satellite-like. They figured out the truth and scurried out. Figuring out the truth put them in their place and they scurried to put us in ours" (103). It was, in fact, their circumnavigating exploration that first taught the European powers that time was neither universal nor static. As early as 1522, Spanish sailors from Magellan's crew realized, according to Ian Bartky, that they had "lost" a day on their return home.[48] Bartky offers numerous accounts of European explorers struggling to understand the time differences they encountered when traveling to their colonial "possessions in the Far East."[49] Thus, transoceanic colonial travel gave rise to the need for date lines and time lines. Europeans' encounter with the temporal instability inherent in the process of empire seems at odds with—or perhaps actually complementary to—the changelessness and immobility both ascribed to and enforced on the peoples Europeans encountered, those who became the colonized and the enslaved. Johannes Fabian has noted the tendency of European anthropology toward "denial of coevalness to the [non-European] cultures that are studied."[50] That static, or "frozen," to adapt Fabian's term (81), state assigned by anthropologist and colonizer constitutes the "/d/" affixed to

Parks's "roun." Fabian concludes that "a clear conception of allochronism is the prerequisite and frame for a critique of racism" (182 n. 13). Or, as Parks puts it, "through each line of text I'm rewriting the Time Line."[51]

In the context of a time line rewritten, Parks's phrase "the death of the *last* black man" signifies at once the final death—that is, the last black man left alive in the whole entire world (an implicit endangered black man argument)—*and* the most recent, in that he is just the latest black man to die, with many more to follow him. The nearly compulsive repetition within the form of the play supports the latter interpretation. Among the sparse stage directions are: "*(A bell sounds twice)*" (103); "*(A bell sounds once)*" (105); "*(A bell sounds four times)*" (110); "*(A bell sounds three times)*" (111). The repetition and revision in dialogue, what Parks terms her "Rep & Rev,"[52] echo the multiple tolling bells; Black Man With Watermelon intones: "The black man bursts into flames. The black man bursts into flames" (103). Parks thereby joins Gaines and Wright in delivering content that shows the apparently timeless nature of racialized justice and punishment, as modern lynching and contemporary capital punishment bleed into one another. Black Man With Watermelon says, "Last meal I had was my last-mans-meal" (106), and he functions as a kind of living ghost throughout the play, one of Wideman's "living bodies of dead men." In the play, only formal penal structures, both literal and figurative, distinguish one kind of unjust death from another. As Black Man With Watermelon puts it, "I had heard of uh word called scaffold and thought that perhaps they might just build me one of um but uh uhn naw just outa my vocabulary but uh uhn trees come cheaply" (118). Regardless of whether the meting out of that death is juridical (scaffold/capital punishment) or extra-juridical (burning/lynching), readers, spectators, and characters all know what's coming. Just like the community in *A Lesson before Dying,* and like the characters in 1910s antilynching plays, Park's characters are familiar with the processes of execution, whether by hanging, burning, or electrocution:

BLACK WOMAN WITH FRIED DRUMSTICK: They comed from you and tooked you. That was yesterday. Today you sit in your chair where you sat yesterday and thuh day afore yesterday and afore they comed and tooked you. Things today is just as they are yesterday cept nothing is familiar cause it was such a long time uhgoh.

BLACK WOMAN WITH WATERMELON: Later oughta be now by
   now huh? . . .
BLACK WOMAN WITH FRIED DRUMSTICK: Thuh chair was por-
   table. They take it from county tuh county. Only got one. Can
   only eliminate one at uh time. Woulda fried you right here on
   thuh front porch but we dont got enough electric. No onessgot
   enough electric. Not on our block. Don't believe in havin enough.
   Put thuh Chair in thuh middle of thuh City. Outdoors. In thuh
   square. Folks come to watch with picnic baskets. . . . (107)

In Park's play, the line "Things today is just as they are yesterday" corresponds to the moments of expectation in antilynching plays wherein black
women knew that when black men in their families were late, lynching
was the likeliest explanation. Inherent in this utter predictability of black
male mortality are injustice and familial destruction, both of which are
expressed through the nearly compulsive repetitiveness in plays by Grimké
as well as Parks. John Edgar Wideman's novel *The Lynchers* intervenes in
this predictable pattern of violence and formal repetition; his four main
black male characters in fact reverse it by planning *and scheduling* the
"lynching [of] a white cop," what they call "a formal lynching. With all the
trimmings."[53] This act (which never actually takes place) would be so
powerful, so counter to the conventional order of things, that the date
planned for the lynching produces "a hole in time destroying the meaning
of the calendar" (451). We can understand this reversal ("a lynching in
blackface") and its "formal" destruction of time as symbolic counterparts
to Parks's aesthetic-political project, in which she aims to rewrite the time
line by compulsively returning to, and thereby condemning, the seemingly endless cycle of black men's violent deaths. Both novel and play, in the
words of one of Wideman's characters, aim "to shatter the arbitrary balance and order" (597, 494).

   Of course, we should be true to Parks's tone as well as her "Rep & Rev"
and other "elements of style," as she terms her formal innovations.[54] Unlike Wideman—not to mention Wright, Gaines, and the antilynching
dramatists—Parks can be funny. For instance, in contrast to Wideman's
immensely weighty "event so traumatically symbolic that things could
never be the same afterwards" (614), the title "death of the last black man
in the whole entire world" is clearly meant to be funny, even if also awful.
If we accept Deleuze's notion that "repetition belongs to humour and

irony; it is by nature transgression or exception," we may find humor embedded in the form of Parks's plays, though perhaps not in the works of
the other authors, whose degree of repetition does not quite match
Parks's.[55] Nonetheless, the play's almost frenetic postmodern form, including its extreme repetition and its linguistic playfulness—as Black Man
With Watermelon says, "some things go on and on until they dont stop"
(112)—ultimately does not establish much distance between Parks's *content* and that of her literary forebears, Richard Wright in particular. *The
Death of the Last Black Man* even includes a character named And Bigger
And Bigger And Bigger, who introduces himself as "Sir name Tom-us and
Bigger be my Christian name. Rise up out of uh made-up story" (115). The
play thereby intentionally extends the story of black male execution we
know from *Native Son*. But Parks's Bigger ends up wearing a choking
noose: "WILL SOMEBODY WILL THIS ROPE FROM ROUND MY NECK GOD
DAMN I WOULD LIKE TUH TAKE MY BREATH BY RIGHTS," rather than dying
in the electric chair (120; emphasis in original). Noose, electric chair, scaffold, tree, and hanging and burning converge in Parks's Rep & Rev tab-
leaux of the killings of black men across time. She even offers a kind of
dramatic ekphrasis as Black Man With Watermelon describes a scene
from a lynching postcard: as he is "swinging" from a noose, "they puttin
uhway their picnic baskets" (119). Parks's visual imagery and neologistic
language together signify that "history" becomes "histree" for the lynched
black man, and the black male characters begin to merge, "Black Man
with Watermelon/And Bigger and Bigger and Bigger" (121, 123). Near
play's end, Black Woman With Fried Drumstick says, "This could go on
forever"; Black Man With Watermelon replies: "Lets. Hope. Not." (127).

To return to Deleuze, the "emancipation of time" he posits that cinema
can deliver via the "time-image" cannot obtain in the theater either (39).
Stage performance means that actors, not image, repeat in time. Dialogue
is spoken again and again, and stage directions are followed again and
again—by actual voices and bodies. Whereas the "motion picture" has the
"power to compress and expand everyday time," as O'Malley pointed out,
drama has the complementary power to inhabit it fully (206). That im-
mersion in time coupled with the repetition and revision in Parks's plays
leads to her break with twentieth-century African American literature's
long-established pattern of wrapping current content in prior forms.
Whereas the novels of Wright and Gaines rely on familiar novelistic conventions of naturalism and realism, Parks exploits experimental literary

forms and the inherent potentialities of drama not only to represent racial trauma and injustice but, as I will argue in this book's conclusion, to envision, perform, and call for a new, more just world. Just so, while Bigger "Tom-us" may reappear, along with the grimly familiar thematic of lynching and capital punishment in *The Death of the Last Black Man in the Whole Entire World*, the play's formal qualities, its word play and postmodern influences, deliver new literary and even political possibilities that in turn suggest that there may be a third way to interpret the play's title: the seemingly impossible possibility of the "last" unjust killing of a black man, and finally, emancipation from time: Lets. Hope. So.

4

"Seize the Time!"

Strategic Presentism in the Black Arts Movement

> I am in the sound
> The sound is in me.
> I am the sound.
>
> —Walter DeLegall, "Psalm for Sonny Rollins"

That many black thinkers from the late 1950s through the early 1970s were preoccupied by time and philosophies of time is highlighted by the formation of the Dasein Literary Society, a circle of black writers originally based at Howard University. The group started forming as early as 1958; they published a literary journal, also called *Dasein*, from 1961 through 1973.[1] The name of both group and journal testifies to the writers' engagement with the work of Martin Heidegger (1889–1976), who understood human subjectivity to be a condition of individuality in and over time and coined the term "Dasein," *being in time*, or *being there*, to describe that condition; in Heidegger's words (in translation), "being-in-the-world."[2] Winston Napier, along with Eugene Redmond and Aldon Nielsen, is among the very few scholars ever to write about the Dasein group, and Napier confirms that Oswald Govan, a Dasein Literary Society founding member and a Howard math major who later became a philosopher-mathematician, "selected the title for the journal, abstracting it from his readings in German Phenomenology."[3] In 1963, the Dasein group published a collection of their poetry titled *Burning Spear: An Anthology of Afro-Saxon Poetry.* "Burning Spear" was the nickname of Jomo Kenyatta, the first prime minister of an independent Kenya in 1963, and then its first president from 1964 until his death in 1978. This anthology title and the group's name situate these writers and their work not only firmly in the 1950s–1960s but also in a doubly international context, as they identify themselves with both an ongoing Western/European philosophical tradition and an ongoing postcolonial/black diasporic one.

The Dasein writers thus mark a distinct shift in African American arts and letters. Unlike Frederick Douglass, Pauline Hopkins, Charles Chesnutt, the antilynching dramatists, Richard Wright, Ann Petry, and Ernest Gaines, the Dasein poets constitute an artistic community "imagined" on the grounds of what Benedict Anderson terms "temporal coincidence," or, more precisely, as the group's name suggests, on Heideggerian *being there.*[4] The Dasein Literary Society supplants strategic anachronism, a sense of being out of step with one's own times, with an equally strategic presentism derived from their active participation in and contribution to the philosophies, aesthetics, and politics of their period: being in the world. This is *not* to say that earlier African American writers had failed to participate in the philosophies and politics of their day. To give just one example, Richard Wright's membership in the Communist Party in the 1930s and his existentialist writings of the 1940s and 1950s identify him very strongly with his era. Still, Wright's characters—not to mention his novels—were generally "outsiders" temporally, racially, or politically. Figures like Bigger Thomas or Cross Damon, the protagonist of Wright's 1954 novel *The Outsider,* do not fit comfortably in their times in much the same way the naturalist novel *Native Son* is formally out-of-synch, drawing at midcentury on a naturalist literary mode characteristic of the works of the white American novelists Norris, Dreiser, and others at the turn of the twentieth century. Even Ellison's formally innovative *Invisible Man,* while it offers us the concluding possibility that the novel's narrator may be speaking for all of us, nonetheless emphasizes an alternative black temporality theorized from a marginal underground: "Invisibility, let me explain, gives one a slightly different sense of time, you're never quite on the beat."[5]

By contrast, Dasein poetry's form and content are deeply invested in the present and even in optimism about that present. While not denying the power of history, the Dasein poets claim and foreground contemporaneity through writings that represent the imminence of (at the least) justice and equality and (at the most) thoroughgoing social and political change or revolution. For instance, Oswald Govan's *Burning Spear* poem "The Lynching" offers thirteen past-tense free verse stanzas detailing the horrifying historical trauma of lynching, stanzas that are then resolved by a concluding quatrain that speaks to the elemental power of present-day black solutions:

A spear burns
in the cool dark earth.
A spear burns
and a tide descends.[6]

In their present-tense understanding and representation of blackness, the Dasein poets stand as neglected predecessors of better known black cultural nationalist figures; in Aldon Nielsen's words, "across three decades the Dasein group appeared and reappeared as a vocal instigator of the new black arts" (77). Granted, it was not until the later 1960s and early 1970s that black nationalism, whether cultural or political, would be fully articulated in the United States. Yet well before the 1966 founding of the Black Panther Party (BPP) in Oakland, California, and well before Larry Neal published his manifesto "The Black Arts Movement" in 1968 and Amiri Baraka published *Black Music* (which included his influential 1966 essay "The Changing Same") in 1967, and well before Baraka declared "It's Nation Time!" in 1970, the Dasein group had imagined *being there* through black art and had linked their poetic forms and content to the tempos and sounds of jazz.

It is especially on these last, literary-formal grounds that we must give the Dasein group their due. Their poetry married form and content in order to forward a new commitment to the times, to the meters and the tempos of the present, as part of the project of forging a continuous black subjectivity. Adapting and extending Alexander Weheliye's concept of "sonic Afro-modernity," or black cultural production that is "producing a flash point of subjectivity gleaned in and through sound," I would argue that the Dasein poets made possible some version, however contingent, of a collective blackness sustained beyond an instant or a flash, and did so in part through their systematic connection of the literary to the musical.[7] And the Dasein poets were certainly not shy about their connection with contemporary (for them) jazz; the back cover of *Burning Spear* proclaims: "These eight poets are a new breed of young poets who are to American poetry what Charlie Parker, Dizzy Gillespie, Thelonious Monk, and Miles Davis are to American jazz." Although perhaps not as eminent as such musical giants, the Dasein group clearly helped lay the groundwork for the aesthetic-political theory of the soon-to-follow Black Arts Movement (BAM), most notably the movement's well-known commitment to music and, more broadly, to oral/aural culture. For example, *Burning Spear* includes "Psalm for Sonny Rollins" by Walter DeLegall, a mathematician. Its opening lines echo Rollins's improvisatory, looping, forward-moving horn style of the late 1950s and early 1960s: "This vibrant, all-embracing, all pervading / Sound which bleeds from the vinylite veins / Of my record."[8] DeLegall's present participles and alliterative *v*s and *l*s lend the poem velocity and musicality as well as an almost improvisatory quality; as the poetic speaker proclaims, "I am the sound," identifying poet and poem with Rollins and his horn-playing in the here and now. Similarly, Le Roy Stone, a sociologist, contributed to *Burning Spear* "Flamenco Sketches (To Miles Davis)," a poem that (arguably) echoes Davis's sibilant, melodic, yet highly rhythmic style from the 1960 album *Sketches of Spain* more than it does the languorous "Flamenco Sketches" from the 1959 *Kind of Blue*. Regardless, Stone's poem applauds Davis's internationalist musical aesthetics that are particularly in evidence on the later album:[9]

> Blue Milan
> New York red in weeping
> Black-draped Chicago mourning
> Tinted all in Spanish suggestions
> Flamenco episodes[10]

Just as Eugene Redmond explains, Stone in this poem, with its geographic span and its percussive syncopation, "reveres Davis' use and knowledge of world music" (317). The Dasein group's union of their poetry with the music of their present, their interest in contemporary international philosophical and political movements, and their imaginative construction of present-day black community would be replicated throughout the 1960s and early 1970s by a range of black cultural and political groups, from the BAM writers to the militantly nationalist BPP.

Such presentism not only links the various forms of black nationalism in this period but also differentiates them from earlier African American and Black Atlantic literature and political thought. Whereas Gronniosaw, Equiano, Douglass, and Jacobs asserted black *sameness* articulated via Western literary and rhetorical forms, Black Arts/Black Power–era writing and political activism asserted black *distinctiveness* via African American vernacular and musical forms. Of course the black nationalisms of the 1960s and 1970s, either in their theory or their practice, were not without precedent. As early as the mid- and late nineteenth century, Martin Delany and Sutton Griggs were writing of imagined black nation-states in *Blake* (1861–62) and in *Imperium in Imperio* (1899). And certainly a great deal of black writing of the 1920s self-consciously linked African American subjectivity to oral cultural practices, to music, and to international constructions of blackness. Furthermore, the expatriatism of many twentieth-century African American performers and writers—including Josephine Baker, Ada "Bricktop" Smith, Langston Hughes, and Jessie Fauset in the 1920s; Richard Wright and James Baldwin in the 1940s and 1950s; W. E. B. Du Bois, Maya Angelou, James Baldwin, and Dexter Gordon in the 1960s and 1970s—testifies to a wide range of international African American experiences and communities across decades. Similarly, the Marxist sympathies, and sometimes Communist Party membership, of a number of African American writers of the twentieth century—Du Bois, Hughes, McKay, Wright, and Ellison among them—testifies to the engagement of individual African American writers with international political theory throughout the twentieth century.

Nonetheless, the era of Black Arts and Black Power remains unique in African American cultural history for its sustained, widespread, collective, intentional, and explicit intertwining of the literary with the oral and musical, and the political with the cultural and the international. As Eugene B. Redmond noted in *Drumvoices,* a landmark 1976 history of African American poetry:

> One major difference between the cultural/political upsurges of the twenties and the sixties/seventies was location: the renaissance was centered literarily, if not always geographically, in Harlem; but its recent successors can be found in every North American community with a substantial black population. Another difference was in degree of artistic-political consciousness. To be sure, the cultural and political arms of the [Harlem] renaissance were, on occasion, interlocked. But such marriages never reached the current state of "wholeness" and "continuity." (347)

Redmond may overstate somewhat the centrality of Harlem for the New Negro Movement and understate somewhat that movement's political commitments, yet he is on target about the "continuity" that the Dasein poets first articulated and that soon came to characterize the Black Arts era that was reaching its end at the time of Redmond's writing. Redmond's term "continuity" effectively encapsulates the complex dynamics of multiple 1960s and 1970s black cultural and political nationalisms. Black Arts writers and Black Power activists alike understood their projects to be temporally and geopolitically *continuous* with: black musical and oral/vernacular culture, other domestic revolutionary and protest movements, and other non-U.S. nationalisms and postcolonial developments of their time. We can find across the range of the multiple and various, often competing, black nationalisms in the United States of the period the same investment in, and representation of, being in time, *being there*. If Dasein represents a particularly literary and university-based version of presentist black community, then the BPP could be seen as a particularly political and community-based version, though one that possessed stronger and more active cultural and academic "arms" than is often acknowledged.

The internationalist underpinnings of the Black Panthers' political thought, on the other hand, are both generally accepted and well known. Huey Newton and Bobby Seale (the party's founders), Eldridge Cleaver, and Stokely Carmichael were all, in Jane Rhodes's words, "profoundly influenced," not only by "the powerful writing and rhetoric of Malcolm X" but also by the writings of Karl Marx, Frantz Fanon, and Che Guevara, along with *Quotations from Chairman Mao Tse-Tung*, a list that comprises what Rhodes succinctly terms "the core revolutionary texts of the day."[11] Eldridge Cleaver confirms that he "sought out" Marx's books and that he "fell in love with Bakunin and Nechayev's *Catechism of the Revolutionist*," while Stokely Carmichael and Charles V. Hamilton note the centrality of Fanon's thought for their development "of the concept of black power."[12] Huey Newton in fact identified internationalism as part of what set the BPP apart from other black nationalisms of the day, and he diagnosed the "hang-ups" of black cultural, as opposed to political, nationalists with what he saw as their failure to think internationally beyond Africa:

> Ron Karenga and some other nationalist groups seem to be hung up on surviving Africanisms, or what we call cultural nationalism. Cultural nationalism deals with a return to the old culture of Africa and that we are somehow freed by identifying and returning to this culture, to the African cultural stage of the 1100's or earlier. Somehow they believe that they will be freed through identifying in this manner. As far as we are concerned, we believe that it's important

for us to recognize our origins and identify with the revolutionary Black people of Africa and people of color throughout the world. But as far as returning, per se, to the ancient customs, we don't see any necessity in this.[13]

The Black Panthers' activism generally did match the presentist and internationalist outlook Newton here outlines. For example, the Panther newspaper, the *Black Community News Service,* was "to play a central role in the construction of an imagined community of black revolutionaries across the United States and eventually across the globe," as Rhodes points out (97). The weekly paper kept the black community alert, in the present, to police brutality and actions taken against the Panthers and announced the party's platform and "rules" as well as upcoming meetings.[14] The very first issue called for action in protest of the killing by a police officer of Denzil Dowell, a black resident of North Richmond, California: "BROTHERS AND SISTERS WE MUST UNITE. MANY OTHER MURDERS AND BRUTAL BEATINGS HAVE TAKEN PLACE WITHOUT US DOING MUCH OF ANYTHING. BUT LET'S STOP IT *NOW!* WITH SOME REAL NITTY GRITTY *POLITICAL ACTION.*"[15]

The January 4, 1969, issue announced the Panthers' free Breakfast for School Children program, one of the literally present-time, ongoing daily (and successful) actions of the party.[16] The increasingly internationalist orientation of the BPP was reflected, as well, in the renaming of the newspaper as the *Black Panther Intercommunal News Service (BPINS)* in early 1971. "Intercommunal" was Huey Newton's neologism, created as a result of his realization that "the United States is an empire [rather than a nation], [and] that would make it impossible for us to be internationalists. We are no longer internationalists, we're not afraid about that. Matter of fact we will try to shed light upon it, and we will define the new transformation and the phenomena, and we will call ourselves 'Intercommunalists.' Because nations have been transformed into communities of the world."[17]

Elaine Brown, information minister and later chairperson of the party, described *BPINS* as "report[ing] on the condition of blacks inside the United States as well as on liberation struggles of oppressed people throughout the world."[18] Likewise, David Hilliard, a BPP founder and its former chief of staff, observed in a recent interview: "We were a global movement."[19] However, as accurate as Newton's description of the presentism and internationalism of the BPP may have been, his rejection of "cultural nationalism" as a possible means to social or political change is not nearly as reflective of actual Panther activities.

Indeed, Newton's dismissal of cultural nationalism—in his words, "the only culture worth holding is revolutionary culture"—should be treated with some skepticism.[20] First, his stated views on culture may have been inspired as much by schisms and power struggles within Black Power as they were by actual ideological differences. As of Newton's 1969 writing, Ron (now Malauna) Karenga was heading a BPP rival, the US Organization. Perhaps more important, Newton was definitely downplaying the BPP's interest and investment in culture as part of their political agenda; in fact, presentist politics and cultural enterprises of various sorts were regularly linked in BPP activities. For example, "Seize the Time," one of the party's key slogans, was the title of Bobby Seale's 1970 book chronicling the formation of the BPP; it was also the title of a 1969 album recorded by Elaine Brown. The album, recently rereleased as a CD, includes ten songs written and sung by Brown, including "Seize the Time," "The Panther," "Very Black Man," and "Assassination." Perhaps surprisingly, the songs are perhaps best described as typically late-1960s, summer-of-love soft rock, or perhaps pop soul/R & B, yet with (as the titles suggest) explicitly political and revolutionary lyrics, as in "Seize the Time": "You've never even fought/For the liberty you claim to lack/ . . . /Oh, Seize The Time."[21] Seize the Time was, as well, the name of the record label on which the Black Panthers' very own soul/R & B group, Lumpen (as in lumpenproletariat), recorded. In an interview in 2009 with James Mott, an original member of Lumpen, Rickey Vincent asked Mott: "What did Huey [Newton] think of the Lumpen?" Mott responded: "He thought that we were very viable . . . [the] cultural aspect was . . . also a way of communicating [through] music. . . . Getting the message of the party across [through Lumpen] was very viable as far as Huey was concerned."[22]

Moreover, while Newton downplayed the presence of this cultural "arm" of the BPP, he also overstated the cultural nationalists' preoccupation with the past and the exclusivity of their interest in Africa. Certainly, recovering and revaluing African history and heritage were core pursuits for many black cultural nationalists. But even Karenga could at times sound rather like Newton, as in his 1968 declaration that "all art must reflect and support the Black Revolution, and any art that does not discuss and contribute to the revolution is invalid."[23] Likewise, many BAM writers echoed the BPP's message about the importance of the present and of international connections in addition to those between the United States and African nations. Larry Neal in his 1968 manifesto "The Black Arts Movement" stated that the "Black aesthetic" is "broader than" the "African–American cultural tradition," in that "it encompasses most of the useable elements of Third World culture."[24] Similarly, as of the early 1970s, Amiri Baraka was moving away from his call for a black nation within the United States and was writing, instead, of "Afrikan Revolution":

> Afrikan People all over the world
> Suffering from white domination
> Afrikan People all over the world
> Trying to liberate their Afrikan nation(s)
> Afrikan People all over the world[25]

Like the Dasein poets before him, Baraka uses literary-formal means to deliver a presentist, global message. *It's Nation Time,* a short 1970 Third World Press publication of three poems by then "Imamu" Amiri Baraka, concludes with "It's Nation Time," a poem that carries urgency, action, confidence, and unity in its imagery and in its insistent present tenses, participial forms, compressed words, and rapid tempo:

> Time to get
> together
> time to be one strong fast black enrgy space
>   one pulsating positive magnetism, rising
> time to get up and
> be[26]

As in Walter DeLegall's earlier poetry, here the lack of capitalization and punctuation, the assonance of the short *a,* and the alliteration and consonance of the *p* and *s* all contribute to a sense of swift possibility and pending change. Similarly, "the black man is the future of the world," "when brothers take over the school," "come together in unity unify / for nation time" (21, 22): these lines document and laud the student protests and sit-ins that were happening during the period and that sparked the start of black studies programs at colleges and universities across the nation. At the same time, such political-academic enterprises are linked, via Baraka's own literary-poetic enterprise, to the musical, the oral, and the performative:

> Come together in unity unify
> for nation time
> it's nation time . . .
>> Boom
>> Boom
>> BOOOM
>> Boom
>> Dadadadadadadadadadad
>> Boom
>> Boom
>> Boom
>> Boom
>> Dadadadad adadadad
>>> Hey aheee   (soft)
>>> Hey ahheee   (loud)
>> Boom
>> Boom
>> Boom
> sing a get up time to nationfy (22)

The poem establishes transnational and transcultural black identity and spiritual power—Christ, "krishna," Shango, hermes, moses, budda [sic], and "Rasta farari" are all black in this poem—and it does so on the grounds of tempo and time:

> chant with bells and drum
>> its nation time (24)

Overall in "It's Nation Time," Baraka is calling for a black nation inaugurated by music. He didn't have to wait long for a response.

Baraka's "chant" was taken up swiftly and directly by Joe McPhee, a free jazz artist whose 1971 album *Nation Time* was "a tribute to author, playwright, poet and music critic Ameer [sic] Baraka (Le Roi Jones)," according to McPhee's original liner notes. McPhee, playing tenor sax and trumpet, wrote the title piece, "Nation Time," as a "24 bar composition," but in the live performance recorded for the album, according to the notes,

> the 24 bar construction is abandoned . . . in favor of a more free, spontaneous interpretation, to allow for audience interpretation. Each player is free to choose the musical route he prefers. There is no set chordal sequence upon which to base the improvisations, and *only the time and rhythm patterns were predetermined.* The second section, built on another riff figure and shuffle rhythm pattern, is a spontaneous group improvisation.[27]

Like Baraka in his poem "It's Nation Time," McPhee and his musicians blend individual oral/aural performances into a unified whole on the basis of time. The piece begins and ends with a call to the audience: "What time is it??!!" The response: "Nation time!!" with the very last sounds we hear highly rhythmic, regular, martial rolls of the drum punctuated by high hat. This musical call for "the building of a Black Nation" was performed in a perhaps surprising setting: Vassar College's Urban Center for Black Studies, where McPhee taught a course titled "Revolution in Sound." McPhee's music thus linked free jazz not only to the world of Black Arts and Black Power but also to the academic world. His was an intellectual and cultural practice in the name of presentist black nationalism. McPhee and his band perform for their audience Karenga's "rhythmic reality of a permanent revolution" (2090)—that is, a musical version of the black nationalism Stokely Carmichael theorized in 1967: black people "will not be stopped in their drive to achieve dignity, to achieve their share of power, indeed, to become their own men and women—in this time and in this land—by whatever means necessary" (185).

The remarkable "conversation" between Baraka and McPhee is just one among many such exchanges in the Black Arts/Black Power era, when individuals who blended the literary, the musical, and the political were more the rule than the exception. Whereas Paul Robeson stands out as a rare performer-intellectual-activist of the 1920s, the 1960s saw the rise of quite a number of musical political activists and political musical performers, from the BPP's Elaine Brown and Lumpen's Walter Mott to Nina Simone, Archie Shepp, and Sun Ra, who even contributed a number of poems to *Black Fire,* a 1968 anthology of "Afro-American writing" edited by Amiri Baraka and Larry Neal. Robin D. G. Kelley observes that the activist think tank the Afro-American Institute, founded in 1962 by members of the radical black organization Revolutionary Action Movement, "even recruited the great drummer Max Roach to help organize a panel entitled 'The Role of the Black Artist in the Struggle for Freedom.'"[28] Just a few years later, the Black Panthers started Lumpen explicitly in order to spread the revolutionary message.[29] In a recent interview with Rickey Vincent, Michael Torrance, another original member of Lumpen, explained: "We were Panthers first [before we were musicians], by no means were we entertainers. . . . We were a cultural-educational cadre." But the fact remains that the Lumpen were serious and talented musicians and performers, and they were clearly, despite Torrance's insistence otherwise, entertainers, and they were good ones. Torrance continues: "We [the Lumpen] had a lot of choreography; we wanted to take the model that was popular and recognizable to the people in the community, particularly the black community . . . like the Temptations but with strong rhythm like James Brown."[30] And of course, as a number of music scholars and historians have noted, black popular music of the period, including James Brown's, was occasionally in the business not just of making money but, sometimes at least, of delivering political messages.[31] Many listeners heard subtle, and sometimes not so subtle, statements of pride, nationalism, urgency—even calls for uprising—in popular songs, including Brown's 1968 "Say It Loud, I'm Black and I'm Proud" and especially Martha [Reeves] and the Vandellas' 1965 hits "Dancing in the Street," "Heatwave," and "Nowhere to Run," that offered a sound track to the long hot summers of the late 1960s. In addition, as Brian Ward has suggested, such songs might have more effectively helped black listeners imagine a unified, black national identity by dint of their sheer popularity than did some of the "New Jazz" that was far more explicitly part of a black cultural nationalist project yet reached a far smaller audience. As Ward puts it, "popular music did shape people's view of the world, their sense of selfhood and community," and it "did contribute to the ways in which ordinary people arranged their beliefs, values and priorities" (15).

Of course, connections between political movements and music were neither new in, nor were they unique to, the Black Arts and Black Power era.[32] There have been many instances of political and activist song in the genealogy of African American music and performance, for example

Billie Holiday's "Strange Fruit," any number of blues songs about alienated labor from the 1910s on, and the antebellum sorrow songs that most scholars of the form agree were often coded plans for escape from slavery.[33] Still, the exceptionally strong and self-conscious connections between music and the various forms of black nationalism and activism in the 1960s and 1970s have been well documented.[34] Black Arts Movement historian and literary scholar James Smethurst rightly notes that "the Black Arts conception of a popular, revolutionary African American cultural avant-garde [was] rooted in a continuum of African American vernacular music" (39). Certainly, Black Arts writers and Black Panthers alike were quite conscious of the role vernacular music had to play in the period's range of black nationalisms. Baraka, in his influential 1966 essay "The Changing Same," argued that "Rhythm and Blues is part of 'the national genius' of the Black man, of the Black nation. It is the direct, no monkey business expression of urban and rural (in its various stylistic variations) Black America."[35] In this context, it is worth underscoring the fact that Lumpen was a *soul/R & B* group—even though we might have expected the resolutely anticapitalist Black Panthers to steer clear away from the more commodified forms of popular culture. For example, they famously loathed "blaxploitation" films. In Bobby Seale's words: "The Black Panther Party denounces this silver coated form of oppression."[36] But apparently even the BPP realized that soul and R & B might be a quite effective way to reach "the masses" with a revolutionary message. Yet it was jazz and experimental musicians, for example Archie Shepp and Sun Ra, who were consistently and outspokenly committed to imagining new black identities and expressing them through their musical inventions. Indeed, Baraka, as much as he claimed to value R & B, privileges the political intentionality, transnationalism, and intellectual presentism of 1960s avant-garde jazz musicians, as in his review of Archie Shepp's 1964 album *Four for Trane* (i.e., John Coltrane), in which he focuses on the tenor sax player John Tchicai: "Like Shepp, Tchicai carries the world-spirit in his playing, what is happening now, to *all of us*, whether we are sensitive enough to realize it or not. Contemporary means that; with the feeling that animates our time. Shepp, Tchicai and the other players on this album do just that."[37] Baraka continues his temporal-musical/black cultural nationalist theorization in his discussion of four Albert Ayler albums, *My Name Is Albert Ayler* (1963), *Spirits* (1964), *Spiritual Unity* (1964), and *Bells* (1965). For Baraka,

Albert Ayler is the atomic age. Sun-Ra, who was supposed to be heard on this album, but was not because of the missionary's vagaries, is the Space Age. These two ages are co-existent . . . .

[T]he album is also heavy evidence that something is really happening. Now. Has been happening, though generally ignored and/or reviled by middle-brow critics (usually white) who have no understanding of the emotional context this music comes to life in.

This is some of the music of contemporary black culture. The people who make this music are intellectuals or mystics or both. The black rhythm energy blues feeling (sensibility) is projected into the area of reflection.[38]

Baraka links, almost without breath or pause, "contemporary black culture . . . rhythm energy blues feeling" with his appreciation of "something [that] is really happening. Now."

Such relentless insistence on the present and on certain ideals of "black culture," would, inevitably, have its costs. The masculinism and heterosexism of a number of BAM writers, taken all too often to the point of misogyny and homophobia, and the anti-Semitism embedded in a number of the movement's writings have all rightly been targets of critical ire for quite some time.[39] The movement has been called to task not only for such rigid and discriminatory notions of black identity but also for its dismissal of history, including and even particularly African American cultural and musical history.[40] As Adolph Reed put it in his classic essay "Black Particularity Reconsidered," the "nationalist elaboration of Black Power . . . froze . . . into an ahistorical theory of authenticity."[41] In their drive toward Nation Time, BAM writers actually rather enthusiastically cut loose the legacy of the New Negro writers. Larry Neal offered one of the most definitive affirmations of the movement at the expense of the Harlem Renaissance: "The Black Arts Movement represents the flowering of a cultural nationalism that has been suppressed since the 1920's. I mean the "Harlem Renaissance"—which was essentially a failure. It did not address itself to the mythology and the lifestyles of the black community. It failed to take roots, to link itself concretely to the struggles of that community, to become its voice and spirit."[42]

Philip Brian Harper understands the Black Arts writers' denial of any indebtedness or similarity to the New Negro Movement as stemming from an "anxiety of influence" and a wish to see their movement not only as "historically distinct" but also as distanced from the bourgeois values and accommodationism they ascribed to African American writers of the 1920s.[43] I would add that it was the black nationalists' relentless presentism that, in and of itself, contributed to their occluded historical vision and their outsized sense of their own exceptionalism.

And it may be true that *early* African American literary history held few models for the deep musical-literary-political interconnections of the 1960s and early 1970s. Antebellum African American writers engaged surprisingly rarely with musical, or more broadly, oral traditions and cultural practices. Frederick Douglass's brief sorrow song passage in *The Narrative of the Life* (1845) and Harriet Jacobs's sporadic use of black and white lower-class dialect and her brief mention of slaves singing in church in *Incidents in the Life of a Slave Girl* (1861) are among the few examples. But significant and more numerous precedents for the Black Arts writers' literary, if not political, use of oral, vernacular, and musical forms began to emerge in the United States around the turn of the twentieth century, with Charles Chesnutt's 1890s conjure stories, Sutton Griggs's inclusion of orations in his 1899 *Imperium in Imperio,* Paul Laurence Dunbar's "dialect" poetry, and Du Bois's transcription of sorrow songs in the last chapter of his 1903 *Souls of Black Folk.* African American writers' adoption and adaptation of oral and musical forms became broader and more thoroughgoing during the Harlem Renaissance, with the publication of Langston Hughes's jazz poetry, McKay's "dialect" novels, Zora Neale Hurston's vernacular fiction and drama, and James Weldon Johnson's spiritual and poetry collections, for example *Gods' Trombones* (1927). In James Weldon Johnson's words, "genuine folk stuff," "such folk sources as the blues and the work songs . . . are unfailing sources of material for authentic poetry."[44] As his words here demonstrate, while Amiri Baraka, Haki Madhubuti, Sonia Sanchez, and Nikki Giovanni in the 1960s and 1970s often chose literary forms inspired by the content and tempos of oral/aural and folk black culture, the New Negro writers had done just that four decades earlier.

Langston Hughes may be the figure who most thoroughly disrupts Larry Neal's narrow dismissal of the Harlem Renaissance. Hughes had only recently passed away when Neal published his 1968 manifesto, and he remained a productive and politically aware and committed artist virtually to the end of his life. In 1963, Hughes and the Chicago poet Margaret Danner recorded an album, *Poets of the Revolution,* that was released in 1964 on Black Forum, a spoken-word label of the Motown recording company. On this album, Danner and Hughes discuss their poetic process and perform their poetry, including Danner's perhaps best known poem, "To a Cold Caucasian."[45] Hughes's voice was being recorded at around the peak of the Dasein poets' activities and on the eve of the emergence of the BAM, and that timing is fitting, for as Aldon Nielsen has observed, "like Coleman Hawkins in jazz, Hughes was a bridge between generations of black artists" (41). Danner, too, was a bridge figure; as Eugene Redmond tells us, she—along with Gwendolyn Brooks, Margaret Walker, and a few others—was "among the older group of writers who vigorously took up the banner of the new mood" of the 1960s (303). Yet most of the younger Black Arts writers evinced little interest in crossing that bridge.

In the end, the BAM's dismissal of the Harlem Renaissance, rather like Richard Wright's earlier dismissal of it,[46] implies that the Black Arts figures were exceptional in ways that don't match history. Philip Brian Harper has made a similar point about Addison Gayle's delineation of Black Arts writers' audience. In his 1971 book *The Black Aesthetic*, Gayle proclaimed that unlike Harlem Renaissance writers, "today's black artist . . . has given up the futile practice of speaking to whites, and has begun to speak to his brothers."[47] Harper aptly observes that the BAM's claim to be speaking exclusively to black people, despite attempts to position the movement as "historically unique," actually "establishes itself as a historical repetition, insofar as, nearly fifty years before, a black theorist of the Harlem Renaissance made a very similar claim about the nature of that movement" (179). The black theorist whom Harper has in mind is Alain Locke, who in a 1925 essay, "Youth Speaks" (included in *Survey Graphic*'s "New Negro" number in March 1925), declared: "Our poets have now stopped speaking for the Negro—they speak as Negroes. Where formerly they spoke to others and tried to interpret, they now speak to their own and try to express."[48] But Harper might just as easily have been thinking of Langston Hughes, who in his 1926 essay "The Negro Artist and the Racial Mountain," published in the *Nation*, wrote that "jazz to me is one of the inherent expressions of Negro life in America" and that in "many of" his own poems, he tried "to grasp some of the meanings and rhythms of jazz."[49]

It turns out that, despite some Black Arts writers' repudiation of the Harlem Renaissance, the movements share more than an interest in audience and in folk-oral cultural and musical sources. Their theoretical underpinnings, too, are often remarkably alike. First, like the black cultural and political nationalists of the 1960s and 1970s, writers of the Harlem

Renaissance understood their politics and aesthetics to be of a piece with other nationalisms of their period. In his own 1925 manifesto "The New Negro," Locke explicitly analogizes a movement centered in Harlem to other modern nationalist, particularly cultural nationalist, movements:

> In Harlem, Negro life is seizing upon its first chances for group expression and self-determination. It is—or promises at least to be—a race capital. That is why our comparison is taken with those nascent centers of folk-expression and self-determination which are playing a creative part in the world to-day. Without pretense to their political significance, Harlem has the same rôle to play for the New Negro as Dublin has had for the New Ireland or Prague for the New Czechoslovakia.[50]

This linking of the New Negro with other cultural nationalisms, particularly the Irish Renaissance, was repeated by a number of other Harlem Renaissance figures, including James Weldon Johnson.[51] As Brent Hayes Edwards has argued, understanding their intellectual and political work as taking place within an international context "is a constant thread in the work of black intellectuals" of the 1920s.[52]

The Harlem Renaissance shares with 1960s and 1970s black nationalism not only such self-conscious transnationalism but also an awareness of its own contemporaneity. If, to use Edwards's terms, the New Negro Movement was engaged in "the practice of diaspora," in the forging of a transnational black subject, then, as with the Black Arts and Black Power thinkers, that subjectivity necessarily depended on time as well as space. Inasmuch as geography becomes less decisive within the "inherently cosmopolitan and diverse" notion of black subjectivity that, according to Edwards, characterizes the Harlem Renaissance along with other period movements, for example Pan-Africanism and Négritude (113), it must be, then, on other grounds—race, color, and temporality chief among them—that collective black subjectivity is being forged. Just so, in the 1920s as in the 1960s, a transnational black community was being imagined through an "awareness of being imbedded in secular, serial time, with all its implications of continuity," to quote Benedict Anderson (205), who in turn is echoing, if unintentionally, Eugene Redmond's 1976 term "continuity" (347). In order to theorize a modern black diaspora that must have been based on something along the lines of Anderson's and Redmond's temporal continuity, Edwards appropriately looks to Johannes Fabian's notion of "*coevalness*" (185), which Fabian defines explicitly in terms of time: "coeval, i.e., share the same Time" (30). Yet Edwards redefines, perhaps even misappropriates, Fabian's term as being primarily spatial in nature, as signifying "the cohabitation of this particular metropolitan space in all its contradictions" (185). Similarly, Edwards focuses on music as a central "practice" of a black diaspora in the 1920s, arguing, for instance, that in Claude McKay's "*Banjo,* a black transnational community is defined more than anything else by a certain relationship to music" (190), while paying little attention to music's *temporality.* Edwards's conclusion that "black internationalism . . . is less like a sturdy edifice or a definitive program than like the uncertain harmony of a new song" (318), as persuasive and poetic as it is, overlooks the fact that harmony constitutes only one aspect of song. As a quotation from George Antheil on the very last page of *The Practice of Diaspora* attests, "black music is 'so intricate in rhythmic pattern, so delicately balanced in contra-rhythms and proportions'" (318) that time, in the form of tempo and rhythm and sustain, is necessarily among its predominant formal qualities. Therefore, to the degree that 1920s black intellectuals, artists, and activists endorsed the notion of a transnational, even extra- or postnational ("intercommunal") "African rhythm of life,"[53] the rhythmic, the temporal *must*—along with the spatial, the geographic—be theorized as a necessary constituent of black diasporic identities. Indeed, we cannot easily separate the temporal and the spatial. Certainly we can understand why scholars of African American and black diasporic literature and music might be reluctant to focus on time and tempo, given the very long legacy of racist stereotypes about rhythm. To give just one such instance, as Brian Ward notes, during the early civil rights period, "white obsession with the pace or tempo of black music was part of a broader concern with its rhythmic potency," with a bodily and sexual fetishization of black culture underlying that white obsession (249).

Yet rhythm and tempo served, as well, a clearly intraracial agenda in the United States in the 1960s and early 1970s, just as they had in the 1920s. African American cultural theorists in both periods outlined a newly possible and newly achievable black present—what Karenga called "the rhythmic reality of a permanent revolution" (2090) and what Locke called "quickened centers of the lives of black folk" that find expression in "a renewed race-spirit that consciously and proudly sets itself apart."[54] The similarities between the two movements unfold from this initial, shared understanding of newness and distinctiveness articulated by an avant-garde leadership seemingly already located at the cutting edge of their time. Locke in 1925 announced "a new group psychology" among "American Negroes" that was to be stirred by "the new intellectuals among them."[55] In their 1967 book *Black Power: The Politics of Liberation,* Stokely Carmichael and Charles V. Hamilton proclaimed their own "aim to define and encourage a new consciousness among black people" (viii). Carmichael and Hamilton's assertion that "one must start from premises rooted in truth and reality rather than myth" (viii) could just as easily, with only slightly altered terminology, have appeared in "The New Negro," wherein Locke states that "the old Negro had long become more of a myth than a man" (3). Locke wants to move beyond "the obsolete," with the Great Migration figured as "a deliberate flight not only from countryside to city, but from medieval America to modern" (5, 6). Karenga wants black art to "commit us to a future that is ours" because "whatever we do, we cannot remain in the past, for we have too much at stake in the present" (2089, 2090). Alain Locke says of "the Younger Generation" of "New Negro" artists that they "bring the artistic advance of the Negro sharply into stepping alignment with contemporary artistic thought, mood, and style. They are thoroughly modern, some of them ultra-modern, and Negro thoughts now wear the uniform of the age."[56] In sum, when African American intellectuals, activists, and artists have collectively imagined, and to some, however limited, degree achieved a sense of equality—explicitly in terms of aesthetic/cultural nationalism or separatism—their representations and philosophies of time take on a new quality. We find in both the 1920s and the 1960s an imagining of black subjectivity and simultaneity, here-ness and now-ness, expressed via connections between oral/musical and print cultures and through a conscious association with other revolutionary, cultural-national, or postcolonial struggles of the times: "Seize the Time!"

Of course, we must acknowledge that black intellectuals in the 1920s and 1960s were seizing different times and different tempos. As Weheliye has observed, studies of black literature in relationship to oral and musical forms all too "frequently posit music and orality as static constants, mapping one particular form of music, such as the blues onto all of black culture, or locating a pre-technological orality in black cultural history" (7). The blues of the 1920s, like the New Negro Movement, cannot be understood apart from the Great Migration, immigration from the West Indies, the return of black veterans from World War I, segregation throughout the

United States, race riots in a number of American cities, and widespread white racial terrorism. And in the 1920s, *Plessy* remained the law of the land, *Birth of a Nation* was rereleased, the Dyer antilynching bill failed in the Senate, and the state of Virginia passed the Race Registration Act. In sum, as I have argued elsewhere, during the time of the Harlem Renaissance, racial segregation "served as the nation's primary post-Reconstruction legal and social modality."[57] Thus, to be fully presentist in this period was to confront an at once ongoing and long-standing, federally codified project of keeping African Americans without access to anything resembling full citizenship or justice—that is, being kept back in time. Revisiting the past and revising dominant versions of it begin to seem like reasonable political and formal strategies, not just for the anti-lynching dramatists, but even for such a generally presentist poet as Langston Hughes. Although best known for his invention of jazz and blues poetry, Hughes, like Grimké and Douglas Johnson, also mined the past for poetic form. In his 1927 poem "Song for a Dark Girl," Hughes parodied the immensely popular 1859 minstrel tune "Dixie," exploiting its conventional and repetitive, even trite, form to deliver the traumatic content of lynching: "Way Down South in Dixie / . . . / They hung my black young lover."[58] Hughes obliterates the original's bouncy nostalgia, correctly replacing the repeated, violent murders of black men, and the trauma that then repeatedly results for black women, at the center of southern history and its popular culture. Hughes's form here, particularly the refrain—along with Du Bois and Johnson's turn to sorrow songs and to rural black folk culture, indeed their cultural turn altogether—makes a great deal of sense when understood in the context of political and social realities for African Americans in the 1920s. A revised and usable past was crucial for withstanding a traumatic present wherein the cultural sphere remained far more available and far less dangerous than a political one. Certainly, political activism and demands for civil rights were not safe in the 1960s either. Yet by the time of the Dasein group's formation in 1958, lynching had become a rare enough (though by no means bygone) occurrence that the 1955 lynching of Emmett Till helped galvanize the civil rights movement. And while segregation may have remained the nation's de facto modality, it was no longer its de jure one. The *Brown v. Board of Education* decision in 1954, the Civil Rights Act of 1964, the Voting Rights Act of 1965, Thurgood Marshall's ascent to the Supreme Court and the election of Edward W. Brooke (the first African American senator since

Reconstruction) in 1967, the election of Shirley Chisholm (the first African American woman in Congress) in 1968: all substantiate the Black Arts figures' commitment to presentism.

The Black Arts writers and Black Power activists also had the advantage of being situated among many other international and domestic activisms and activists—anticolonial struggles across the globe (especially in Kenya, for Dasein), the many facets of the civil rights movement in the United States, Malcolm X and the Nation of Islam, the antiwar movement, the New Left, women's liberation, the gay rights movement, the American Indian Movement, and so on: all were under way or were flourishing by the late 1960s. Even the perennially optimistic Alain Locke, by contrast, had to bracket any "pretense to . . . political significance" for the New Negro Movement when he analogized Harlem to Dublin and Prague.[59] In a sense, the BAM writers and artists could afford to live more fully in the present than could the Harlem Renaissance writers and artists; their 1960s political ambitions were shared by so many others historically marginalized and oppressed both within and outside the nation's borders. Their more sustained optimism makes sense as well, with audible anger replacing despair,[60] New Jazz and R & B taking the place of the blues, and highly vocal demonstrations across the country taking the place of such events as the 1917 silent march in Harlem—together, these black activisms signify what Weheliye terms "sonic modernity," one way of "becoming-in-the world for modern black subjects in the West" (50).

Ironically, despite that unprecedented sense of *being there* in the BAM, it seems to share one final element with the Harlem Renaissance: failure. Larry Neal didn't mince words in calling the Harlem Renaissance "essentially a failure" (2050). Likewise, one of the main theoreticians of the movement, Addison Gayle, held out the possibility that this movement, having corrected what he perceived to be the errors of the Harlem Renaissance, would "escape the fate of its predecessor in the nineteen twenties, and endure" (1918). But accusations of failure and error have in fact been regularly leveled at the BAM, starting from shortly after its ending on up to the present.[61] If its ultimate project was to forge a strong and enduring collective black subjectivity, then the movement's exclusionary, disciplinary tendencies had always carried with them the seeds of failure.[62] For instance, as Philip Brian Harper has brilliantly argued, when Baraka claimed to be "Calling all black people" in his 1969 poem "SOS," he wasn't *really* calling all black people, because not all African American people in 1969 would have responded to the term "black," much less identified with a black nationalist project of any sort (182–83). Such rhetoric of authenticity was deeply and inextricably linked to the BAM's sense of its own currency, its thoroughgoing presentism. Clearly, not all black people were keeping Nation Time in the 1960s; even some who *thought* they were apparently were not.

In December 2000, Amiri Baraka wrote a review in *JazzTimes* of McPhee's 1971 *Nation Time* on its 1999 rerelease as a CD. The review was recently reprinted in Baraka's collection *Digging: The Afro-American Soul of American Classical Music* (2009). In the review, Baraka dismisses both musician and album, and he seems actually to take offense at McPhee's "tribute" to him thirty years earlier: "McPhee is often in danger of being the other pole of what happens to influence without depth, impact without complete understanding of WHY the paradigmatic expression emerged in the first place. It is ironic that the title of the CD and the first piece carry a phrase that this writer first introduced, as a political statement animated by the Black Liberation Movement."[63] Baraka dismisses what he terms McPhee's "essentially rhythm and blues shaped mainstream musical approach" (contradicting his own earlier valorization of R & B) and concludes that his album *Nation Time*

> is limited by a confused and incomplete *use* of his materials. And behind this settles overall into a restatement of funk clichés hoisted occasionally by flashes of "the new." So that despite the Call for the New, R & B clichés obstruct the shaping of something really new. Still, when he blue screams our old Call "What Time Is It?" which was to be answered by the album's title, it does put one in mind of more dynamic times, would that they were more completely expressed in this music.[64]

Here Baraka dismisses McPhee for not being fully with the times, for not being truly *new*; only the sparking of Baraka's own nostalgia makes the CD not a total failure. Baraka's allusion to "more dynamic times" underscores the extraordinary temporal-cultural-political nature and appeal of Black Arts and Black Power, but his distaste for that which is not "really new" speaks as well to the movements' shortcomings. Baraka faults McPhee for "his essentially rhythm and blues shaped mainstream musical approach." If it was that difficult for a cool black male jazz musician to be sufficiently—

at least according to Baraka—with the times, then the chances for the average R & B-listening "cat on the block," to use Baraka's own terms, were pretty slim.[65] Equally unlikely was the possibility that a more coherent and complete expression of those "more dynamic times"—provided, perhaps, by Archie Shepp, or Elaine Brown, or Lumpen, or Sun Ra—would in turn have led directly to widespread social and political change. Granted, such change seemed far more possible in 1971 than it had in 1929, when the Harlem Renaissance was nearing its end. Even so, it wasn't long after the publication of Baraka's book *It's Nation Time* and the release of McPhee's album *Nation Time* that the presentism and optimism of the period, along with the Black Arts/Black Power era and its sense of *being there,* came to a fairly swift end. In the words of one of Wideman's damaged and cynical characters in his 1973 novel *The Lynchers*:

> The others can wear their hair and clothes differently, sing, shout, call one another brother and believe themselves identical with the new wave, part of a new world, containing and contained by it. We have lost any vision beyond a wavering faith in something better than the misery we have lived through. We are certainly not any part of a vision of something better. We are not even vessels of transition.[66]

Indeed, there had been clues even earlier that the black nationalisms that were at their height as of the late 1960s might not, to use Gayle's word, "endure."

In August 1970, an extraordinary series of conversations took place between Margaret Mead and James Baldwin. The two met for seven and a half hours of talk that took place over the course of two days and were transcribed in the 1971 book *Rap on Race.* This "rap" stands as just one of many remarkable moments in the late 1960s and early 1970s that help to disclose the depth and range of the period's ambivalences surrounding blackness in the United States; the disciplinary nature of 1960s black nationalism could neither address nor accommodate those ambivalences. This meeting between two public intellectuals—one the most famous U.S. anthropologist of her day (perhaps ever) and the other considered by many the foremost U.S. black writer of his day—produced some memorable dialogue about the political unrest and social change of 1970. At one point, Mead remarks, "The kids all say—and they're pretty clear about it—that the future is now. It's no use predicting the year 2000."[67] Baldwin agrees with her, and Mead continues: "It's what we do this week that matters." Again, Baldwin agrees, and Mead expands: "Right now, this minute." Baldwin replies, "That's the only time there is; there isn't any other time" (61). Baldwin here neatly sums up what I take to be the prevailing temporal-political-aesthetic climate during the era of Black Power and the Black Arts. But the truth of the matter is that there is *always* another time, and that other time can wield just as much power in the moment as does "right now, this minute." And once again, as in Baraka's disregard for McPhee's version of Nation Time, a reviewer tells a far less cohesive and agreeable (but still temporal) story about this rap on race.

Just as remarkable as Baldwin and Mead's "rap" is the fact that Anatole Broyard, of all people, reviewed it—and reviewed it harshly. Broyard, well known as "a book critic, essayist and editor for *The New York Times* for 18 years until his retirement in June 1989,"[68] is now perhaps equally well known for having passed as white throughout his journalistic career, despite his having been from an African American, if light-skinned, New Orleans family. In his review, Broyard was quite ruthless toward Baldwin, accusing him of exhibiting "nervous shrillness" and of being "almost operatic."[69] At the same time it delivers those veiled slurs about Baldwin's sexuality, the review expresses an impatience bordering on contempt for Baldwin's part of the "rap": "clause upon clause in what seems to be merely rhythms, without cognitive content" (37). Even if Broyard's assessment were accurate about Baldwin's words (which it is not), it completely misses the import of "rhythms" as in and of themselves productive of meaning both in Baldwin and Mead's conversation and within the context of black art and political thought in 1970. After all, the last section of *Rap on Race*, titled "August 27th 11 P.M.," turns on Baldwin's opening gambit (in reply to Mead's question "Now what's been bugging you all day?"): "Enormous question. For me, an enormous question. I still don't know how to put it, quite, but it has something to do with time present. This time and *time*" (165, 167). It may not be surprising that Broyard sees rhythm, based in time but not necessarily on melody, as devoid of meaning. But we cannot help but be astonished at the final sentence of Broyard's review: "While the black experience belongs only to blacks, the truth belongs to everybody" (37). Given that Broyard is probably the most famous person to pass for white in the latter half of the twentieth century, this moment in the review is, to put it mildly, ironic. The racial lie that Broyard lived may help explain an even more ironic moment in the review, wherein he paraphrases (not quite faithfully) Mead's challenge to Baldwin's skepticism about the benefits of mass production: "We can't undo the past, and the steps that got us here have to be incorporated into where we are going next" (37).[70] Both Baldwin and Broyard resist the past's pull, but for different reasons. Baldwin agrees with Sanger that the past cannot be undone, though with the clear caveat that he doesn't "want to go back anywhere!" because going back would mean returning to more oppressive, more segregated times for black people.[71] For Broyard, on the other hand, no, the past cannot be undone, but if is he is lucky, it will not be uncovered and will stay in the past (61). The strategic presentism of Broyard is personal and professional and, in at least some ways, deeply negative. For avowedly black activists, artists, writers, and musicians of the day, on the other hand, strategic presentism, at its best, was, in at least some ways, collective and political as well as optimistic. Of course, that optimism would not be sustained; while it *did* last beyond Weheliye's "flash," it did not last beyond the early 1970s, and that failure to endure was recorded precisely where we might expect: in words, in music, in tempos.

In 1975, during the waning days of the Black Arts era, Gil Scott-Heron and Brian Jackson and the Midnight Band released the album *The First Minute of a New Day*. They included on it a track called "Pardon Our Analysis (We Beg Your Pardon)" that combined spoken word by Scott-Heron with solo piano accompaniment by Jackson. "Pardon" is a response to, and analysis of, President Gerald Ford's pardon of Richard Nixon. Scott-Heron intones: "They call it due process and some people are overdue," registering the (temporal) despair that was prevalent in the wake of 1960s violence as well as the cynicism that was widespread in the wake of the Watergate scandal.[72] Despite the apparently revolutionary cultural production, intellection, and activism of the prior decade—to which Scott-Heron himself had contributed—socially and racially differential justice and time appeared to be still solidly in place as of 1975. *The First Minute of a New Day,* despite its seemingly optimistic and forward-looking title, is actually steeped in pessimism; other lyrics include "It's winter; winter in America / and all of the healers have been killed or betrayed";[73] and "The world is dark, we look to the horizons; / reflections of the sunset yesterday. / Man is in a state of loss, subjected to an evil force. / It hurts so bad the sun has stopped to pray."[74] And in the end, even the album title speaks more to a return to an alternative, and possibly subaltern, temporality than to the emergence of an altered national or transnational temporality that would welcome and make space for innovative black art. As Scott-Heron says in the liner notes to the 1998 reissue of the album as a CD: "They told us we'd have to get up 'pretty early in the morning' to bring something new to the music business. So we got up at midnight. Midnight is 'the first minute of a new day.'" As of 1975, the Midnight Band is no longer seeking *coevalness*, to return to Fabian's term. Yet just a few years earlier, in 1970, Scott-Heron issued a rousing call to revolution, a revolution that was not going to be "televised" but would happen "LIVE." The cynicism and disappointment of Scott-Heron about a revolution that did *not* happen, about the fact that black activist musicians and writers did not establish a sense of collective black subjectivity, *being there*, beyond a decade or so—would ultimately be expressed in African American literature as well. As we will see in the next chapter, a postnationalist, postmodern era witnesses a return to strategic anachronism, in the form of African American hard-boiled detective fiction in the 1990s.

5

Being Black There

Contemporary African American Detective Fiction

Since 1990, Walter Mosley, Barbara Neely, Eleanor Taylor Bland, Anthony Gar Haywood, Nichelle Tramble, and Valerie Wilson Wesley, among a number of other African American authors, have chosen to write not just one detective novel but a series of detective novels. In response to that ever-expanding list of authors and works, quite a few valuable essays and book-length studies of contemporary African American and "ethnic" detective fiction have been published in recent years.[1] Yet for all the attention being paid to African American detective fiction, the reasons for its contemporary flourishing remain a mystery. Few critics have engaged the question why so many African American authors in the 1990s and early 2000s have turned to this particular genre. Paula Woods, a groundbreaking scholar of this type of fiction, has argued persuasively that the use of black detective-protagonists "lets readers know that African Americans are not just the victims or perpetrators of crimes but are also those who try to correct the balance that murder upsets."[2] In considering why so many writers are *currently* working in the genre, however, Woods only speculates briefly: "Perhaps as an outgrowth of the hunger Americans of all colors have developed for black writing, African American mystery writers have also begun to claim the spotlight."[3] Nicole King does get at the "when" in her analysis of several African American novels published in the 1980s—a period, she asserts, that "called forth a resurgence of nostalgic affirmations of black community."[4] She concludes that her chosen novels, including Walter Mosley's *Devil in a Blue Dress,* show the period's "desire to assert 'blackness' . . . as well as the virtual impossibility of representing it as wholly unified or stable."[5] Certainly, given the failure of 1960s and early 1970s black cultural and political nationalisms to establish forms of collective black identity that could be sustained beyond the era of Black Arts and Black Power, King's argument seems to be on target. But as compelling as it is, that argument does not take genre fully into account. Doris Witt perhaps comes closest to solving the mystery, arguing that the detective work of Blanche White, Barbara Neely's serial protagonist, "is very centrally a decoding of contemporary United States body politics, as inflected by sexuality, gender, ethnicity, race, class, age, and (dis)ability."[6] Yet Witt's argument applies not to African American detective fiction in general but solely to Neely's novels and, even more specifically, to Neely's novels in contradistinction to "the urban male-oriented writings of Walter Mosley."[7] Certainly, the Blanche White series—with its female detective, sometimes rural settings, and focus on Blanche's children and lovers— does not fit comfortably into the masculinist "hard-boiled" subgenre of detective fiction that clearly includes Mosley's Easy Rawlins series; yet the crime genre, more broadly conceived, serves some of the same functions for both authors.[8]

Mosley and Neely, along with a number of other African American writers, have chosen a past genre because it suits their literary and political— and inter- and intraracial—purposes particularly well. First, in writing crime novels, contemporary black writers, much like the antilynching dramatists in the 1910s and Richard Wright and Ann Petry in the 1940s, are enacting a strategic (literary) anachronism in order to comment on a distinct lack of progress regarding race within judicial and penal systems in the United States. If for Petry and Wright the Reform Era left Harlem and Chicago's South Side behind, for Mosley and Neely the civil rights era and decades of "urban renewal" left Watts and Roxbury behind. In other words, contemporary black authors are using crime fiction as the ideal form through which to expose and narrate the still-lived experience of being "criminal by color," particularly in poor and working-class urban settings.[9] Despite the Easy Rawlins novels' historically specific settings, then, the past will *not* stay in the past for Easy, and the series investigates and discloses just how much remains the same for him in Los Angeles, even across decades. For Easy, the "first minute of a new day" in Watts feels a lot like the first minute of yesterday and tomorrow. In other words, African American detective fiction since 1990 signals an aesthetic-political abandonment of the Black Arts and Black Power writers' strategic presentism.

Unlike the Dasein poets, Mosley's protagonist finds that a Heideggerian philosophy of time just doesn't work for him. He cannot *be there*, because he is always being *black* there. Unlike 1960s' theorizing of blackness as a source of identity that is of a piece and compatible with other nationalisms and postcolonial movements of the time, the late twentieth century's literary and cultural theory, social science, and biogenetics have undone race itself. As a result, the nature of modern and postmodern black or African American identity has become an increasingly irresolvable mystery, one that the detective form seems to accommodate.[10] Many, and perhaps most, contemporary African American detective novels present readers with questions regarding the possibility of black community, but Neely's novels in particular try, and generally fail, to answer questions about how to establish blackness outside the forces of the law. In the words of her protagonist-detective, Blanche White: "Did white people have any idea how much energy and hope and downright stubbornness it took to live and work and try to find some fun in a place where you were always the first to be suspected, regardless of the crime?"[11] In sum, Mosley and Neely's turn to detective fiction makes a great deal of sense once we begin to trace the nature of the contemporary interracial and intraracial mysteries they are investigating under cover of the murder plot. Those mysteries—one concerning ongoing racially differential justice, the other concerning the elusiveness of contemporary black collective subjectivity—ultimately resolve in much contemporary African American detective fiction (and its criticism) into a single stubborn, racially inflected mystery surrounding families and genealogies, literal and literary, material and philosophical.

Walter Mosley has inherited, and also revitalized, the hard-boiled subgenre of detective fiction that originated decades earlier with the 1930s–1940s novels of Dashiell Hammett and Raymond Chandler. We must note that none of these writers' chosen form bears an accidental relationship to his period. As a number of critics have argued, Hammett's and Chandler's novels cannot be understood apart from their political, social, and literary contexts. In *Gumshoe America*, Sean McCann describes 1930s hard-boiled detective fiction as a Depression-era "cultural complaint" about the "poverty of liberal theory."[12] Arising out of "populist cynicism and its air of fatality," hard-boiled fiction has exposed "the classic mystery tale" as "a political myth, illegitimate because it no longer corresponded to the complex realities of an urban, industrial society" (3, 18). According to McCann, if classic mysteries of the nineteenth century, like the Sherlock Holmes stories, represented the genius-detective as triumphantly reasserting late Victorian legal and social order over and against the lawlessness of individual desires, then 1930s hard-boiled mysteries, like the Sam Spade and Philip Marlowe novels, represent the philosopher-detective as cynically discovering that modern legal and social orders are neither redemptive nor consolatory. In fact, he discovers that they may be both incompetent and malignant, particularly toward vulnerable individuals (89–91). Regarding Chester Himes, McCann concludes that the hard-boiled genre's "traditional preoccupation" with the failures and injustices of the law offered "a perfect means to dramatize the intimate relations between racism and American democracy" at midcentury, resulting in Himes's keen novelistic "vision of American society as a violent and absurd racial carnival" (252).

As of the 1990 publication of the first in his series of detective novels, *Devil in a Blue Dress*, Mosley entered and expanded that carnival, along with the hard-boiled tradition. Indeed, despite the Easy Rawlins novels' 1990–early 2000s publication dates, their protagonist operates very much like the detectives in Hammett and Chandler's novels, as a few critics have argued. With a "lone wolf" private investigator negotiating a complex and corrupt social landscape, the Easy Rawlins series of novels even takes place, like those of Mosley's predecessors, in Los Angeles. Yet in spite of the many parallels between his novels and those of Hammett and Chandler, a great deal of scholarship on Mosley's writing (and on contemporary African American detective fiction in general) has centered on the degree of *difference* it attains from white detective fiction—and therefore, at least according to critics, its degree of both formal subversion and social progressiveness.[13] Gilbert Muller insists that "the most significant influence on Mosley is not so much the pantheon of white writers of detective fiction as it is Chester Himes" and calls Mosley and Himes "transcontinental twins," despite the facts that Himes's crime novels are set in Harlem rather than Los Angeles and feature two police officers (not private detectives), Coffin Ed and Gravedigger Jones.[14] Similarly, Helen Lock insists that Easy Rawlins "is a lot more than simply a darker-skinned version of Philip Marlowe or Sam Spade."[15] For Lock, Mosley's novels represent an "African American experience of double-consciousness, especially in the urban America of the period [in which they are set]."[16] While reaching a very different conclusion, Roger Berger also carefully measures Mosley's novels as potential "texts of difference," reading them as "metacritical allegories that reflect a fundamental ambivalence about his own intervention into white (detective) discourse."[17] Berger argues that their "black characters and locations . . . and their generic 'violations' of the hardboiled detective story" do in fact produce difference from white antecedents. But he decides that inasmuch as Mosley's Easy Rawlins novels "deploy the Chandlerian hard-boiled detective," "Mosley cannot fully disentangle himself from the reactionary politics that are embedded in the genre."[18]

Critics have been just as uneasy with Himes's potential for being like white authors, and they have long struggled with his assertion that he wrote quite traditional detective stories and "just made the faces black."[19] For example, immediately after supplying that well-known quotation from a John W. Williams interview with Himes, Sean McCann counters it: "Given Himes's inventiveness with the genre, that remark must be taken as one of the better examples of false modesty in the history of popular writing" (252). Yet permitting both Himes and Mosley their sameness, as well as their difference, may well clarify the stakes in their return to a "white" genre born in and of the 1930s. If we agree with McCann that all hard-boiled detective fiction of the 1930s functions as a period-specific "cultural complaint," then we should be able to understand Mosley's Easy Rawlins novels (and African American detective fiction in general) in much the same way. The "complex meditation[s]" of Hammett, Chandler, and Himes "on the hopes and disappointments of New Deal liberalism" (308) are matched by Mosley's ongoing meditations on political, social, and legal promises, repeatedly made and repeatedly broken, within a pre– and post–civil rights era United States. The majority opinion in the 1954 Supreme Court decision *Brown v. Board of Education* called for integration "with all deliberate speed."[20] This vague timetable, with its contradictory blend of patience and urgency, ultimately framed a failed project. Mosley's (and others') return to a quintessentially modern (and quintessentially cynical) genre underscores that failure and offers an implicit argument that we have yet to earn the "post" in postmodernity. We have not solved the fundamental mystery of the liberal democratic state: how to achieve liberty and justice for each and for all, or even simply how to integrate schools and neighborhoods. Sameness (just as much as difference) becomes, then, a deeply political and historically engaged literary argument, with Mosley rightly taking his place alongside Chandler and Hammett, his literary "ancestors," to use Ralph Ellison's terms, in a genealogy of hard-boiled detective fiction writers.

That genealogy also establishes that Mosley is only most obviously writing hard-boiled detective fiction; he is also writing historical fiction. Indeed, he is writing *doubly* historical fiction—that is, his novels are historical at both metageneric and local-content levels, with period mattering just as much as genre in the Easy Rawlins series. As one interviewer observes, "Mosley thinks of novels as documents of the history of the time and believes that people are more likely to read a novel for an understanding of a historical period than a history book. So he strives for a kind of fundamental accuracy."[21] Mosley's ongoing, color-coded Easy Rawlins series began with *Devil in a Blue Dress* (1990), set in 1948, followed by *Red Death* (1991), set in 1951; *White Butterfly* (1992), set in 1956; *Black Betty* (1994), set in 1961; *A Little Yellow Dog* (1996), set in 1963; *Bad Boy Brawly Brown* (2003), set in 1964; *Little Scarlet* (2004), set in 1965; *Cinnamon Kiss* (2005), set in 1966; and *Blonde Faith* (2007), set in 1967.[22] But the temporal layers we see in this list do not in and of themselves necessarily distinguish Mosley's novels from other detective fiction. Tzvetan Todorov, following Van Dine and Burton, has argued for a "duality" of narrative timelines in all detective novels. As Todorov puts it, the "whodunit . . . carries not one but two stories: the story of the crime and the story of the investigation."[23] Throughout the Easy Rawlins series, Walter Mosley adopts yet also supplements the temporal duality Todorov associates with detective fiction; in each book, we encounter not just two stories and two time lines (crime and investigation) but at least two additional time lines and stories resulting from Mosley's juxtaposition of the modern and the contemporary in terms of genre, setting, and publication date. And to the degree that the contemporary turns out to look much like the modern—in fact, to be the *same*—Mosley's novels work as literary-political statements. He chooses to return in the 1990s and early 2000s to a genre born of 1930s discontent in order to write novels set in the 1940s–1960s, thereby enacting a complex process of literary anachronism that describes and inscribes both past and present-day injustice and discontent.

Black Betty, for example, takes place in 1961 but was published in 1994. The plot turns on Easy's search for the missing title character, who had been working as a domestic servant for a wealthy white family. Easy is hired by the family to find Betty, ostensibly in order that she might receive an inheritance following the death of the family's patriarch. In his pursuit of her, Easy travels from Watts to a Beverly Hills gated community and back, encountering and uncovering police brutality and a great deal of white-on-black violence along the way. Clearly, the novel is commenting simultaneously on Los Angeles—and the United States—both of its setting and its publication date.[24] As we read, we cannot help but draw parallels between Mosley's early 1960s Los Angeles, which will soon erupt in the 1965 Watts uprising, and the Los Angeles of thirty years later, which will rupt again in 1992 as a result of economic and judicial injustice. Yet the time in which *Black Betty* is *set* had appeared to be a time of promise, particularly for African Americans. At the outset of the story, Easy says, "I tried to think of better things. About our new Irish president and Martin Luther King; about how the world was changing, and a black man in America had the chance to be a man for the first time in hundreds of years."[25] The naming of Kennedy and King as metonyms of hope suggests that the narrative itself knows that any hope will soon be dashed. That is, just as we the readers are well aware that both figures will be assassinated, the narrative, in a kind of cynical prescience, knows it too. Indeed, Easy's optimism quickly falters: "I wanted to feel better but all I had was the certainty that the world had passed me by—leaving me and my kind dead or making death in the dark causeways" (*BB* 46). In Watts in 1961, even the sense of a possibility "of better things" could not be sustained. Thus, in Easy Rawlins's neighborhood, it's always "winter in America / and all of the healers have been killed or betrayed," to use Gil Scott-Heron's words from 1975.[26] Alternatively, in Henri Bergson's terms, the future is "closed" for those living in Watts. The question Mosley implicitly poses is whether there has ever been an "opening" for them in the twentieth century; have poor people in Watts attained élan vital in the decades since the first Watts uprising?

The period when *Black Betty* was written and published, the early 1990s, not unlike the early 1960s, appeared to be a time of promise—and again, especially for African Americans. A man Toni Morrison would later famously and controversially, if somewhat indirectly, term "our first black president" ("Blacker than any actual black person who could ever be elected in our children's lifetime") was about to be elected.[27] Of course, Morrison was wrong. But in any case, as of 1992, African American *writers* in particular had cause for optimism about the new, reading president. As the *New York Times* noted in December 1992, the Clintons "read books of all sorts . . . [a]nd that is the most striking feature of a cultural profile of the first-family-to-be."[28] Even before the election, Bill Clinton had been profiled as a voracious reader, with mysteries among his favorites. In August 1992, then *Boston Globe* journalist Michael Frisby described a campaign flight with Bill Clinton during which the candidate "admitted to being an avid book reader and cited two of his recent favorites as the mystery

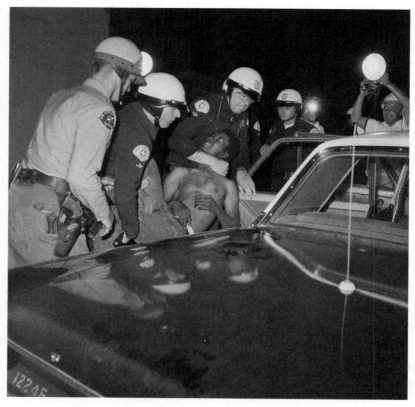

African American man being forcefully arrested during Watts uprising. 1965. Original caption: "8/12/1965—Los Angeles, CA: Policemen force a rioter here into a police car during second night in a row of rioting. The rioters, led by a hard core of 300 hoodlums, were controlled by heavily armed police." Bettmann Archive. Courtesy of Corbis Images, Corbis Corporation, New York, N.Y.

detective novels *Devil in a Blue Dress* and *Red Death* by Walter Mosley."[29] Clinton was even photographed on the campaign trail while holding a copy of *White Butterfly*, Mosley's then most recent Easy Rawlins novel. At the time, Clinton told reporters covering the campaign that Mosley was his favorite mystery writer.

In his very next novel, Mosley offered a response to the "first fan," as well as a commentary on Clinton's 1992 campaign image as a common man, and on his political promises of expanded opportunities for all Americans. Frisby also noted, in covering a September 1992 political rally,

that Clinton "promised yesterday to bring a new approach to government . . . [saying], 'I have done my best for more than a year now to offer
the American people a new approach, one that goes beyond trickle-down
economics without going back to tax and spend'"—in the journalist's
words, the candidate was "returning to a theme."[30] He was, after all, "The
Man from Hope" in the famous and extraordinarily effective video from
the 1992 Democratic convention; the very first words of this stirring video
are spoken by Bill Clinton himself: "I was born in a little town called Hope,
Arkansas."[31] As if in direct reply to that candidate, soon to be president—
who signed the North American Free Trade Agreement into law in 1993
and would in 1996 sign the "Personal Responsibility Act" (i.e., welfare
reform)—Easy declares in the second chapter of the 1994 *Black Betty*:
"hope is the harshest kind of dreaming" (*BB* 57). Easy's rather hopeless
version of "hope" reflects his restricted social position that in turn shapes
his particular methods of detection: "Hunches," he explains, "are a desperate man's way to hope" (*BB* 330).[32] Easy's livelihood, itself a mode of
understanding and moving in a highly racialized urban American landscape, renders "hope" unreliable as either an epistemology or a means of
upward social mobility. Such riffing on Clinton's campaign rhetoric of
birthplace-as-policy detects and discloses the nonuniversality of such
narratives of bootstrapped success as the one that took the candidate
from Hope, Arkansas, to the White House.[33] Easy concludes that "a better
day might have been coming, for some people—but not for everyone"
(*BB* 46).

In the 2004 installment in the series, Easy even suspends his own
moral code because of persistent racial injustice: "It hadn't felt right. . . .
But the denizens of Watts were under the law with no say. . . . I would have
put Mouse [Easy's ultraviolent best friend] in the White House if I could
have."[34] In other words, despite Toni Morrison's intriguing theory, Mosley, through Easy, reminds us that there are substantive differences between a figure like Easy Rawlins or Raymond Alexander (Mouse) and one
like Bill Clinton. It still makes a difference whether a man is poor and black
in Los Angeles or poor and white in rural Arkansas. For example, Easy
describes his chillingly familiar encounter with the Los Angeles Police
Department:

Six men! Policemen. There were around the car and in the doors
before I could even think.

> I was dragged from the front seat and thrown to the asphalt.
> "Spread 'em!"
> "Get the keys. Search the vehicle."
> They went through my clothes and cuffed my hands behind my back.
> "Hey, man! What'd I do?" I shouted.
> That got me a nightstick pressed hard across the back of my neck.
> "You just shut up," an angry voice whispered in my ear. (*BB* 125)

The police take Easy to jail, where they beat him: "My chin sure hurt later when I woke up in my new jail cell. My chest hurt too, and my arm and the back of my hand. A big knot had swollen up above my diaphragm and my side ached awfully. He must have hit me after I was out. That's the only way I could understand it, all those bumps and bruises" (*BB* 133). The echoes of the Rodney King beating here seem to suggest that at least some things are liable to stay the *same*, across time, for the black man in Los Angeles—and therein lies at least some of the political power of the Easy Rawlins series. As Roger Rosenblatt argues of Richard Wright's fiction, "time is only useful when one's life is changed during or by it";[35] or, as Easy says, "no matter how far back you remember, there's a beatin' there waiting for you" (*LS* 48). However, we must acknowledge that while *sameness* helps produce the literary and political power of Mosley's and other African American authors' detective fiction, so too does *difference*.

Not all critics have privileged the differences between Mosley and his protagonist and white hard-boiled detective fiction authors and their protagonists. For example, Helen Lock succinctly explains that Easy, like the classic hard-boiled detective, "operates in a frequently murky borderland between good and evil [and] is thus an essentially liminal figure."[36] Just as Lock suggests, Easy does possess the typical hard-boiled detective's liminality in that he dwells between regions, classes, and discourses, between legality and illegality, and between legitimacy and illegitimacy. However, I would extend and complicate her argument. Yes, Easy's liminality resembles Sam Spade and Philip Marlowe's, but it is, at the same time, both racially specific and highly individual. Easy's *version* of being "in between" is, in fact, precisely what sets him apart from Chandler's and Hammett's detectives and permits him to exceed their cultural and racial scripts. His sameness—in this instance at least—is different. Theodore Mason agrees, asserting that for Easy, "the borders between 'races' and between genders"

Screengrab from George Holliday, "Rodney King Beating Video" at 26 seconds. March 3, 1991. http://www.rodney kingvideo.com.ar/.

are "the site not only of the criminal act but also . . . the site of culturally transgressive possibility."[37]

Easy in fact crosses a number of borders over the course of the series. We learn at the very beginning of the first novel that he is a black World War II veteran who has migrated from Houston to Los Angeles.[38] That collective (raced and gendered) experience of the Great Migration and of segregated wartime service is perhaps best represented by Easy's flexible speech, yet that speech also reflects the contingencies of his own individual experience, intelligence, and personality. For example, in each of the books, he can and does shift smoothly among various forms of black vernacular and to standard English when he needs to. In *Black Betty,* Easy says of wealthy white clients: "I spoke in a dialect that they would expect" (*BB* 122); and in *Bad Boy Brawly Brown,* he says of a young African American revolutionary: "my diction and grammar slid into the form I wanted Junior to hear."[39] Here, Junior and Easy share a racial identity, but Junior cannot detect (or reproduce) Easy's linguistic shifts any more than can the rich whites in *Black Betty.*

Even more important, what Liam Kennedy terms Easy's "social . . . mobility" far exceeds that of Sam Spade or Philip Marlowe, even if that mobility is, as Kennedy observes, "mold[ed]" by race.[40] Throughout the series, Easy befriends and occasionally works with a variety of black people (mixed race, African American, and Afro-Caribbean), as well as with white, Mexican, Asian, and Latino people; he even adopts a Mexican boy, Jesus, and a biracial (black and white) girl, Feather. Such crossracial alliances and family structures unquestionably distinguish Easy from Hammett's and Chandler's detectives. Suggestively, Easy generally forges those alliances on the basis of a shared distrust of white power structures, and typically as those structures are represented by and concentrated within the police. When his friend the Japanese American librarian Miss Eto is being stalked, Easy asks her "Why don't you go to the cops?" (*BB* 78). "Oh, no," she replies, "Never go to the police." Easy immediately tells us "Maybe that's why I helped her" (*BB* 78). Quite unlike white detectives from Holmes to Marlowe, Easy is not connected in any sustained fashion (at least not in the first six novels of the series) with the police.[41] We cannot imagine Sam Spade unashamedly declaring "In the morning, the fear of the police returned" (*BB* 270). In fact, Easy is thoroughly, consistently, and, it turns out, quite reasonably distrustful and fearful of the police. After all, he tells us from the very beginning: "I had played the game of 'cops and nigger' before" (*DIABD* 69). Throughout the series, Easy repeatedly shares, articulates, and documents "the kind of terror that poor people have for the cops" and connects with others across lines of race because of that common experience (*BB* 268). Easy's white ally, the "crazy and naturally criminal" expert burglar Alamo Weir, is someone he met when they "spent two days in jail" together (*BB* 78, 222). Alamo tells Easy not to "be too mad" at some poor white men who have just hurled racial slurs at him, explaining: "Those boys in there don't know what it's like. They ain't never seen what a white man truly is. They think it's all TV and *Look* magazine. They don't know that it's white men who cut off their balls" (*BB* 223). Easy then declares, "I liked Alamo. He was insane but he had a clearer view of the world than most men do" (*BB* 223). Easy's declaration points to the ways race and class make a difference in crime and in crime fiction—in the case of race, so much so that even if Chester Himes and Walter Mosley both had simply "made the faces black" in their novels, they would have necessarily altered the meaning and power of the genre.

At the literal center of *Black Betty*, Easy says, "I've never really been what you would call a friend to the LAPD" (180). To paraphrase D. A. Miller, the police, along with the novel, *mean* differently when the main characters (and especially the detective) are black. To date, most criticisms of *The Novel and the Police* have centered on Miller's argument that the novel as a genre functions as part of the disciplinary mechanisms surrounding bourgeois subjectivity; Miller says of mid-nineteenth-century English novels: "Whenever the novel censures policing power, it has already reinvented it, in *the very practice of novelistic representation*."[42] In other words, in his view, the "genre of the novel *belongs* to the disciplinary field it portrays.[43] A number of literary scholars have objected to such a reading of the novel as essentially and always disciplinary, as being just part of an overall social-regulatory system.[44] But here I am less concerned with Miller's view of the novel as nonliberatory or nonprogressive than I am with his neglect of race. The Victorian novels on which he bases his argument were being published at precisely the same time as the earliest African American novels, yet both the genealogies and the criticism of the two sets of texts have been and generally remain quite separate. Indeed, only a handful of critics have targeted Miller's thesis in the context of his narrow racial, national, and temporal textual selections. In an insightful essay, Yumna Siddiqi challenges Miller by pointing to postcolonial novels, such as Arudhati Roy's *The God of Small Things* and Amitav Gosh's *The Circle of Reason*, which "cast suspicion on the repressive apparatuses of the state."[45] To the degree that there are always targets of colonial or racial policing who do not match the form of subjectivity desired by the state and produced by Miller's chosen novels, his theory cannot hold. As Siddiqi aptly observes, in many postcolonial novels, "the forces of police criminalize the protagonists."[46] Likewise, quite a few contemporary African American detective novels represent a protagonist who is both detective and perceived criminal because of race, thereby complicating Miller's conclusion about the novel's always-state-interested cultural and disciplinary work. Of course, Miller would be well within his rights to point out that both Siddiqi and I take his argument out of temporal context; his thesis, after all, pertained to *Victorian* novels. However, the intertwining of race and criminality that we find in Mosley's and Neely's novels did not begin with contemporary African American detective fiction.

From its very origins (again, at precisely the same period as Miller's Victorian novels) and on into the present, African American fiction has articulated and analyzed the intersection of crime and color in the United States. A character in Frederick Douglass's 1853 novella *The Heroic Slave* says of the black protagonist: "Here is indeed a man of rare endowments, a child of God, —guilty of no crime but the color of his skin."[47] Half a century later, in Pauline Hopkins's 1900 short story "Talma Gordon" (one of the earliest examples of African American crime fiction), a white man rejects his passing-for-white fiancée, who is suspected of murder, crying, "I could stand the stigma of murder, but add to that the pollution of Negro blood! No man is brave enough to face such a situation."[48] Much later, Chester Himes turned the tables by declaring in his 1976 autobiography: "I could not name the white man who was guilty because all white men were guilty."[49] Now, contemporary detective fiction offers a concentrated, extended means to expose and explore the continued construction of race via crime and its policing (even as the fictionality of race has been largely accepted). In Neely's 1994 novel *Blanche among the Talented Tenth*, for example, the characters bond over distrust of the police, despite profound color and class conflicts. Thus, the police themselves construct blackness. The dark-skinned, working-class protagonist-detective Blanche White "shared" with the light-skinned wealthy academic Mattie a "lack of faith in the police."[50] "In her experience," Blanche explains, regardless of their circumstances, "black people who called the cops stood a good chance of being abused instead of assisted" (*BATT* 122–23). Even when they don't "call the cops," black people, Blanche knows, must always see their behavior from the perspective of the police. As she says in the first novel of the series: "A running black person was still a target of suspicion."[51]

Easy Rawlins, also in the first novel of the series, likewise tells us: "It was fifteen blocks to John's speak and I had to keep telling myself to slow down. I knew that a patrol car would arrest any sprinting Negro they encountered" (*DIABD* 76). This passage shows that Easy Rawlins has been shaped, not just in his reactions and his outward behavior by the police, but in his inner being as well. His is a raced emotional and epistemological interior: he *fears* the police because he *knows* what they can and will do to him. Like the slaves in Douglass's *Narrative* and like Sojourner Truth in her *Narrative*, Easy is suspended in a raced temporality and a raced epistemology that together are causal for his quotidian material and emotional experiences. And if Frederick Douglass and Sojourner Truth were countermanding Hegel, then Mosley, unlike the Dasein poets of the early 1960s, is actually countermanding and supplanting Heidegger. Easy isn't just *being there*; he is being *black* there. He resides very much in the same present-day temporality as do the police, yet he also experiences a kind of temporal double consciousness that in turn determines his pace.

And, significantly, he shares this complex temporality with others in his community, who likewise share his state of *being black there*. As Easy says in the most recent and possibly last novel of the series:

> Black folk of my generation and before had to be able to see around the corner to ensure their safety. We couldn't afford to suffer surprise. I had a card that told anyone who was interested that I was a detective, but I was no more a private eye than John or Gara or any soul sitting in that dark, dark room. Each and every one of us was examining and evaluating clues all the time, day and night.[52]

Over the course of Easy Rawlins's life throughout the series, many, many black people fail to gain either the temporal or the spatial perquisites of postmodern subjectivity, so they must all remain detectives, "all the time." In the neighborhoods where Easy lives, primarily Houston's Fifth Ward and South Central Los Angeles, almost no one lives or works at, or even near, the cutting edge of modernity, much less postmodernity. *Postmodern Times,* if we had a contemporary Charlie Chaplin, would likely show us the film's star caught in a cubicle, not a cog. But as of the 1960s, when Lyotard, DeMan, and Derrida were helping usher in postmodernism, Mosley's characters are still working in the factory—that is, if they're lucky. *Devil in a Blue Dress* actually begins with Easy being fired from his job building airplanes in a defense plant.[53] He becomes a detective, reluctantly, because he needs a job, and the usual workaday world available to black men, as for Bigger Wright in the 1930s, simply holds no appeal for him (*BB* 162). As Easy tells us, in his community being "'retired' . . . back in 1961, meant you worked 'part-time' forty hours a week and paid your own insurance" (*BB* 64). Thus, "Dasein" does not describe working-class African American men's subjectivity as represented in the Easy Rawlins novels as much as would a term such as "arbeit-sein" (to be/being in work) or "da-arbeiten" (working there). Throughout the Easy Rawlins novels, Mosley is concerned with the ways that time measures at once changelessness and a lived, laboring temporality particularly for working-class African American men. For them, being is *working* in time. But, as Easy discovers, it is also *dying* in time and over time.

Mortality undergirds modern philosophers' analyses of time. The limit of our existence, death itself, connotes temporality as well as the nature of human subjectivity. Heidegger in his definition of the individual human subject asserted that *"no one can relieve the other of his own dying."*[54] Just so, Derrida asserts in *The Gift of Death*: "Death is very much that which nobody else can undergo or confront in my place. My irreplaceability is therefore conferred, delivered, 'given,' one can say, by death."[55] Although Easy Rawlins may not precisely relieve or undergo others' deaths, he does share the sense of always-possible and ever-present mortality with others of his "kind"—"leaving me and my kind dead or making death in the dark causeways"—to such a degree that his mode of *being there* in Los Angeles, in 1961, challenges both Heidegger's and Derrida's "given" that human subjectivity, human individuality, depends on the un-share-ability of death. The result is a curious kind of atemporality, or *not* being in time—in other words, a lack of change over time *collectively* for poor black men in Los Angeles permits them even to "share death." Death becomes not a process of "individuation,"[56] as Derrida would have it, but a process of collectivization, of community. This keen awareness of shared mortality—the predictability of one's people's death in and across time—is perhaps the most profound and stirring thematic thread in African American literature, and in African American history.

Once again, in Mosley's exploration of the racialized psychological terrain of his protagonist and of his protagonist's community, we can see a literary politics of sameness and difference at work. Easy spends time in altered or liminal states, apparently just like the detectives who preceded him. Sherlock Holmes had his opium fogs and his trance-like episodes of intense concentration; Sam Spade and Philip Marlowe had their moments of ruminating and philosophizing (so often parodied now). Easy Rawlins's characteristic liminal states include fear, rage, and, most of all, dreams. As of the first page of *Black Betty,* he is dreaming (43–44), and the novel as a whole is punctuated by his recurrent dreams and nightmares. But Easy is not simply dreaming; throughout, he is dreaming of the past. The book begins with Easy's dream of his past experiences with the title character, Black Betty, and it ends with his telling us: "I'd been thinking about the young people I remembered in my dreams" (*BB* 280). Unlike past detectives' altered states, then, Easy's also constitute liminal *temporal* states; he is suspended between past and present as he dreams, thereby reinforcing and expanding the political commentary initiated by his resemblance to past hard-boiled detectives.

Easy has lived through and observed World War II and the postwar years, the beginnings of the civil rights and Black Power movements, the assassination of John F. Kennedy, the Vietnam War, and the 1965 Watts riots. He thus embodies the memory and past of a particular community. His allegorical role becomes clear in *Little Scarlet,* set in 1965 Los Angeles:

> it was as if there was a strong wind at my back. I had resisted it all through the riots: the angry voice in my heart that urged me to go out and fight after all of the hangings I had seen, after all of the times I had been called nigger and all of the doors that had been slammed in my face. I spent my whole early life at the back of buses and in the segregated balconies at theaters. I had been arrested for walking in the wrong part of town and threatened for looking a man in the eye. And when I went to war to fight for freedom, I found myself in a segregated army, treated with less respect than they treated German POWs. I had seen people who looked like me jeered on TV and in the movies. I had had enough and I wasn't about to turn back, even though I wanted to. (*LS* 18–19)

In fact, both author and protagonist are explicitly seeking to represent stories and characters often neglected by mainstream histories of American and African American culture. Mosley plainly states: "I want to map that migration through the deep South and to the West of black people. Because one of the things—and this is because we haven't been that involved in the center of the literary world, people of color—a lot of our histories are left out of the fiction."[57] Similarly, Easy Rawlins knows he must withstand the powerful and corrupt social and economic forces arrayed against him in his search for Black Betty, for, if he fails, "Who would have survived to be witness against [these] crimes?" (*BB* 129). He must live long enough to tell the story. Here, the urgent mission of the detective is not so much to solve the mystery as it is to survive so as to investigate and narrate, to remember and relate a history of race relations in the United States from the perspective of the common person who has lived that history. Easy notes and values not just the grand gestures and acts of a public civil rights struggle but the minor, private acts of resistance to white power and privilege. He describes one such act of resistance as "a little piece of history that happened right there in that room and went unrecorded" (*BB* 220). Easy thus functions as a kind of time traveler who adds to, revises, and reenvisions an interracial and multiracial history articulated through a nonhistorical persona.

The history Easy is documenting is national and familial—and ongoing. Just as we cannot help but link his early 1960s Los Angeles setting to early 1990s Los Angeles, we cannot help but connect his interracial history with our present. For example, the plot of *Black Betty* turns on the disclosure of a secret interracial family. Betty, while employed as a maid by the wealthy white Cain family, bore two children as a result of rape (or, at the very least, coerced sex) by the family's patriarch, Albert Cain. On his death, Cain leaves Betty nearly all his property, apparently as atonement, yet his white family breaks the will in a trial that leaves her "destroyed," disinherited, and made "to seem like a whore who had beguiled Albert Cain" (*BB* 359). Even when made public, then, the truth of the sexual exploitation of a black woman and the resulting interracial family cannot shake the legal genealogy of whiteness. This story should sound familiar to us, and it demonstrates that if literary history often continues to insist on racial separateness, then so too does much relatively current political history. It was only recently that Strom Thurmond's secret interracial family came to light; Essie Mae Washington Williams, too, "went unrecorded," publicly and formally, until December 2003, when she came forward after the senator's death. Yet she was his first child, born in 1925 when Thurmond was twenty-two, as a result of his affair with his family's black maid, who was sixteen at the time. Though his mixed-race family took priority in time, it certainly did not take priority in official narratives of Thurmond's personal or political history. Indeed, despite the fact that his "mixed" past apparently was a kind of open secret in Washington, none of his obituaries from the summer of 2003 mentioned what a *Slate* writer has termed "the most interesting of his sundry racial legacies."[58] Thus, the Easy Rawlins series travels back in time to recover and record a national genealogical history that all too often remains in need of disclosure and official documentation.

To complicate matters further, there is yet another kind of time travel taking place throughout the Easy Rawlins series. In Mosley's fiction, the detective narrates each of the novels from some indefinite point in the future, looking back on the events as they occurred. This narrative strategy produces a twofold challenge: to contemporary political complacence about the ongoing realities of race in the United States, and to traditional literary theories about narrative time. Because we as readers can never precisely locate Easy, as narrator, in time, and because the injustices he encounters in the stories are unchanging throughout the series, Mosley's novels exceed not only Todorov's "duality" theory of detective fiction but also the temporal model of perhaps the most influential theorist of narrative time, Gérard Genette. Genette's well-known grid of A, B, C, D, E + 1, 2, 3, 4, 5 (signifying the chronological order of events being related by a narrative overlaid with their sequencing in a narrative) cannot accommodate temporal layers that include a first-person narrator speaking in the present tense about a collective past that is sustained into and by the present.[59] Even Genette's elaboration of the grid via many kinds of "analepses, or 'returns'"—not to mention "prolepses," "ellipses," and "iteration"—is insufficient, because Genette's theories only work when *events* occur and recur in the lives of individuals and families—as in his example from *A la recherche du temps perdu* of Marcel's two visits to Paris in 1914 and 1916 (51). But when *conditions,* material and social, do not simply recur but remain the same for certain groups across time, Genette's theories of narratology, despite their postmodern publication dates, fail on the grounds of bourgeois individualism and notions of progress that D. A. Miller associates with Victorian novels. Easy Rawlins is no Mr. Bucket, but he is no Marcel either. Genette's grid, however beautifully elaborated, just doesn't fit a character like Easy, who changes and ages as he fully inhabits and fully shares a world like South Central Los Angeles; nor does it fit a series like Mosley's, wherein the mystery of how to attain nonracialized justice remains static from book to book. In Genette's terms, Easy's narration is, impossibly, at once subsequent/reminiscent and prior/prophetic.[60]

This complex combination of change and stasis permits Easy, as character and narrator, to comment on *and* to predict: the period of the novels' action, the present of the novels' publication date, the nature of his community, and his own development. And Easy does in fact change and learn, despite the unchanging nature of his social and racial surroundings. Mosley reports: "When I write the Easy Rawlins series—the character has to change. . . . You know you can't just make him a different person in every book."[61] One of Easy's most significant changes regards gender. A number of critics have noted a troubling masculinism in the Easy Rawlins novels, arguing that this commonality with hard-boiled detective fiction of the past hinders their progressiveness. Doris Witt holds up Neely's novels "as an alternative to the 'boys in the hood' fixation of much of early 1990s United States culture, a fixation that contributed to the enthusiastic reception of Mosley's Easy Rawlins and his loyal, if violent friend Mouse."[62] *Black Betty* in particular invites such feminist critique. In the book, Easy is perpetually searching for Betty, the mysterious pursued who is deferred until nearly the end of the novel (she first appears on page 294 of a 360-page edition of the novel). In the beginning, Easy describes her as "a great shark of a woman" desired by virtually all the men in the book (*BB* 49). By novel's end, she is threatened and infantilized, exposed and defeated; she is rendered "pitiful" (*BB* 344). Along the way, we learn that Betty constitutes the origin of Easy's own sexuality; he says that "the first time [he] had sex" was with her (*BB* 247). It is crucial to note here, however, that Easy is *not* referring to an actual sexual experience with Betty but to an experience of voyeurism: as a child, he once watched her having sex with a man, and his extreme arousal at the sight is what made it his "first time" (*BB* 247). This simulacrum of a sexual experience points to the falseness that underpins Easy's pursuit of Black Betty as an embodiment of authentic, essential, and irresistible black female sexuality. From the start, Easy's fundamental error is to frame and define the Black Betty he seeks as his own fantasy. She is from and of his past, and even back then, his experience of her was restricted to indirect and perhaps faulty perception; she is his projection and his memory.

But we must not rush to an equation of 1930s hard-boiled masculinism with Easy's 1960s gender politics written down in the 1990s. For one thing, Easy seems to be aware that putting Black Betty to use in this way may be exactly his problem. As he thinks back about his failures, Easy wonders: "Maybe it was because I never learned to respect women" (*BB* 174). It's as if the modern-in-the-postmodern African American male detective realizes, in narrating 1961 from a future vantage point, that what he most sorely lacked was the second-wave feminism that was then emerging and was about to flourish, and that a modern legacy of feminism may be the crucial element that contemporary African American men must remember and put to use. This is precisely the lack that haunts Richard Wright's work: his failure to accommodate and benefit from the black feminism that had preceded him in the works of figures ranging from Anna Julia Cooper and Victoria Earle Matthews to Nella Larsen and Zora Neale Hurston and that was even more immediately available to him in the works of his contemporaries Ann Petry and Gwendolyn Brooks. And just as Bigger Thomas looks at his girlfriend and imagines her as a threat to be removed, Easy Rawlins seeks a dangerous black woman who initially is nothing more than his projection and who, in the end, is a nonpresence. Granted, the novel doesn't murder her, as *Native Son* "murders" Bessie Mears, but *Black Betty* certainly renders Betty powerless, just as soon as Easy finally comes into contact with her.

The problem here is that he's looking for the wrong woman; in a sense, Easy Rawlins should be looking for Neely's Blanche White rather than his Black Betty. Both are dark black women working as domestics for wealthy white families; both have been raped by men in those families (we learn in the first novel of Neely's series about her detective-protagonist's earlier rape). But quite unlike Betty, Blanche, who is herself a product of the 1960s, is neither rendered "pitiful" nor "destroyed." In fact, as of the most recent installment in the series, *Blanche Passes Go* (2000), she successfully takes revenge on her rapist. In Mosley's recent Easy Rawlins novels, the detective seems to be in the process of learning the kind of lessons in black feminism that Blanche could teach, with powerful women of color occupying more of his time and attention. In *Bad Boy Brawly Brown* (2002), set in 1964, Easy reports that his new girlfriend, Bonnie Shay, "was on my wavelength. And she was an independent thinker" (60). "Bonnie," he says, "was in every way my equal" (*BBBB* 222). Suggestively, an even more recent Easy Rawlins novel, *Cinnamon Kiss* (2005), ends with a sense of optimism, not on political or social grounds, but on the personal grounds of a nonsexual friendship between a black man and a black woman: "You watch out, girl," says Easy, "You just might make me into a happy man."[63] The series seems to be suggesting that the familial and interpersonal, if not the political, provides a site for progress, for the achievement of Bergson's "open future," and therefore real hope for the black community that remains steadily at the center of the Easy Rawlins novels.

Yet Mosley's novels, even as they revolve around a separate and vital black community, do not posit or create a singular blackness. As Nicole King argues, Mosley "use[s] intra-racial class difference, especially middle-class aspirations, to refute the romance of grand narratives of blackness."[64] For example, the processes of migration and class differentiation so well documented in the Easy Rawlins series have characterized postemancipation African American historical experience, especially in the twentieth century; as a result, Easy's experiences show how the notion of *an* African

American identity has become increasingly elusive. Once he leaves Houston's Fifth Ward, his community rapidly expands to include not only cross-racial friendships and alliances, but ever more varieties of blackness as well. For example, his cherished girlfriend in the 2002 installment of the series is not African American but Caribbean, and she represents for him another complex, potentially diasporic, version of blackness. Easy explains that Bonnie "was born in British Guyana but her father was from Martinique, so there was the music of the French language in her English accent" (*BBBB* 2).

Of course, Mosley's novels are not alone within contemporary African American detective fiction in functioning on this complex, intraracial level. Neely, like Mosley, is writing a series of detective novels that explore the nature, indeed the very possibility, of black community at a time when the idea of a unified blackness has been discredited. It may be at least in part because of the series's seemingly anachronistic, even possibly reactionary, preoccupation with reforging black identity that they have remained largely outside current academic discourse; Mosley's novels, by contrast, have been the subject of a great deal of both popular and academic interest. Nevertheless, the two series have much in common. Like Mosley's Easy Rawlins novels, Neely's four detective novels seek to represent, in allegorical fashion, a narrative of recent black history. They have followed the migration of its protagonist, Blanche White, from her southern hometown of Farleigh, North Carolina, to black neighborhoods in urban settings (Harlem and Roxbury) in a kind of contemporary reenactment of the Great Migration. And, in *Blanche Passes Go* (2000), Blanche returns South, just as many African Americans are currently doing, suggesting that the series as a whole offers a kind of compressed version of twentieth-century and early twenty-first-century migratory trends.[65] Throughout her travels, and in both the North and the South, Blanche encounters a great deal of white racism, but unlike Easy Rawlins, she finds intraracial conflict surrounding gender, color, and class to be among her most troubling experiences. In *Blanche among the Talented Tenth* (1994), the second novel in the series, Blanche commiserates with another dark-skinned woman, explaining that prejudice from other African Americans "hurts more than anything any white person could ever do to us" (*BATT* 128). In fact, how to achieve black unity is the paramount mystery throughout the Blanche White series, and it clearly overshadows the actual crimes.

Yet for Barbara Neely, the detective form remains crucial because it suits her explicitly political/popular purposes. As she puts it: "I realized the mystery genre was perfect to talk about serious subjects, and it could carry the political fiction I wanted to write. In a way, I feel the genre chose me."[66] When asked by an interviewer about her plans to extend the Blanche White detective novel series, Neely replied that she will continue writing the books "as long as I have issues that I want to harangue people about."[67] In the end, her novels function as vehicles through which to "examine race and class from the point of view of a working-class black woman" and to seek answers to perhaps irresolvable questions regarding the nature, past and present, of blackness.[68]

Neely's doubly ironically named protagonist-detective Blanche White is a "deep black," size sixteen, forty-something domestic worker (by choice), whose self-proclaimed nosiness repeatedly leads her into mystery and often into danger (BATT 1). Blanche clearly represents an unprecedented sort of detective: black and female and working-class—and that tripartite identity drives the novel's content. The title of Neely's 1994 novel Blanche among the Talented Tenth testifies to the book's preoccupation with a color-coded and classed version of African American experience and history. In the novel, Blanche White is vacationing at Amber Cove, a long-standing upper-class African American resort community in New England (likely modeled after Oak Bluffs on Martha's Vineyard). Another "brown-skinned," working-class woman also vacationing at the resort terms the Amber Cove residents "as hincty a bunch of Talented Tenths as you'd ever want to see" (BATT 65). Apparently, Du Bois's term could not possibly include either Blanche's black companion, who loud-talks and wears bright colors, or Blanche herself (BATT 65). Deeply cynical about the community's class and color politics, Blanche approaches Amber Cove with her own version of blackness functioning as the measure of authenticity. She observes that she is "the only guest present with any true color" (BATT 40); and she misses "the fire of the red-and-purple loving black people she knew," "the shoulder, hip [and] hand language that spoke volumes among black people," and the "staples of the black diet as she knew it" (BATT 58). She concludes that at Amber Cove, "the things, besides color, that made a person black were either missing or mere ghosts of their former selves" (BATT 58). But Blanche's racial measuring does not go unchallenged either within the text (by other characters) or outside it (by us, the readers).

At Amber Cove, Blanche encounters mostly light-skinned middle- and upper- class African American characters, and all seem destined to fail her tests of racial authenticity. First, Blanche encounters Mattie, a famous black feminist historian, whom she initially identifies (and identifies *with*) as a model of the strong black woman, a "diva" in Blanche's words (*BATT* 25, 41). But Mattie ultimately fails Blanche's tests of raced and gendered authenticity. Not only is Mattie married to a white man, another academic, but we later discover that Mattie has a son who was born as the result of her years-earlier affair with a black man, a son whom she refuses to acknowledge publicly. As in Mosley's *Black Betty,* then, here too we see a secret racial family; but in this case, the secret affair and child are intraracial (black) and the official, documented family interracial (black and white). This twist testifies to the preoccupation of the novel—indeed the entire Blanche White series—with the obstacles to creating and sustaining black identity and connection. In *Blanche among the Talented Tenth,* repressed genealogical history, even when uncovered, cannot successfully forge a unitary blackness any more than it can forge an official, public interracial history in *Black Betty.* In fact, when Blanche confronts Mattie with her knowledge of the affair and the secret black son, Mattie abruptly severs their apparent connection, as if it were a "retractable bridge" (*BATT* 220). Blanche, in turn, promptly rejects Mattie, explicitly in terms of gender and race (and perhaps class as well): "I see why nobody's ever called you girlfriend before. You don't even know what the word means" (*BATT* 221).

Blanche's second possible "connection" in the novel does give her some hope that she might be able to establish a long-term relationship with another black person. While at Amber Cove, she meets Tina, a young woman as dark as Blanche herself, who grew up "in the projects" of North Philadelphia, has recently graduated from Brown University, and plans to teach poor children in Boston (*BATT* 93, 95). With her long braids, beautiful full features, and deep black skin, Tina looks, says Blanche, like a "bronze head" or like the face on an "African coin" (*BATT* 67). Indeed, Tina functions in the novel as a signifier of racial value; and as she exchanges hands during the course of the novel—going from ally of Blanche to fiancée of a light-skinned, bourgeois young man—her racial and gender value decreases, as does her interest for Blanche. When Tina announces her engagement, all Blanche feels is "disappointment," because "she didn't think Durant was good enough for Tina" (208, 181). Blanche's "investment" in Tina rapidly dwindles, and, as with Mattie, "distance . . . stretched between them" in the end (94, 229). Blanche's own ill-starred romance with the light-skinned Stuart, a longtime Amber Cove resident and Maine native, ends even more dismally when he is unmasked as the bad guy of the book (although not as a murderer). Ultimately, Blanche makes no new connections, and her friendship with her "home girl" Ardell remains the only relationship she keeps from the beginning to end of this novel—and from the beginning to end of the entire series. Thus, Blanche is not a flexible, liminal detective figure who successfully spans social categories. This failure to connect with other people, particularly other black people, distinguishes the Blanche White series from the Easy Rawlins series, where widely varied friendships and characters are sustained from novel to novel. As a result, the Blanche White novels appear far less sanguine, at least to date, about the interpersonal and familial as routes to sustained hope or stable community for African Americans. Indeed, the series in general, and *Blanche among the Talented Tenth* in particular (published the same year as Mosley's *Black Betty*), seem to be suggesting the near-impossibility of forging black community across lines of class, gender, age, color, and region.

Of course, in addition to such vexing questions that pervade *Blanche among the Talented Tenth,* there is an actual mystery going on. A long-standing and widely detested member of the Amber Cove community, Faith Brown, has been mysteriously electrocuted while bathing in the tub in her cottage. The investigation surrounding her death is conducted by Blanche, who arrives at Amber Cove just after it happens. Thus, the novel does include Todorov's dual narrative time lines of crime and investigation; but like the Easy Rawlins novels, *Blanche among the Talented Tenth* deploys additional temporal layers. During her investigation of the electrocution, Blanche discovers that Faith's foremost hobby was to collect compromising history about her fellow Amber Cove residents. Nearly everyone at the resort had an ugly secret from the past, it seemed, and therefore a motive for killing Faith. Yet, remarkably, it turns out that Faith's death was accidental; there was no murder at all, although neither the reader nor Blanche realizes that fact until near the end of the book. So if there was no murder, then what is the true mystery in *Blanche among the Talented Tenth?* It is tempting to conclude that the novel does really want to investigate who—or what—has "killed faith." The narrative pivots on the painful reality of a fractured and tense African American community in Amber Cove, "a place where," Blanche explains, "none of the color codes could be ignored" (227). An authentic mystery emerges from the fact that "color codes" still hold power, even as late as the 1990s, when race and color distinctions have ostensibly been proven spurious. For Blanche, mystery inheres in the project of how to achieve that which she nonetheless urgently desires (despite the contemporary and apparently liberating truth that race is a fiction): an intact and healthy African American community, along with unprejudiced, egalitarian love relationships between African American women and men, neither of which she has ever experienced.[69] Unlike Easy Rawlins, Blanche has not, as of the latest book in the series, settled down with anyone and does not derive much hope from her love life. In *Blanche Passes Go*, she does have a somewhat successful romance with the railroad man Thelvin, but it is marred by his jealousy; ultimately, she decides to return to Boston, committing neither to the South nor to Thelvin.[70] In the end, Blanche is left with no clear-cut solution to the mystery of how either black community or heterosexual black love might be sustained. Indeed, she even has a recurrent dream, just like Easy, but her dream speaks of isolation rather than a communal past: "The people were gone; even their voices were gone. And in the way of dreams, she knew that they were gone forever. That she had seen and heard her last human being; that she was alone in a way that made her understand the word as she had never done before" (*BATT* 210–11). Her dream, she comes to understand, was at once about the "future," about "now," and about "memories"—with each period characterized by people "moving farther and farther away" (*BATT* 223).

Blanche fails to sustain connections with other African Americans in part because her disciplinary rhetoric of authenticity, much like that of the Black Arts Movement in the late 1960s, cannot lead either to community or to solution. Authentic blackness is by definition a receding mystery, the ever-detected yet never-found. Nevertheless, the pursuit of that mystery remains a frequent subject of contemporary African American detective novels, even if the pursuit is in some sense anachronistic. Easy Rawlins notes of the aftermath of the 1965 riots: "that was the beginning of the breakup of our community" (*LS* 77). The Blanche White novels are preoccupied with that "breakup" but date its origin differently. In *Blanche among the Talented Tenth* (whose very title speaks of a mixture of time periods), Blanche responds to her "brown-skinned" companion's use of the term "Talented Tenth" by laughing and replying "It's been a long time since I heard that old DuBois's thing about the light-brights being the natural leaders of their darker brethren" (65). Of course Blanche is right, the term is an old one: W. E. B. Du Bois first used it in an 1897 essay to describe his model of modern elite racial leaders whose duty it was to uplift the race—not only socially, but politically and economically as well.[71] Steeped in bourgeois social sensibilities but also in progressive politics, Du Bois's Talented Tenth model was neither simply elitist nor predicated simply on lightness of skin; indeed, it was not simple at all. Blanche misremembers and, I would argue, misapplies the term "talented tenth" to Amber Cove's class- and color-struck vacationers, whose shallow materialism and doomed aspirations toward whiteness reflect only dimly and partially Du Bois's complex picture of racial uplift by a well-educated and progressive black leadership. In a sense, then, Blanche is doing the same thing that the dead Faith Brown had been doing: digging up and remembering an ugly, and neither whole nor wholly accurate, version of an African American past. By failing to take into account the full range of Du Bois's intellectual and political work (she remembers his elitism but not his socialism; his own light skin tone but not his expatriation to Ghana; his prudish tastes but not his suffragism), Blanche cannot ever hope to solve the numerous race-, gender-, and class-based questions that arise during the course of the novel. Blanche wonders why she is content to let Tina take over all the child-care duties. She wonders why she is treating Tina poorly once the dark-skinned young woman has declared her allegiance to her insufficiently black or masculine (according to Blanche's standards) fiancé. She wonders how she can get the white domestic worker who cleans her cottage to trust her. She wonders how a handsome, light-skinned African American man could be attracted to her, a dark-skinned woman who is not thin. Ultimately, Blanche fails to provide answers to any of these provocative questions regarding social categories, perhaps because her own judgments and historical elisions echo Mattie's earlier repression of her intraracial family.

The answers to such questions as those Blanche asks herself may lie in the novel's blend of the modern and the postmodern (after all, Blanche in 1994 is *still* relying on Du Bois's "Talented Tenth" to understand social differences). Blanche herself embodies a black past. Like Easy, she "still remembered the police beatings in the sixties."[72] In a way, she represents the protagonist-detective as anachronism, implying that a recovery of past political perspectives might be just the solution required in the present. When her adoptive son Malik asks when she stopped straightening her hair, Blanche replies: "It was the sixties. I was lucky enough to be in on the tail end of a time when some black folks were saying our dark skin and kinky hair have to be beautiful because they are ours. So, there was a lot of nappy hair out there when I decided to give up the straightening comb. It was more than a fad for me" (*BATT* 152). Blanche offers at once, paradoxically, a historied and atemporal alternative that challenges contingent stylings of blackness. As she tells us (via free indirect discourse), "In the sixties, women who looked like her became status symbols to be draped on revolutionary black arms like a piece of kinte cloth. Now she mostly saw black couples of the same color and darker men with lighter women" (*BATT* 36). Black Power and the slogan "Black is beautiful" should return, according to Blanche, but they must now consist of more than male-centered fashion statements. Thus, with her generous proportions, natural hair, dark skin, and self-designed version of ancestor worship, the detective seems to be offering a possible solution to the mystery of black community, one that centers on prior cultural and bodily expressions of blackness (*BATT* 61). For Blanche, it once again should be "Nation Time," minus the "black patriarchal prescriptions."[73]

Her temporal-political solution points us, once again, to the real mystery at the heart of the Blanche White series and to a provisional explanation of the current flourishing of African American detective fiction. The continued frustration of black community throughout the Blanche White novels and the continued interracial injustice in the Easy Rawlins novels result, in both series, from an incomplete recovery of African American and U.S. intellectual and familial genealogies. Blanche White misremembers Du Bois even as she calls for a return to the past; Easy Rawlins shows us that the nation has often suppressed or denied its interracial past (and therefore reexperiences it) even as he lacks his own era's feminism. Both characters and both series logically operate via an anachronistic process that, though flawed, serves to imagine possible solutions that are both literary and political, and both intraracial and interracial. Indeed, Blanche and Easy's dreams of the past and present, their liminal states, offer something more than those of past detectives. Even if their vision is not perfect, contemporary African American detectives see more clearly than did Sam Spade and Philip Marlowe—at least when it comes to solving genealogical mysteries and diagnosing early twenty-first-century social ills in the United States. Most obviously, they uncomfortably insist on the continuing social reality and power of race—what Houston Baker, following Baraka, has termed "'real-side' referentiality"—despite the postmodern fact that race is fiction.[74] But the novels also construct alternative models, not only of the detective-protagonist but also of epistemology and history, of community and family, and of time and philosophy. This is not to say that Blanche and Easy are ideal detectives, and scholars of the novels rightly remain critical of what are often the limited and limiting terms of their detection processes.[75] Nevertheless, Blanche and Easy successfully investigate not just murders but national, family, and literary histories—by *being black there.*

Political Truths

This is the Space Age
The age beyond the earth age:
A new direction
Beyond the gravitation of the past.

—Sun Ra, "The Cosmic Age"

Despite the clear centrality of time in the African American literary tradition, it has remained relatively neglected as a category of analysis. To my knowledge there has been only one other book-length study of time in relation to black writing, Bonnie J. Barthold's groundbreaking *Black Time: Fiction of Africa, Caribbean, and the United States* (1981).[1] Barthold argues that a "focus on time" in black fiction, which she defines as any fiction written by a black author of African descent, shows how diasporic black writing can be considered as a whole, united by form and content, or by what she calls "structure" and "substance."[2] Examining novels by Chinua Achebe, George Lamming, Jean Toomer, William Attaway, Ayi Kwei Armah, Toni Morrison, and Wole Soyinka, Barthold concludes that these authors' shared preoccupation with time "demonstrate[s] a continuity of vision among a diversity of black writers—African, Caribbean, American, men and women from the late nineteenth-century to the present" (197). As a result, a focus on time serves to overcome what Barthold terms the "fragmentation" of traditional literary scholarship that, in her view, all too often separates African from Caribbean from American, past from present, and form from content (198). Barthold's persuasive readings suggest that time studies can indeed help take us further along the paths not only of nation-based literary studies but of black diasporic literary and cultural studies as well. By contrast, Kenneth Warren has identified "the difficulty of sustaining, from a new world perspective, the imaginative contemporaneity of Africa and the 'West' and of black elites and masses" as the paramount obstacle to forging a strong, collective diasporic black identity not only during the Harlem Renaissance (his explicit topic) but also, he implies, in any period.[3] How can we square these two notions: time represented literarily and experienced materially as a foundation for "imagining" or "practicing" diaspora, versus time as constituting precisely the shoals on which diaspora founders?

In this Conclusion, I would like to try to shift the terms of this debate by suggesting that an actual, sustained achievement of diaspora is not as crucial as the *desire* for it, expressed via the imagination and theorization of black "contemporaneity" or continuity, as in the Black Arts Movement (BAM) and the Harlem Renaissance. Such sustained challenges to white supremacy and concomitant imaginings of collective black subjectivity have emerged perhaps most vividly when national borders have been experienced or have been perceived to be at their most permeable. Writers of the Harlem Renaissance, for instance, did begin to imagine and try to construct transnational black "contemporaneity" (393). First, the art of the period was often international in content. A neglected Rudolph Fisher novel of the late Harlem Renaissance, *The Conjure Man Dies: A Mystery Tale of Dark Harlem* (1933), takes as its central character an African immigrant whose identity produces the "dark mystery" of the title, while Claude McKay regularly featured Caribbean immigrants in his novels. Of course, the transnational wasn't solely representational in the period. The influential Harlem presence of non-U.S.-born political and artistic figures, McKay and Marcus Garvey, for example, suggests that the New Negro Movement, even though seemingly concentrated within New York and the United States, was inherently transnational. Likewise, the extensive travels and even expatriatism of so many literary, political, and musical figures of the era—from Du Bois to Ada "Bricktop" Smith—took the Renaissance with them across national borders, while the movement's main theoreticians, including Alain Locke and James Weldon Johnson, repeatedly framed it as one among a number of cultural nationalisms of the period. Indeed, as Brent Hayes Edwards has amply demonstrated, the "practice of diaspora" underpinned the New Negro Movement much more than has often been acknowledged.

Granted, Warren does make a strong case for the movement's failure to achieve its imagined transnational and Pan-African ideals in the face not only of "overwhelming" geopolitical obstacles but also of "the ambiguities that inhere in diasporic thought" itself, ambiguities (e.g., those regarding the relationship of Africa to African Americans) that in turn both produce the possibility of diaspora and render its realization impossible (393). And it is true that Countée Cullen's poetic question "What Is Africa to

Me?" never seems to have been answered, certainly not within the bounds of "Heritage," the well-known poem in which he poses that question. Similarly, the nature of the relationship between "the black elite and masses," to use Warren's terms, or between the "Talented Tenth" and "ordinary Negroes," to use Du Bois's and Hughes's terms, was never resolved satisfactorily by the writers of the Harlem Renaissance.[4] Nonetheless, the *desire* to achieve that resolution—that is, the very projects of collectivity and of diaspora—distinguishes the period. Like the 1920s, the BAM of the 1960s and 1970s represents another era when an imagined (and, perhaps to some degree realized) transnational "contemporaneity," a *strategic presentism,* emerges.

But I do not then wish to argue that African American literature of other periods is in any sense lesser. The *strategic anachronism* of late nineteenth- and early twentieth-century African American novels, for instance, is every bit as powerful as the presentism of the Harlem Renaissance and the BAM. Indeed, Pauline Hopkins may be the most adept writer in the entire tradition at exploiting print culture's varying temporalities to suit her literary-political purposes. By serializing several of her novels in the *Colored American,* Hopkins took advantage of journalism's ability to cover contemporary events at the "nadir" and of the novel's ability to represent multiple generations and locales—that is, its "chronotopes," Bakhtin's term for "the intrinsic connectedness of temporal and spatial relationships that are artistically expressed in literature."[5] Just so, Hopkins writes of the seemingly perpetual racial oppression that shaped the experiences of black and mixed-race American families over very long periods of time and across regions, even as she imagines the sustained vitality of those families. Such a temporal-political thematic—of the past inhabiting the present, and of a troubled present leading into an imagined better future—occurs throughout the African American literary tradition and across genres.

This is not to say that all genres work in the same ways throughout the tradition. Novels' characteristic narrative and temporal structures, such as the marriage plot and the murder mystery, have enabled African American writers to elaborate on and extend slave narratives' analyses of race, legal status, and the measure of time. The repetition that marks theatre performance permitted the antilynching dramatists to comment on the decades-long "brutal carnival," to use Pauline Hopkins's terms, of lynching.[6] The relatively fast pace and production process of journalism drive the plots of Chesnutt's *Marrow of Tradition* and other turn-of-the-century novels as well as Wright's midcentury *Native Son*. Even back in Phillis Wheatley's day, quickly produced broadsides and newspapers, along with the custom of occasional poetry, meant that colonial poetry partook of some of the temporal dynamics and advantages of journalism and therefore served to document the quotidian political and intellectual experiences of the era. As Benedict Anderson puts it, in the eighteenth century "the printer's office emerged as the key to North American communications and community intellectual life," a fact that helps explain Wheatley's rapid rise to prominence (although her attainment of freedom took rather longer).[7] Over two centuries later, Toni Morrison in her novels has deployed yet another sort of "strategic anachronism," a converse sort (as contrasted to that of Hopkins, Grimké, and Wright) in which historical content is represented via innovative literary forms of and in the present; as in Mosley's novels, this strategy permits simultaneous critical-aesthetic analysis of two periods.[8] In sum, authors throughout the African American literary tradition have always understood, juxtaposed, and exploited the differing temporalities inherent in print culture's various forms in various eras. But they have been equally alert to the ways they have been kept waiting—and their choice of literary form often mirrors that delay, what we might term the "temporal damage" rendered by racialized injustice across centuries. But there are signs that some African American writers may be starting to imagine ways to heal that damage.

Suzan-Lori Parks begins *this book*: "Standard Time Line and Standard Plot Line are in cahoots!" She ends it as well. Between November 13, 2002, and November 12, 2003, Parks wrote a play a day. Rather like Pauline Hopkins before her, Parks strategically combined temporalities through the complementary processes of writing, putting into print, and then producing on stage the work(s) that resulted: *365 Days/365 Plays*. The entire work was published in book form in November 2006 and was performed between November 13, 2006, and November 12, 2007, in "The 365 National Festival," with performances taking place in many widely varying venues across the United States. An elaborate network of hub theaters, knit together with other theaters and sundry spaces, provided spaces where actors performed a week's worth of the plays throughout the year, with all performances free and open to the public. As Parks and the producer, Bonnie Metzgar, put it, the plays were performed "in theaters both grand and modest, in schoolrooms, storefronts, nursing homes and alleyways."[9]

Poster from Outsider's Inn Collective's performance of Suzan-Lori Parks's 365 Days/365 Plays, Seattle. Copyright Vladimir Verano and Outsider's Inn Collective. Courtesy of Vladimir Verano.

In printed form, this 376-page work of mostly one- to two-page one-act plays represents and performs *time* as its primary theme, along with the excavation of the past (a Parks preoccupation) and the perpetuity of war. With plays about a rapidly closing "Window of Opportunity," a condemned prisoner's last meal, and a train passenger being excluded from the first-class coach in the twentieth and twenty-first centuries, *365* perfectly encapsulates the concerns of *Each Hour Redeem*: time, justice, and aesthetic form. In the piece "The Great Depression," two characters, The One and The Other One, are waiting and waiting, seemingly for rain:

> THE OTHER ONE: Don't get antsy.
> THE ONE: Im not *antsy*—Im just—
> THE OTHER ONE: Antsy.
> THE ONE: "Tired of waiting," I'd call it. (71)

Parks's plays frequently perform waiting as well as impatience with ongoing injustice and with the past's seemingly relentless grasp on the present. In the play for February 29, Parks takes Black History Month as her topic; the characters Panther and X have the following dialogue:

> PANTHER: Its Black History Month.
> x: Was.
> PANTHER: Past Is Present.
> x: Right on. (139)

Parks's plays often emerge out of such a blending of time periods—"past is present"—in a particularly conspicuous form of strategic anachronism. She even includes Past, Present, and Future as characters in her play for March 18 (154–55). Parks has defined the writing method she terms "Rep & Rev," or repetition and revision, as

> a concept integral to the Jazz esthetic in which the composer or performer will write or play a musical phrase once and again and again; etc.—with each revisit the phrase is slightly revised. "Rep & Rev" as I call it is a central element in my work; through its use I'm working to create a dramatic text that departs from the traditional linear narrative style to look and sound more like a musical score.[10]

Rep & Rev serves as a formal analogue to the nearly compulsive returns to crucial moments from the past that make up so much of the content of Parks's plays. Her 2002 Pulitzer Prize–winning play *Topdog/Underdog*, like her earlier work, *The America Play* (1994), pivots on repetitive reenactments of the assassination of Abraham Lincoln.

Parks's *365*, too, returns to this historical event and to strategic anachronism. In the play for November 26, titled "Mrs. Keckley and Mrs. Lincoln" and set in 1865, the president's wife and "her Negro dressmaker" hear a gunshot (25, 27). Mrs. Keckley assures Mrs. Lincoln that it was "just the sound of a car backfiring" (27). This moment combines an absurd, even funny intentional anachronism (everyone knows there were no cars in the 1860s) with documented historical facts. For example, both characters are actual historical figures: Mary Todd Lincoln, the president's wife, and Elizabeth Keckley, a former slave who worked her way to freedom as a seamstress. Keckley was well known during her lifetime as both dressmaker and friend to the first lady and as an activist on behalf of the black community of Washington, D.C. She also wrote an autobiographical narrative chronicling her life: *Behind the Scenes. Or, Thirty Years a Slave and Four Years in the White House* (1868), an extraordinary book that, in James Olney's words, "is not altogether a slave narrative and not exactly an autobiography . . . nor is it a romance or a sentimental novel," though it "partakes" of all of these.[11] Keckley, not unlike Parks, perceives the literary power inherent in the past and in a combination of temporalities:

> I am now on the shady side of forty, and as I sit alone in my room the brain is busy, and a rapidly moving panorama brings scene after scene before me, some pleasant and others sad; and when I thus greet old familiar faces, I often find myself wondering if I am not living the past over again. The visions are so terribly distinct that I almost imagine them to be real. Hour after hour I sit while the scenes are being shifted; and as I gaze upon the past, I realize how crowded with incidents my life has been.[12]

This passage, along with the book's title, suggests that Olney might well have added drama and performance to his list of genres and literary modes shaping Keckley's narrative. Just so, the recurrent, multiple forms of violence that Park calls on actors to perform find their antecedents in the multiple interrelated violences that simmer beneath the pages of Keckley's narrative and that structure it: the violence done to slaves, the violence of the Civil War, the assassination of the president, and the post–Civil War violence visited on the emancipated. Keckley notes that "Wilberforce University, a colored college near Xenia, Ohio, [was] destroyed by fire on the night that the President was murdered" (203). For Parks, such connections, only apparently paradoxically, point to a possible way out of the repetitive violence and injustice of the past. In the play for December 27, "2 Examples From the Interconnectedness of All Things," "2 griot" tell a story about ghosts from the past and "future folks" who join together to help a runaway slave's family to escape: "the ghosts of the past and the future saved them" (64–65). The play ends as "the Cops . . . beat the 1st griot—not to death, not enough to cause a riot—but just enough to make us all doubt the interconnectedness of all things" (65). Thus, after its performance of a union of past and present for the sake of freedom and good deeds, this play changes course, taking up Walter Mosley's concerns about the ways that repetitive violence inflicted on a black community can perpetuate temporal damage. The play reminds us of the Rodney King uprising, and we are reminded as well of Easy Rawlins: "no matter how far back you remember, there's a beatin' there waiting for you."[13] Parks considers and represents the difficulty of forging positive anachronism rather than reactive or strategic anachronism; she realizes how very difficult it is to overcome Pauline Hopkins's law of reversion.

Yet Parks and her plays do not remain moored either in time or in pessimism. In *365*, the stage directions are often quite temporally specific or, alternatively, paradoxical and fantastic: "4 people speak simultaneously for specific lengths of time. Speakers should follow prompts. Use a conductor to keep time" (111). "At this very moment, the stage is flooded with recently freed slaves" (233). "Eons pass within an instant . . . evolution happens double-triple time" (150). "The action continues and repeats forever" (163). "A large man on stage. He's been there since the beginning of time, or at least since the beginning of the plays, or at least for a few minutes" (261). Parks even includes a play titled "Top Speed" (150–51). Her regular acknowledgments of the past's ongoing presence, coupled with her profound and ongoing experimentations with time, offer the promise of healing temporal damage—or perhaps simply a renewed possibility for the simultaneity that was imagined during the Harlem Renaissance and the BAM. On the other hand, Parks may once again simply be offering us the fantastically, impossibly happy endings that Hopkins did.

Still, one wonders if Parks's own version of simultaneity more closely resembles the optimism of the BAM, when writers and performers alike believed that the Revolution might happen "live." Parks herself says:

> After years of listening to Jazz, and classical music too, I'm realizing that my writing is very much influenced by music; how much I employ its methods. Through reading lots I've realized how much Repetition and Revision is an integral part of the African and African-American literary and oral traditions.
>
> I am most interested in words and how they impact on actors and directors and how those folks physicalize those verbal aberrations. How does this Rep & Rev—a literal incorporation of the past—impact on the creation of a theatrical experience?[14]

In this remarkably rich and efficient passage, Parks peaceably unites print culture and oral tradition, jazz and classical music, vernacular and theory, and performance and physicality. Suggestively, the final play in *365* is titled "365 Days/365 Plays" and, in its entirety, consists of the following:

> Lights bump back up to white-hot.
> Zoom.
> Onstage, the manuscript of *365 Days/365 Plays*. (376)

The abiding existence of the print form of the work, the possibility of endless performance, and the actuality of performances across the nation over the course of a year—together, these "elements of style," as Parks might describe them, present us with a powerful blending of: author, director, and actor; print, oral, and visual culture; aesthetics and temporalities; communities and nation.

Granted, the work does not let us forget about the ongoing reality and threat of seemingly perpetual, trans-historical, internecine and international conflict and violence. The stage directions (really more a poem) for the second of two May 10 plays read as follows:

> Gang warfare: Crips against Bloods, Red States against
> Blue States, North against South, Spanish against English,
> Russians against themselves, Chinese against themselves,
> you know, South Koreans against Northern brethren,

> Germans against the world, then against the Wall,
> Irish against the English, English against the French,
> Chinese against Tibetans, us against them, U.S. against Iraq,
> Hutu against Tutsi, Serbs against Croats,
> Israeli against Palestinian, etc., you know, you know,
> you know how it go, back through the beginning of time
> and unfortunately out into the future. (202–3)

Parks's *365*, taken as a whole, nonetheless expresses remarkable optimism. As Parks and Metzgar modestly put it, "the 365 Festival is not building a new community; it is revealing community where it already exists" (401). Moreover, quite a few of the plays present new ways of parsing time. In "Beginning, Middle, End," a character named Traditionalist intones:

> Beginning, Middle, End
> Beginning, Middle, End. (23)

The only other character in the play, Fresh One, replies:

> End, Beginning
> Beginning, Middle
> Middle, End
> Middle, Fiddle
> Faddle, Paddle
> yr own canoe. (23)

The play goes on to connect these different notions of time with aesthetic form, as the two characters debate the relative merits of tradition versus innovation. Fresh One says: "When I started out I looked to traditional forms. But the situations I wanted to explore, the characters I wanted to embrace didnt fit—you get the picture?" (23). Traditionalist replies that his/her "stuff" does fit traditional forms (24). Fresh One responds: "Then be traditional. Its not a CRIME"; and Traditionalist replies: "But being fresh is criminal"; to which Fresh One responds: "In some circles" (24). The stage directions then read: "The Traditionalist takes out a piece of chalk. He considers writing the following stage direction: 'The Traditionalist draws a circle around the Fresh One'" (24). "Riot Police" then come on the scene and beat The Fresh One; perhaps unexpectedly, they then beat the Traditionalist (24, 25). This play captures a formal dilemma facing any artist, but it may be particularly apposite for African American writers and artists. Phillis Wheatley failed to impress Thomas Jefferson because he found her poetry conventional and unoriginal. Yet how would Jefferson have responded had Wheatley's poetry been as innovative for her time as, say, Emily Dickinson's was for hers? Certainly, Wheatley would have been attacked either for being a "traditionalist" or for being a "fresh one." But Parks has been rightly rewarded for being a "fresh one," even as her play refuses to judge the traditionalist: both can be at risk.

In the end, *365* posits the possibility of positive and healing resolution, however hard-won. First, the project includes multiple allusive connections with plays and playwrights in a very long Western literary tradition, from *Oedipus Rex* and *Macbeth* to *The Seagull, Death of a Salesman,* and *Waiting for Godot,* while it just as clearly participates in an African American literary tradition in a way that imagines the possibility of, finally, "being there." Parks even conceives of a synchronizing and blending of times and peoples and nations *on board a train,* of all places. "The Lake Shore Limited," the February 7 play, begins with a character named "Train Conductor" yelling "The Lake Shore Limited!! All Ahbbooooooard!" (112). The stage directions then read:

> The stage fills with hundreds of thousands of people. From different ethnic groups, races, social classes, dressed for different seasons, from different epochs, some in native dress of countries that have never been heard of, some from planets and solar systems and galaxies as yet undiscovered. Some with great bundles and packages, some empty-handed and bareheaded with empty pockets. All united in their desire to board the train. But there is no train. They wait with smiles which, after a while, melt and turn grimy like old snow in upstate New York. (112–13)

The very next line is spoken by a character named Man: "The goddamned train is late" (113). Parks, with characteristic sardonic humor, punctures the utopian possibility outlined in the first part of the stage directions. Yet the play also calls for "Patience," rather than violence—"I feel like shooting somebody right now," followed literally by the word "Patience"—while rejecting "words [that] are numerous and meaningless" (113). The play ends with further stage directions that depend on an interaction among print, sound, light, and bodily performance to make meaning: "The Man, now with a capital M, continues talking, and like the miracle of daybreak, the hopeless faces are refreshed. He continues talking, most likely just repeating what he's already read, as the mood grows quite buoyantly patriotic and the lights fade" (113). Parks here calls political fictions out for both their hollow power to placate and their substantial power to perpetuate injustice. In *365*, she wants not something "like" daybreak (or the first minute of a new day) but rather an authentically new time, "the minutes between night and dawn," when "the air is fresh and clean" and "everything is possible," beyond the gravitation of the past (352). In the end, Parks seems to be calling for fewer yet more meaningful words—that is, for *political truths*.

Notes

Introduction

1. "Preface," *Phillis Wheatley, Complete Writings*, 5.
2. Wheatley, "To the University of Cambridge."
3. Ibid.; emphasis in original. Of course, "redeem" also carries a religious meaning in this poem.
4. Benedict Anderson, *Imagined Communities*, 24.
5. Pratt, "Progress, Labor, Revolution," 56.
6. Dimock, *Through Other Continents*, 3, 2.
7. Ibid., 2, 3.
8. McCallum, "Timezone Endgame," 143.
9. Dimock, *Residues of Justice*, 10.
10. Hopkins, *Contending Forces*, 297; emphasis added.
11. Fabian, *Time and the Other*, 30.
12. *Dred Scott v. John F. A. Sandford.*
13. Ibid.
14. Truth, *Narrative*, 64–65; further citations will be parenthetical in the text.
15. Hegel, *Philosophy of History*, 99.
16. Mark M. Smith, *Mastered by the Clock*, 16, 133.
17. Ibid., 112. Additional quoted material is from the original source: *Alabama Planter*, "Management of Slaves," 193–94.
18. Douglass, *Narrative of the Life*, 29.
19. Jacobs, *Incidents*, 49.
20. McCallum, "Timezone Endgame," 143.
21. Hopkins, *Hagar's Daughter*, 11.
22. Hopkins, *Winona*, 317. *Hagar's Daughter* was published serially in the *Colored American*.
23. Logan, *Negro*, title page, 316, 339.
24. Holmes, *Common Law*, in *Essential Holmes*, 237.
25. Chesnutt, *House behind the Cedars*, 81, 183.
26. Dunbar, *Sport of the Gods*, 1; further citations will be parenthetical in the text.
27. Chesnutt, *Marrow of Tradition*, 154.
28. Douglass, *Heroic Slave*, 135.

29. Du Bois, "Winter Pilgrimage," 15.

30. Locke, "Enter the New Negro," 631.

31. Ibid., 631.

32. English, *Unnatural Selections*, 128.

33. Bergson, *Time and Free Will*, 176.

34. Ibid., 212, 207.

35. Ibid., 207.

36. Vaughan, "Introduction: Henri Bergson's *Creative Evolution*," 7.

37. Deleuze, "Lecture Course," 72.

38. Grosz, "Thinking the New," 44.

39. Kern, *Culture of Time and Space*, 199–201.

40. Quoted in ibid., 201.

41. Grimké, *Rachel*, 27; further citations will be parenthetical in the text.

42. Stein, *Mexico*, 307.

43. Zox-Weaver, *Women Modernists*, 59–60.

44. English, *Unnatural Selections*, 217. This production of the play took place at Myrtilla Miner Normal School, an institution that would eventually become part of the University of the District of Columbia in the 1970s.

45. Stein, "Composition as Explanation," 457.

46. Note that the Black Panther Party Legacy and Alumni have titled their website "It's About Time."

47. Le Poidevin and MacBeath, introduction to *Philosophy of Time*, 1–2.

48. Mosley, *Little Scarlet*, 48.

49. Mosley, *Life out of Context*, 1; further citations will be parenthetical in the text.

50. Parks, "From Elements of Style," 11.

51. Parks, "Possession," 5.

52. Dubey, *Signs and Cities*, 8.

53. Heise, *Chronoschisms*, 1.

54. Dohrn-van Rossum, *History of the Hour*, 245–47.

55. Mark M. Smith, *Mastered by the Clock*, 18.

56. Kern, *Culture*, x.

1. Ticking, Not Talking

1. Gates and McKay, preface to *Norton Anthology*, xxx.

2. "Lucy Terry," headnote in *Norton Anthology*, 186.

3. Hill et al., preface to *Call and Response*, xxxiii; Rochelle Smith and Sharon L. Jones, preface to *Prentice Hall Anthology*, xvi.

4. Hegel, *Philosophy of History*, 93; further citations will be parenthetical in the text.

5. Gilroy, *Black Atlantic,* 50; further citations will be parenthetical in the text.

6. Michelle M. Wright, *Becoming Black,* 29.

7. Douglass, *Narrative of the Life,* 21; further citations will be parenthetical in the text as *NL.*

8. Douglass's claims to be undocumented are not strictly true in the case of every slave. Some antebellum plantation journals did record slave births, illnesses, and deaths, and even sometimes described slaves' labor and activities of daily living, but they usually did so in the context of plantation business practices and profits and losses.

9. Gates, *Figures in Black,* 90; further citations will be parenthetical in the text.

10. Benedict Anderson, *Imagined Communities,* 204; emphasis in original.

11. Pratt, *Archives of American Time,* 163, 165.

12. Mark M. Smith, *Mastered by the Clock,* 5, 50; further citations will be parenthetical in the text.

13. Mumford, *Technics and Civilization,* 14.

14. Bartky, *Selling,* 33.

15. O'Malley, *Keeping,* 67. See also Bartky, *Selling,* 56, 59–60.

16. O'Malley, *Keeping,* 75; Bartky, *Selling,* 67, 78, 89.

17. Bartky, *Selling,* 89.

18. O'Malley, *Keeping,* 88; see also Bartky, *Selling,* 89, 105.

19. Bartky, *Selling,* 114; further citations will be parenthetical in the text.

20. McCrossen, "By the Clock," 558.

21. Gates, *Signifying Monkey,* 131; further citations will be parenthetical in the text.

22. Bruce, *Origins of African American Literature,* 20–21.

23. For just a few examples, see DeLombard, "'Eye-Witness to the Cruelty'"; Lampe, *Frederick Douglass: Freedom's Voice*; Yancy, "Geneva Smitherman"; Babb, "'Joyous Circle.'"

24. For example, in a 2006 article, "Equiano's 'Loud Voice,'" Jesse M. Molesworth argues that "speech acts of all forms—praying, swearing, cursing, and so forth—burst unremitting from the page in black Atlantic writing of the eighteenth century" (123). As this article suggests, widespread, ongoing interest in "speech acts" within early African American literature testifies to just how influential *The Signifying Monkey* and the Talking Book remain. A Project Muse database search on August 2, 2010, yielded well over 250 articles since 1988, including thirty published in 2009 and 2010, that at least cite *Signifying Monkey*; most lean heavily on it or discuss it at some length.

25. Nielsen, *Black Chant,* 19.

26. Wheatley, "To the University of Cambridge," 11.

27. Jefferson, *Notes on the State of Virginia,* 266–67.

28. Gronniosaw, *A narrative of the most remarkable particulars,* 10; further citations will be parenthetical in the text.

29. Equiano, *Interesting Narrative*, 63; further citations will be parenthetical in the text.

30. Granted, we cannot understand the economic dynamics here as strictly capitalist, since capitalism, classically defined, presumes free wage labor rather than slave labor.

31. Vargas Llosa, *Writer's Reality*, 97; further citations will be parenthetical in the text. I thank Rod Ferguson for drawing this passage to my attention.

32. Dohrn-van Rossum, *History of the Hour*, 317.

33. Douglass, *My Bondage and My Freedom*, 140; further citations will be parenthetical in the text as *MBMF*.

34. Quoted in Mark M. Smith, *Mastered by the Clock*, 43.

35. Jacobs, *Incidents*, 15–16.

36. Douglass, *Life and Times*, 605; further citations will be parenthetical in the text as *LT*.

37. C. L. R. James, *Black Jacobins*, 392.

38. Gikandi, *Slavery and the Culture of Taste*, 87.

39. Ibid., 87.

40. I refer here to President Kennedy's well-known quip, "Washington is a city of southern efficiency and northern charm." See Manchester, *Portrait*, 200.

41. "Santo Domingo," box 28, folder 1 of 5, p. 5, Frederick Douglass Papers, Manuscript Division, Library of Congress.

42. Ibid., 6–7.

43. Although Gregg D. Crane has rightly read Douglass as possessing a "cosmopolitan perspective," his argument that "Douglass embodied and argued for the world citizen as the model republican" is somewhat less persuasive, given Douglass's enthusiastic participation in the affairs of the nation as a marker of his own accession to American citizenship; see Crane, *Race, Citizenship, and Law*, 87.

44. Pitre, "Frederick Douglass and the Annexation of Santo Domingo," 390.

45. McCallum, "Timezone Endgame," 143.

46. Walcott, "Lost Empire," in *White Egrets*, 36.

47. See Levine, *Dislocating Race and Nation*, 229–31, for discussion of Douglass's support of the annexation policy, his subsequent disillusionment with that policy, and his later, complex discussion in *Life and Times* of his views on Haiti and his ambassadorial post.

48. Hopkins, *Contending Forces*, 297.

2. "Temporal Damage"

1. Andrews, *To Tell a Free Story*, 271, 276.

2. There is scholarly disagreement regarding the genre of *Our Nig*. Henry

Louis Gates identified it as a novel on his rediscovery of the book and its 1983 re-publication. William Andrews and Mitch Kachun lean toward its "autobiographical rather than fictional character," preferring to call it a "novelized autobiography" (editors' introduction to *Curse of Caste,* lvi n. 4). P. Gabrielle Forman and Reginald Pitts, on the other hand, lean toward the book's novelistic qualities, terming it "a sophisticated hybrid of autobiography and prose fiction" and identifying Wilson as "the first African American woman to publish a novel" (introduction to *Our Nig,* xxiv).

3. Sundquist, *To Wake the Nations,* 11; further citations will be parenthetical in the text. William James, "What Pragmatism Means," 382, 390.

4. Webb, *Garies and Their Friends,* 111; further citations will be parenthetical in the text.

5. Holmes, "Lecture III. Torts—Trespass and Negligence," 124.

6. *Plessy v. Ferguson.*

7. Foster, introduction to *Minnie's Sacrifice,* xxxv.

8. Crane, *Race, Citizenship, and Law,* 6; further citations will be parenthetical in the text.

9. Hartman, *Scenes of Subjection,* 22; further citations will be parenthetical in the text.

10. Griggs, *Imperium in Imperio,* 158; further citations will be parenthetical in the text.

11. William James, "What Pragmatism Means," 380.

12. Carby, introduction to *Magazine Novels of Pauline Hopkins,* xxxii.

13. For analyses of the politics surrounding Hopkins's association with the *Colored American,* see: Nellie Y. McKay, introduction to *Unruly Voice,* 7–8, 10; Bergman, " 'Everything We Hoped She'd Be.' "

14. Watt, *Rise of the Novel,* 60.

15. Armstrong, *How Novels Think,* 10, 3.

16. Ibid., 10.

17. Hopkins, *Winona,* 317; further citations will be parenthetical in the text.

18. Niswonger, "Study in Southern Demagoguery," 115, 118.

19. "Gov. Jefferson Davis, the Arkansas Gentleman," 1.

20. Ibid., 1.

21. "Topics of the Times," *New York Times,* 8.

22. "Governor Jeff Davis," *Macon Telegraph,* 4.

23. Niswonger, "Study in Southern Demagoguery," 118 n. 10; Hopkins, *Winona,* 287n.

24. Hopkins, *Contending Forces,* 348; further citations will be parenthetical in the text.

25. William James, "What Pragmatism Means," 378.

26. Peirce, "How to Make Our Ideas Clear," 132; further citations will be parenthetical in the text.

27. Menand, *Metaphysical Club*, 355.

28. Purcell, "On the Complexity of 'Ideas in America,'" 969.

29. See Menand, *Metaphysical Club*, 369–75, for a discussion of the contexts and reasons for pragmatism's origins and rise in this period. Menand argues, in part, that the movement fit well with the nation's new "economic arrangements": "The period of pragmatism's efflorescence, 1898–1917, was a period when the values of corporate management, public oversight, and political reform were in ascendance. The intellectual elite was finished with the Gilded Age, and so, for its own reasons, was the business elite" (371). James and Dewey "spoke to a generation of academics, journalists, and policy makers eager to find scientific solutions to social problems, and happy to be given good reasons to ignore the claims of finished cosmologies" (372). Menand goes on to link pragmatism's appeal with the reform movement and in turn to the reform movement's failure to support African American civil rights. In Menand's words, "the price of reform in the United States between 1898 and 1917 was the removal of the issue of race from the table" (374). He suggests that pragmatism's evenhandedness and resistance to ideology and absolutes rendered it congenial for a period interested in abandoning impassioned devotion to abstract causes, such as abolition at midcentury or justice for African Americans at century's end (374). Menand makes a strong case for the racist application of pragmatic thought; I argue that there are racialized ways of thinking embedded in the philosophy's very origins.

30. Russell, "Pragmatism," 109.

31. William James, "What Pragmatism Means," 388; emphasis in original.

32. Russell, *Power*, 210.

33. Menand, *Metaphysical Club*, xi; further citations will be parenthetical in the text.

34. William James, "Will to Believe," 727.

35. Chesnutt, "Literature in Its Relation to Life," 114.

36. Peirce, *Collected Papers*, 51.

37. Peirce, "Philosophy and the Conduct of Life," 29.

38. Wilson, preface to *Our Nig*, 3; Armstrong, *How Novels Think*, 10.

39. Peirce, "Philosophy and the Conduct of Life," 29.

40. Ibid., 38.

41. William James, "What Pragmatism Means," 380; emphasis in original.

42. Chesnutt, "Literature in Its Relation to Life," 113–14.

43. Ibid., 114.

44. Holmes, *Common Law*, 237; further citations will be parenthetical in the text.

45. James Weldon Johnson, *Autobiography of an Ex-Colored Man*, 59; emphasis in original.

46. Houser and Klouser, foreword to *Essential Peirce,* xii; Peirce, "Of Reasoning in General," 14; emphasis in original.

47. Peirce, "Doctrine of Chances," 151–52.

48. Ketner, *Peirce and Contemporary Thought,* 147.

49. Peirce, quoted in Sebeok and Sebeok, *"You Know My Method,"* 17–18; further citations will be parenthetical in the text.

50. Chesnutt, *Marrow of Tradition,* 74; further citations will be parenthetical in the text.

51. Chesnutt, *House behind the Cedars,* 114; further citations will be parenthetical in the text.

52. Peirce, "How to Make Our Ideas Clear," 128.

53. Holmes, "Path of the Law," 161.

54. For instance, Matthew Wilson remarks of Chesnutt's *House behind the Cedars*: "Chesnutt was pointing out to his audience that . . . 'race' is not an essence based on blood, but rather an imaginative construction" (introduction to *Paul Marchand,* xxvii); similarly, Julie Nerad points to "Hopkins's attempts to destabilize the primary social categories of race and gender" ("'So Strangely Interwoven,'" 367).

55. W. E. B. Du Bois in *Souls of Black Folk* (1903) also echoes Chesnutt's Jim Crow scene from *Marrow*: "If you wish to ride with me you must come into the 'Jim Crow Car.' There will be no objection,—already four other white men, and a little white girl with her nurse, are in there. Usually the races are mixed in there; but the white coach is all white. Of course this car is not so good as the other, but it is fairly clean and comfortable. The discomfort lies chiefly in the hearts of those four black men yonder—and in mine. . . . Below Macon the world grows darker; for now we approach the Black Belt,— . . . The 'Jim Crow Car' grows larger and a shade better; three rough field-hands and two or three white loafers accompany us, and the newsboy still spreads his wares at one end" (76).

56. Wong, *Neither Fugitive nor Free,* 261.

57. *Plessy v. Ferguson.*

58. Ibid., 262; emphasis in original.

59. See Crane (*Race, Citizenship, and Law,* 206–9) for an interesting alternative reading of the Jim Crow car scene in *The Marrow of Tradition.* Crane focuses on Chesnutt's "liberty of contract theme" and "freedom of association" rather than his engagement with legal pragmatism and juridical constructions of blackness. Crane concludes that the novel is challenging "identity as politics" represented by "Jim Crow law" (209).

60. See Crane for a more "positive" reading of this section of the novel (*Race, Citizenship, and Law,* 210–11, 214). Crane interprets it as Chesnutt's useful deployment of "a kind of public contractual language" rather than a "negative" form of "assimilation" (211, 210). Crane persuasively points to "consensual politics and

jurisprudence" as Chesnutt's and his character's primary and crucial goal, rather than either distance from other black people or proximity to whites (211).

61. See Hazel Carby's classic study *Reconstructing Womanhood,* as well as her introductions to Hopkins's three magazine novels, for a thorough discussion of the publication history of the four novels. As Carby points out in *Reconstructing Womanhood,* only *Contending Forces* was published in book form, in 1900, "by the Colored Co-operative Publishing Company of Boston, which also published her other three novels, in serial form, between 1900 and 1904 in the *Colored American Magazine*" (121).

62. Hopkins, *Of One Blood,* 607; further citations will be parenthetical in the text.

63. Hopkins's preoccupation with "blood" as a vehicle of identity may invite such approaches, and granted, her novels generally star light-skinned, tragic African American characters whose tangled interracial genealogies drive coincidence-filled, romantic, and sometimes bizarre plots. But Hopkins is only most obviously writing racial melodrama and domestic fiction. Also the first African American detective fiction writer, she is as concerned with the racialized workings of the law as she is with the workings of black and mixed-race households. For recent examples of Hopkins scholarship emphasizing biological discourses of the body and race, see the following: Putzi, "'Raising the Stigma,'" McCoy, "Rumors of Grace," Stevenson, "Of One Blood, of One Race," Somerville, "'Prettiest Specimen of Boyhood,'" Leslie Lewis, "Towards a New 'Colored' Consciousness," Nerad, "'So Strangely Interwoven,'" Harris, "Not Black and/or White," and Beam, "Flower of Black Female Sexuality." For an important exception, see Patricia D. Watkins's brilliant essay "Rape, Lynching, Law, and *Contending Forces,*" which stands as a significant exception in the body of recent Hopkins criticism. Watkins rightly argues that Hopkins in her novels "attempts to help blacks gain civil rights by offering an alternative interpretation of reality so that courts might recognize the nature and gravity of injuries caused by racism" (539).

64. Hopkins, *Hagar's Daughter,* 237; emphasis in original. Further citations will be parenthetical in the text.

65. The trope of the tragic mulatto (or mulatta), a doomed or troubled mixed-race character (often the protagonist), is among the most common figures in early African American novels, beginning with the very first, *Clotel.* The figure continued to appear throughout the nineteenth and into the twentieth century in African American-authored texts. Even Danzy Senna's contemporary novel *Caucasia* (1999) could be considered part of this tradition. There is extensive scholarship on the tragic mulatto/a in African American literature; some scholars have interpreted the figure as representing internalized racism, while others have viewed the figure as a way of challenging the reality of race, or as a way of revealing the internal contradiction of racism, or as a means of examining the intersection of race

and sexuality, among other interpretations. For just a few examples, see Sollors's *Neither Black nor White*, Goldstein and Thacker's edited collection *Complicating Constructions*, and Carby's *Reconstructing Womanhood* (especially 88–93).

66. Erika Lee, *At America's Gates*, 25; further citations will be parenthetical in the text. As Lee points out, Chinese people represented a small proportion of the overall immigration numbers for that decade—just 4.3 percent—yet their presence, particularly in regions where they were concentrated, elicited a disproportionate amount of racist and xenophobic anxiety.

67. Louis Menand explains that Peirce "shared his father's views on slavery"— that is, in favor of it—and "despised Charles Sumner," who was, in Peirce's own words, "'one of the absurdest figures of vanity I have ever laid eyes on'" (*Metaphysical Club*, 161).

68. For a discussion of 1870 Senate debates on race and citizenship, including quotations from Sumner, see Meyler, "Gestation of Birthright Citizenship." It's worth noting that Hopkins's choice of "Sumner" as the surname of one of the heroes of *Contending Forces* (appropriately enough, the white one) is probably more than coincidental. Senator Charles Sumner was perhaps the foremost abolitionist in the U.S. Congress, and among his acts during his long political career were the introduction of the Thirteenth Amendment, the nomination of a black lawyer for the Supreme Court, and the introduction of both the Freedmen's Bureau Bill and the bill that, after Sumner's death, became the Civil Rights Act of 1875.

69. In the case, the Butchers' Union Slaughter-House and Live-Stock Landing Company sued the state of Louisiana for having granted exclusive rights for twenty-five years to slaughter animals within the city of New Orleans to a competing white butchers' group, the Crescent City Live-Stock Landing and Slaughter-House Company. While the case did not seem to concern race, it did concern the nature and definition of citizenship and therefore inevitably invoked nineteenth-century legislative and constitutional precedents that themselves turned on race. The Butchers' Union lawyers contended that the Fourteenth Amendment, with its broad language barring states from abrogating individual civil rights, should be extended beyond the amendment's obvious immediate purpose—the guarantee and protection of African American citizenship—so as to decide the case in their favor. In fact, the amendment does not explicitly refer to race, stating simply: "No State shall make or enforce any law which shall abridge the privileges or immunities of citizens of the United States; nor shall any State deprive any person of life, liberty, or property, without due process of law; nor deny to any person within its jurisdiction the equal protection of the laws." But the Supreme Court disagreed with the plaintiffs in the case, with the majority of justices looking back at the Thirteenth and Fourteenth amendments only to limit them, except as regards the "Chinese question" and the question of nonwhite immigrants in general.

70. *Butchers' Benevolent Association v. Crescent City Live-Stock Landing and Slaughter-House Company.*

71. "Membership Has Its Privileges and Immunities."

72. As Robert Kaczorowski ("Revolutionary Constitutionalism") explains, via this decision, the Supreme Court "precluded the national government from protecting citizens in the South during the 1874 revival of political terrorism, and from preventing the establishment of a pattern of domination by Southern Conservative Democrats and white supremacists over Southern blacks and white Republicans. The end result of this decision, as reflected in public policy, was the reduction of Southern blacks to peonage, the creation of Jim Crow, and the demise of the Republican Party in the South" (938).

73. According to Justice Brown, writing in 1896 for the majority in *Plessy*, "the proper construction of this amendment [the Fourteenth] was first called to the attention of this court in the Slaughter-house cases . . . which involved, however, not a question of race, but one of exclusive privileges. The case did not call for any expression of opinion as to the exact rights it was intended to secure to the colored race, but it was said generally that its main purpose was to establish the citizenship of the negro; to give definitions of citizenship of the United States and of the States, and to protect from the hostile legislation of the States the privileges and immunities of citizens of the United States, as distinguished from those of citizens of the States." Like Miller before him, Brown went on to argue that states should enjoy the power to regulate businesses, but going beyond Miller's restriction of the "privileges and immunities" clause, Brown contended that a state may legally and constitutionally segregate its citizens, specifically its "negro" citizens, by race: "The object of the [Fourteenth] amendment was undoubtedly to enforce the absolute equality of the two races before the law, but in the nature of things it could not have been intended to abolish distinctions based upon color, or to enforce social, as distinguished from political equality, or a commingling of the two races upon terms unsatisfactory to either. Laws permitting, and even requiring, their separation in places where they are liable to be brought into contact do not necessarily imply the inferiority of either race to the other, and have been generally, if not universally, recognized as within the competency of the state legislatures in the exercise of their police power." Together, the opinions of Miller and Brown affirmed states' rights to regulate businesses and citizens and races as they saw fit, without much interference from federal courts.

74. Fields, "Ideology and Race," 163.

75. *Yick Wo v. Hopkins.* The majority opinion in the case rightly noted "that no reason for it [the differential enforcement] exists except hostility to the race and nationality to which the petitioners belong, and which in the eye of the law is not justified." The majority concluded: "The discrimination is, therefore, illegal, and the public administration which enforces it is a denial of the equal protection

of the laws and a violation of the Fourteenth Amendment of the Constitution." The liberal judgment of the Court here depends on an intertwining of "negro" and Chinese, just as had the restrictive judgment in the *Slaughterhouse Cases*. Here lies the heart of Pauline Hopkins's "Chinese puzzle": to expand immigrant rights, particularly the rights of noncitizens, by tying them via jurisprudence to precedents regarding "negro" civil rights is also to throw African American citizenship into crisis. We should note that Hopkins is addressing not so much biological as interested legal and constitutional mechanisms of race, ethnicity, and citizenship that render blackness alternatively unexceptional or exceptional (in relation either to whiteness or to other forms of nonwhiteness).

76. *United States v. Wong Kim Ark.*

77. As one legal scholar explains, in *Yick Wo v. Hopkins*, "Justice Field began to present birthright citizenship as a national phenomenon that would supersede even Congress' ability to determine who could and who could not become citizens. Only the Supreme Court's decision in *United States v. Wong Kim Ark* would, however, definitively establish his vision as a Constitutional mandate" (Meyler, "Gestation of Birthright Citizenship," 525).

78. Critical race theorist Michael A. Olivas asserts that "no racial group has been singled out for separate, racist treatment in United States immigration law more than have the Chinese," and he points out that over the course of several years following the 1882 Chinese Exclusion Act, "Congress enacted" ever harsher restrictions on Chinese immigration and "by 1888" had passed an act that "virtually prohibited Chinese from entering or re-entering the United States" ("Chronicles," 13).

79. Gyory, *Closing the Gate*, 1. See also Erika Lee, *At America's Gates*, 24, and Salyer, *Laws Harsh as Tigers*, 12–13.

80. See Salyer, *Laws Harsh as Tigers*, 112–13. Salyer rightly points to "the courts' inconsistencies regarding citizenship," inconsistencies that emerged out of "a tension" between "an expansive liberal and a more narrow ethnocultural definition" of citizenship (207). See the 1893 majority (6–3) opinion in *Fong Yue Ting v. United States*, in which Justice Gray wrote: "Chinese laborers . . . continue to be aliens, having taken no steps towards becoming citizens, and [are] incapable of becoming such under the naturalization laws; and therefore, remain subject to the power of Congress to expel them, or to order them to be removed and deported from the country, whenever, in its judgment their removal is necessary or expedient for the public interest." The opinion also upheld the congressional provision "requiring a Chinese alien, claiming the privilege of remaining in the United States, to prove the fact of his residence here, at the time of the passage of the act, 'by at least one credible white witness.'"

81. For discussion of the period's material and legal discrimination against Chinese Americans, see Torok, "Reconstruction and Racial Nativism," 63–66.

82. William James, "Will to Believe," 732, 734. Interestingly, this essay was originally "an address to the Philosophical Clubs of Yale and Brown Universities" (717).

83. Kaczorowski, "Revolutionary Constitutionalism," 863.

84. For a discussion of the power of legal precedent, particularly a particular precedent's degree of permanence, its resistance to being overruled, see Gerhardt, "Role of Precedent."

85. Hopkins, *Winona*, 317.

86. Holmes, "Path of the Law," 160.

87. Holmes, "Privilege, Malice, and Intent," 1.

88. See, for example, Vandevelde, "Modern Prima Facie Tort," 543.

89. Holmes, "Privilege, Malice, Intent," 1.

90. Hartman, *Scenes of Subjection*, 116.

91. For definitions of constitutional tort and mass tort, see Garner, *Black's Law Dictionary*, 724.

92. See Ignatiev, *How the Irish Became White*; Innes, *Devil's Own Mirror*; and Lott, *Love and Theft*.

93. As Erika Lee shows, anti-Chinese activism was fueled by drawing "similarities between African Americans and Chinese immigrants," with the figures of the Chinese prostitute and Chinese coolie, for example, being "conflated with African American slaves" (27). An inherent part of the process of first "othering" and then excluding Chinese immigrants, then, was blackening them. As Lee further argues, other immigrant groups targeted for exclusion after 1882 (e.g. Mexicans and southern and eastern Europeans) were often likened to the Chinese. "Both the rhetoric and the tools used to exclude the Chinese," Lee explains, "were repeated in later debates over immigration," thereby creating a kind of chain of increasingly exclusive and always racialized versions of American-ness and white supremacy (46).

94. Chesnutt, "Remarks," 514.

95. Frances Harper, *Iola Leroy*, 282.

96. Chesnutt, "Future American"; Griggs, *Hindered Hand*, 332.

97. Griggs, *Imperium in Imperio*, 164.

3. "The Death of the Last Black Man"

1. Du Bois, *Souls of Black Folk*, 133.

2. Ibid., 130–34.

3. Hopkins, *Contending Forces*, 297.

4. Hurston, "How It Feels," 1031.

5. Wideman, "Dead Black Men," 150. I thank an anonymous reader of this manuscript for alerting me to this text.

6. Himes, "His Last Day," 51.

7. Although in later years McKay distanced himself from the interpretation of "If We Must Die" as a militant protest against the violence of the "Red Summer," claiming that it was not necessarily a racial poem, it is hard to deny the context of the 1919 race riots as helping to establish at least one meaning of the poem for its readers then and ever since.

8. Richard Wright, *Native Son,* 403; further citations will be parenthetical in the text.

9. Rampersad, introduction, ix. This opening scene in *Native Son* is so well known and studied that it has even been parodied. See the first page of Trey Ellis's *Platitudes* for an example. As Ellis's title suggests, the ringing alarm clock has become a kind of "platitude," a well-worn trope. I thank an anonymous reader of this manuscript for calling this reference to my attention.

10. Rosenblatt, "Bigger's Infernal Assumption," 31.

11. Griffin, *Who Set You Flowin'?,* 103; further citations will be parenthetical in the text.

12. Cohen, *Making a New Deal,* 279.

13. Felgar, "Cultural Work of Time," 99, 100. Felgar is one among a handful of critics to have observed the novel's sustained focus on what he terms "a temporal problem" (99). In addition to Felgar, see Griffin, *Who Set You Flowin'?,* 60, 65–66, 103–7; Smethurst, "Invented by Horror," 36; Barthold, *Black Time,* 62–69; and Sollors, *Ethnic Modernism,* 159.

14. Kern, *Culture of Time and Space,* 244.

15. Cohen, *Making a New Deal,* 281.

16. O'Malley, *Keeping Watch,* 206; further citations will be parenthetical in the text.

17. Smethurst, "Invented by Horror," 35; further citations will be parenthetical in the text.

18. Deleuze, *Cinema 2,* 39; further citations will be parenthetical in the text.

19. Alger, *Struggling Upward,* 135; further citations will be parenthetical in the text.

20. Waterbury Watch, advertisement.

21. Cohen, *Making a New Deal,* 365, 367.

22. Alger, *Ragged Dick,* 3–4; further citations will be parenthetical in the text.

23. Barbara Johnson, "Re(a)d and the Black," 122; further citations will be parenthetical in the text.

24. Had Bigger looked at the *Tribune* in February and March of that year, he would have encountered these headlines about black men: "Shot Plucks a Clew from Fleeing Thief"; "Convict Stabs Michigan City Prison Guard"; and "Railroad Police Slay Negro Robbing Box Car." And throughout the 1930s, scores of *Tribune* headlines advanced what Barbara Johnson termed the "overdetermined" plot of black man as

rapist of white women ("Re(a)d and the Black," 122); "Eight Negro Rapists Given Death Penalty"; "3 Negro Rapists Draw Death as Mob Threatens"; and "Scan Cold Trail for Three Negro Rapist Slayers." Bigger's own plot to blame Communists for his crimes would also have had strong source material in the *Tribune* during the two-week period of the novel's action, as the following 1939 headlines about "Reds" suggest: "Witnesses Bare New Deal Books' Red Propaganda"; Lawyer Expose Spurs Red Quiz into New Deal"; and "Blatant Naziism and Covert Communism." Clearly, the novel's fictional headlines, as in "Red Nabbed as Girl Vanishes," could easily have actually appeared in the *Tribune* in 1939 (*Native Son*, 198).

25. See for example Joyce, "Figurative Web," 177; and Williams, "Use of Communications Media," 532–34.

26. Ibid., 533.

27. Richard Wright, "Blueprint," 268.

28. McKay, "If We Must Die."

29. Raymond Lewis, "1969," and McKay, "If We Must Die," 11.

30. Ernest Gaines, *A Lesson before Dying*, 3; further citations will be parenthetical in the text.

31. Here one cannot help but think of Frederick Douglass's classic 1852 speech "What to the Slave Is the Fourth of July?"

32. Grant Wiggins understands his mission to be "to prove to these white men" that Jefferson is "not a hog, he's a man. I'm supposed to make him a man. Who am I? God?" (31).

33. Jefferson, *Notes on the State of Virginia*, 265.

34. Mead and Baldwin, *Rap on Race*, 68.

35. Matthews, *Black Men*; Gibbs, *Young, Black, and Male*; Felicia Lee, "Black Men"; White, "Endangered Species."

36. hooks, *We Real Cool*, 89; see also Stephanie Brown and Clark, "Melodramas of Beset Black Manhood?"

37. Sabol and Couture, "Prison Inmates at Mid-year 2007," 7.

38. Ibid.

39. Swindle, "Louisiana Justice," BR11.

40. Ibid.

41. See for example, Byerman, *Fingering the Jagged Grain*, 94; Gaudet, "Miss Jane and Personal Experience Narrative," 26; and Aubert, "Ernest J. Gaines's Truly Tragic Mulatto," 74 n. 2.

42. Sam Anderson et al., "What to Read."

43. Ernest Gaines, "Miss Jane and I," 618.

44. Ibid., 619.

45. Parks, *Death of the Last Black Man*, 48; further citations will be parenthetical in the text.

46. Douglass, *Narrative of the Life*, 21.

47. Parks, "From Elements of Style," 10.

48. Bartky, *One Time Fits All*, 9–10.

49. Ibid., 12.

50. Fabian, *Time and the Other*, 35; further citations will be parenthetical in the text.

51. Parks, "Possession," 5.

52. Ibid., 9.

53. Wideman, *Lynchers*, 438; further citations will be parenthetical in the text. I thank an anonymous reader for the University of Minnesota Press for suggesting the inclusion of this novel in this chapter.

54. Parks, "Possession," 5.

55. Deleuze, *Difference and Repetition*, 5.

4. "Seize the Time!"

1. As Aldon Nielsen points out, Dasein did not die in 1973. Even "as late as 1988," Nielsen explains, *Dasein* enjoyed another in a series of incarnations" (*Black Chant*, 60); further citations of *Black Chant* will be parenthetical in the text.

2. Heidegger, *History of the Concept of Time*, 159.

3. Napier, "Howard Poets," 61. To my knowledge, the only other extended scholarly treatments of the Dasein Literary Group appear in Eugene Redmond, *Drumvoices*, 312–20 (further citations will be parenthetical in the text), and in Nielsen, *Black Chant*, 59–77.

4. Benedict Anderson, *Imagined Communities*, 24; Heidegger, *History of the Concept of Time*, 159.

5. Ellison, *Invisible Man*, 8.

6. Govan, "Lynching," 18.

7. Weheliye, *Phonographies*, 71; further citations will be parenthetical in the text.

8. DeLegall, "Psalm for Sonny Rollins," 8. Note that there is much controversy about the nature of Rollins's constantly evolving style in this period, as in other periods. As Gary Giddins puts it, "Rollins has never stood still long enough for anything to gain on him, and his sound, which took on a husky, scratchy quality in the '70s, commensurate with his electrified rhythm section, has changed almost as many times as his record-label affiliations" (*Riding on a Blue Note*, 121).

9. Note that there is a great deal of controversy about Davis's *Sketches of Spain*, its style and musical quality.

10. Stone, "Flamenco Sketches," 54.

11. Rhodes, *Framing the Black Panthers*, 7; further citations will be parenthetical in the text.

12. Cleaver, *Soul on Ice,* 12; Carmichael and Hamilton, *Black Power,* xi (further citations will be parenthetical in the text).

13. "Quotations from Huey," 13.

14. "Rules of the Black Panther Party," 17.

15. "Why Was Denzil Dowell Killed," 3.

16. "Breakfast for School Children," 7.

17. Newton, "Let Us Hold High the Banner," 54.

18. Elaine Brown, "Significance of the Newspaper," ix.

19. Hilliard, *Black Panther.*

20. Newton, "Quotations from Huey," 13.

21. Elaine Brown, *Seize the Time,* DVD. Ironically, Brown's album was released in 1969 on Vault, a white-owned label. See Ward, *Just My Soul,* 279; further citations will be parenthetical in the text.

22. Mott, interview with Rickey Vincent.

23. Karenga, "Black Art," 2087; further citations will be parenthetical in the text.

24. Neal, "Black Arts Movement," 2040.

25. Baraka, "Afrikan Revolution," 243.

26. Baraka, "It's Nation Time," in *It's Nation Time,* 21; further citations will be parenthetical in the text.

27. McPhee, *Nation Time,* liner notes (unpaginated).

28. Kelley, "Stormy Weather," 73–74.

29. See S. Craig Watkins, "'Black Is Back,'" 192; and Ward, *Just My Soul,* 413–14.

30. Torrance, interview with Rickey Vincent.

31. See Ward, *Just My Soul,* 5–15, and Suzanne E. Smith, *Dancing in the Street.*

32. See Smethurst, *Black Arts Movement,* 29–30; further citations will be parenthetical in the text.

33. See Suzanne E. Smith, *Dancing in the Street,* 12–13, and "Spirituals," 9.

34. See Suzanne E. Smith, *Dancing in the Streets;* Baraka, *Black Music;* Kelley, "Stormy Weather"; Ward, *Just My Soul.*

35. Baraka, "Changing Same," 210–11.

36. "Blaxploitation," 85.

37. Baraka, "Four for Trane," 181; emphasis in original.

38. Baraka, "New Black Music," 199.

39. Farah Jasmine Griffin wonders what positive things might have happened had "black feminist intellectuals" allied more closely with "black nationalist woman intellectuals" ("Conflict and Chorus," 124). E. Frances White notes that 1960s black nationalism, while it "counter[ed] racism," also "construct[ed] conservative utopian images of African American life" ("Africa on My Mind," 13). Wahneema

Lubiano argues that "what replaces the state in black nationalism" is "cultural production and its consumption, and its adherence to black nationalist evaluative criteria," noting that "black cultural nationalism has almost always blocked resistance within its ranks" and has long been in the business of issuing "black patriarchal familial prescriptions" ("Standing In for the State," 159, 163).

40. Karenga, although he clearly valued the legacy of the blues, did not view the blues as a viable source for present-day cultural nationalism; he even went so far as to say that "the blues are invalid; for they teach resignation, in a word acceptance of reality—and we have come to change reality" ("Black Art," 2090). Even as partisan and passionate a blues scholar as Baraka, in balancing legacy (same) with newness (changing), favors keeping up with the times: "Blues was the initial Afro-American music, and bebop the reemphasis of the non-western tradition. And if the latter saved us from the vapid wastes of swing, singlehandedly, the new avant-garde (and John Coltrane) are saving us from the comparatively vapid 50s. And they both utilized the same general methods: getting the music back to its initial rhythmic impetuses and away from the attempts at rhythmic regularity and melodic predictability that the 30's and the 50's had laid on it" ("Jazz Avant-Garde," 92). Baraka always seems to be at his most emphatic and poetic when describing the coolest, most cutting-edge black male jazz musicians, as in this passage from his essay "Apple Cores #4": "Listening to Sonny Murray, you can hear the primal needs of the new music. The heaviest emotional indentation it makes. From ghostly moans of spirit, let out full to the heroic marchspirituals and priestly celebrations of new blackness. I mention Sonny here—and Albert Ayler and Sun-Ra—because their music is closest to the actual soul-juice, cultural genius of the new black feeling. The tone their music takes is a clear emotional reading of where the new music is. And Pharoah, Marion, Charles Moore and the others got into it the other night. And sound ran through us like blood" (154).

41. Reed, "Black Particularity Reconsidered," 52; further citations will be parenthetical in the text. See also Glaude, introduction, wherein Eddie Glaude Jr. notes the tendency of "black nationalists of the period" to have "stepped outside of history" (11).

42. Neal, "Black Arts Movement," 2050; further citations will be parenthetical in the text.

43. Phillip Brian Harper, "Nationalism and Social Division," 180, 179; further citations will be parenthetical in the text.

44. James Weldon Johnson, editor's preface to the revised edition, in *Book of American Negro Poetry,* 6.

45. Suzanne E. Smith, *Dancing in the Street,* 17, 94.

46. In his infamous dismissal of the Harlem Renaissance, Wright contended: "Generally speaking, Negro writing in the past has been confined to humble novels,

poems, and plays, prim and decorous ambassadors who went a-begging to white America. They entered the Court of American Public Opinion dressed in the knee-pants of servility, curtsying to show that the Negro was not inferior, that he was human, and that he had a life comparable to that of other people. For the most part these artistic ambassadors were received as though they were French poodles who do clever tricks" ("Blueprint," 268).

47. Gayle, "From *The Black Aesthetic*," 1916; further citations will be parenthetical in the text.

48. Locke, "Youth Speaks," 659.

49. Hughes, "Negro Artist and the Racial Mountain," 1314, 1313.

50. Locke, "Enter the New Negro," 7.

51. See James Weldon Johnson, editor's preface to the first edition, in *Book of American Negro Poetry*, 41.

52. Edwards, *Practice of Diaspora*, 2; further citations will be parenthetical in the text.

53. Claude McKay, quoted in Edwards, *Practice of Diaspora*, 222.

54. Locke, foreword to "New Negro," xxvi, xxvii.

55. Locke, "New Negro," 10, 7; further citations will be parenthetical in the text.

56. Locke, "Youth Speaks," 660.

57. English, *Unnatural Selections*, 16.

58. Hughes, "Song for a Dark Girl," 104.

59. Locke, "New Negro," 7.

60. See English, "Selecting the Harlem Renaissance" (814–16), for a discussion of pessimism and despair in the Harlem Renaissance.

61. Adolph Reed wrote in 1979 of the "failure of mysticized black nationalism" ("Black Particularity Reconsidered," 58); Eddie Glaude in 2002 noted the movement's "ambiguous legacy" (editor's introduction to *Is It Nation Time?*, 1).

62. As I have argued elsewhere regarding the Harlem Renaissance, the rhetoric of failure for either it or the BAM is apt only if we accept the premise that enduring political or social change is an appropriate benchmark for the success of an aesthetic movement. The rich body of work produced by figures in both movements, in my view, constitutes success, an enduring legacy for both the Harlem Renaissance and the BAM. See English, "Selecting the Harlem Renaissance," 810–14.

63. Baraka, "Peter Brötzmann," 399.

64. Ibid., 400.

65. Baraka, "Changing Same," 214.

66. Wideman, *Lynchers*, 558.

67. Mead and Baldwin, *Rap on Race*, 61; further citations will be parenthetical in the text.

68. Mitgang, "Anatole Broyard."

69. Broyard, "Poet and the Anthropologist," 37; further citations will be parenthetical in the text.

70. Mead does not say "We can't undo the past." She actually says, "If we want to go forward from here, then the steps that got us here have to be incorporated into where we are going next" (Mead and Baldwin, *Rap on Race*, 159).

71. Ibid, 159, 61.

72. Scott-Heron and Jackson, "Pardon Our Analysis."

73. Scott-Heron, "Winter in America."

74. Ali, "Western Sunrise."

5. Being Black There

1. Some relevant book-length studies over the past twenty years include Brady and Maus's edited collection *Finding a Way Home* (2008), Fischer-Hornung and Mueller's edited collection *Sleuthing Ethnicity* (2004), Roth's *Inspecting Jews* (2004), Reddy's *Traces, Codes, and Clues* (2003), Klein's edited collection *Diversity and Detective Fiction* (1999), Gosselin's edited collection *Multicultural Detective Fiction* (1999), Soitos's *The Blues Detective* (1996), Lock's *A Case of Mis-Taken Identity* (1994), and Bailey's *Out of the Woodpile* (1991). For relevant essays, see Roger Berger, "'Black Dick,'" Crooks, "From the Far Side," Kennedy, "Black Noir," Lock, "Invisible Detection," Mason, "Walter Mosley's Easy Rawlins," Muller, "Double Agent," Reitz, "Do We Need Another Hero?," Siddiqi, "Police and Postcolonial Rationality," and Witt, "Detecting Bodies."

2. Woods, introduction to *Spooks, Spies, and Private Eyes*, xv.

3. Ibid., xvii.

4. King, "'You Think Like You White,'" 212.

5. Ibid., 211.

6. Witt, "Detecting Bodies," 166.

7. Ibid., 167.

8. A number of critics have identified Neely's Blanche White novels as examples of "cozy" detective fiction, a subgenre defined as mystery novels in which: little harm comes to the detective or other characters (other than the initial murder), there is little sex or violence, and the setting consists of a confined, often rural place wherein the characters know one another. See, for example, Phillips, "Mystery Woman," 43. Granted, three of the four novels in Neely's Blanche White series seem at first glance to fit this definition. But in the 1999 installment, *Blanche Cleans Up*, Blanche is living in Roxbury and negotiating racism and city-wide corruption in Boston; moreover, Blanche herself is quite tough—mentally and physically—throughout the series. But the fact that she is physically assaulted at least once in every novel and has actually been raped means that the books cannot be considered "cozy," even if they match some of the subgenre's characteristics.

I would argue that they partake of both hard-boiled (Sam Spade) and cozy (Miss Marple) conventions.

9. Mosley, *Little Scarlet*, 235.

10. A great deal of current African diasporic and African Americanist literary scholarship is pressing home the point that "blackness" has never been unitary and that it has always been constructed in particular ways in particular times and places. See Wright's *Becoming Black* for a wonderful example. See also Dubey, *Signs and Cities,* and Edwards, *Practice of Diaspora*.

11. Neely, *Blanche Passes Go,* 288.

12. McCann, *Gumshoe America,* 5, 16; further citations will be parenthetical in the text.

13. Robert Crooks identifies Easy as typical of the hard-boiled hero in that he is "the most scrupulous and decent of the erring humans mired in the blindness of their cultural situations" and, further, that "in this respect Rawlins is hardly distinguishable from Philip Marlowe, Mike Hammer, or Kinsey Millhone" ("From the Far Side," 85). Although Easy becomes a family man during the series, he is—at least as far as his work goes—generally (although not always) a "lone wolf." And Easy is in the business, also like the traditional hard-boiled hero, of negotiating and disclosing an intricate and essentially corrupt urban social landscape. His investigation serves to analyze and diagnose that space, though his diagnosis may not yield a particularly effective prescription. Liam Kennedy succinctly describes this investigative process: Easy, like the typical detective, is "at once a liminal, rootless figure . . . and . . . a classless and self-reliant man," whose detection "renders universal moral principles of truth and justice subjective and presages moral inquiry as the detective's singular response to the atomized urban scenes of modernity" ("Black Noir," 225–26). As for the Los Angeles setting, quite a few critics have observed that the hard-boiled writers themselves have understood and even helped construct that role for the city. Paul Skenazy argues that the hard-boiled Los Angeles novels have worked for decades to "create and dominate many of our insights into the spirit of this city and its citizens" ("Behind the Territory," 104). For Liahna Babener, Chandler delivers a "vision" of Los Angeles as "an empire built on a spurious foundation, decked in tinsel, and beguiled by its own spurious promises," while Marlowe "likens" the city to a "repertory company of liars, cheaters, and imposters" ("Raymond Chandler's City," 132). And now, over the course of Mosley's Easy Rawlins series, "the very landscape of Los Angeles becomes more emblematic of the evil lurking in the hearts and minds of its citizens," as Gilbert Muller argues ("Double Agent," 292). Thus, the hard-boiled detective, from Marlowe to Rawlins, is alone and cynical in the city—indeed, because of the city—and, ultimately, he discovers that his cynicism has been quite justified all along. Just so, Easy says early on in *Black Betty* (1994): "There was nobody I could trust" (167), and

again, near the book's ending, "You can never trust what somebody tells you is true" (278).

14. Muller, "Double Agent," 293.

15. Lock, "Invisible Detection," 77.

16. Ibid., 78.

17. Roger Berger, " 'Black Dick,' " 281.

18. Ibid. Crooks argues similarly that Easy Rawlins's "individualism" renders him like Sam Spade and Philip Marlowe and also therefore renders all of Mosley's novels politically suspect, even antiprogressive, because an individualist ethos "remains crucial . . . for disarming collective resistance" ("From the Far Side," 72). Also see McCann, *Gumshoe America,* for an extensive analysis of the complex politics, neither wholly reactionary nor wholly progressive, of hard-boiled detective fiction of the 1930s–1960s.

19. Williams, "My Man Himes," 48.

20. *Brown v. Board of Education.*

21. Mudge, "New Crime Fiction," par. 12.

22. In 1997 Mosley also published *Gone Fishin',* set in 1939, a "prequel" (Lock, *Case of Mis-Taken Identity,* 2) in the series.

23. Todorov, *Poetics of Prose,* 44.

24. As Gilbert Muller aptly notes, "if Watts in particular or Los Angeles more generally is the point of origin in Mosley's fiction, that demographic point radiates outward to a national boundary or framework that is the province of the novel" ("Double Agent," 289).

25. Mosley, *Black Betty,* 45; further citations will be parenthetical in the text as *BB.*

26. Scott-Heron, "Winter in America."

27. Morrison, "Comment: Talk of the Town," 32.

28. Honan, "Books, Books," 1.

29. Frisby, "Soul-Baring," 81.

30. Frisby, "Clinton Vows," par. 2.

31. Clinton/Gore, *The Man from Hope.*

32. Caroline Reitz has made a similar point about Blanche White, Barbara Neely's protagonist: "Blanche's detective powers . . . are rooted in the social conditions of her existence" ("Do We Need," 229).

33. The sameness of political rhetoric in the 2004 Democratic convention is striking. With "Hope Is on the Way," the Kerry-Edwards slogan, it seems that Mosley could have written *Black Betty* yet again. And given Barack Obama's coinage, "the audacity of hope," it seems that little has changed, at least as far as the Democratic Party's campaign rhetoric goes. We can only hope that Watts will not suffer again in the ways it did in 1965 and 1992.

34. Mosley, *Little Scarlet,* 204–5; further citations will be parenthetical in the text as *LS.*

35. Rosenblatt, "Bigger's Infernal Assumption," 32.

36. Lock, "Invisible Detection," 78.

37. Mason, "Walter Mosley's Easy Rawlins," 173.

38. Mosley, *Devil in a Blue Dress,* 2, 4; further citations will be parenthetical in the text as *DIABD.* Easy crosses other borders (literal and figurative) as well. Over the course of the rest of the novels, he moves up and down the social and economic ladder, going from poor to working-class to middle-class neighborhoods, and from renter to homeowner to landlord and back. He also marries and divorces and becomes a biological and an adoptive father.

39. Mosley, *Bad Boy Brawly Brown,* 49; further citations will be parenthetical in the text as *BBBB.*

40. Kennedy, "Black Noir," 230.

41. In *Little Scarlet,* that dynamic has changed. Throughout the novel, Easy is connected, however reluctantly, with the LAPD, and he even befriends a white police detective. The 1965 Watts setting, in the midst of the uprising, creates new conditions for Easy's relations with whites, including and especially the police. For example, when Easy finds himself "dismiss[ing]" a white police officer, he realizes that "the world was changing so quickly I was worried about making a misstep in the new terrain" (31). At the conclusion of his investigation, Easy is even granted a private detective's license by the Deputy Commissioner of the LAPD (303). This shift in race relations seems to suggest a new optimism building in the series; on the other hand, near the book's ending, Easy observes that "three weeks later the riots were all but forgotten" (304).

42. Miller, *Novel and the Police,* 20; emphasis in original.

43. Ibid., 21; emphasis in original.

44. One of the best examples: Cohn, "Optics and Power."

45. Siddiqi, "Police and Postcolonial Rationality," 177.

46. Ibid., 176.

47. Douglass, *Heroic Slave,* 135.

48. Hopkins, "Talma Gordon," 16.

49. Himes, *My Life,* 102.

50. Neely, *Blanche among the Talented Tenth,* 122; further citations will be parenthetical in the text as *BATT.*

51. Neely, *Blanche on the Lam,* 6.

52. Mosley, *Blonde Faith,* 97–98; further citations will be parenthetical in the text as *BF.*

53. Easy loses his job as a result of his racially-specific relationship to his workplace. When his boss Mr. Giacomo asks him to stay late to check his work,

Easy balks because he is both over-tired and confident that the work was done properly. He is also upset that his boss does not trust his work and his judgment. Easy tells us: "The white workers didn't have a problem with that sort of treatment because they didn't come from a place where men were always called boys. The white workers would just have said, 'Sure, Benny, you called it right, but damn if I could see straight now.' And Benny would have understood that. He would have laughed and realized how pushy he was being and offered to take Mr. Davenport, or whoever, out to drink a beer. But the Negro workers didn't drink with Benny. We didn't go to the same bars or wink at the same girls" (DIABD 62–63). Easy is also angry because the boss calls him and the other black workers by their first names but the white workers by their last names: "Mr. Davenport, or whoever."

54. Heidegger, *History of the Concept of Time*, 310; emphasis in original.

55. Derrida, *Gift of Death*, 41.

56. Halloran, "Performative Mourning," par. 2 (unpaginated).

57. Moyers, "Now," par. 14.

58. McWhorter, "Strom's Skeleton," par. 1.

59. Genette, *Narrative Discourse*, 37; further citations will be parenthetical in the text.

60. Ibid., 216–17; Gennette, *Narrative Discourse Revisited*, 40.

61. Moyers, "Now," par. 14.

62. Witt, "Detecting Bodies," 167.

63. Mosley, *Cinnamon Kiss*, 306.

64. King, " 'You Think Like You White,' " 211.

65. A number of studies and newspaper and television stories have documented this migratory trend. See Arax, "In a Reverse Migration"; "African Americans Returning South"; and U.S. Bureau of the Census, "South Attracts More People."

66. Collette, "Damn, She Done It," par. 2. Further citations will be parenthetical in the text.

67. Cary, "Grandma Just Liked," par. 40. The didactic quality of Neely's novels also goes some way toward explaining critical and scholarly disregard of the Blanche White series. Reviewer Kathy Phillips wonders: "Is the mystery a useful forum for social attack? Presumably the mystery reader is looking for lighter, if not lightweight, fare, and the Blanche novels no longer provide anything of the sort, if the first novel arguably did. . . . While she may be succeeding as a novelist, it is less likely that she is succeeding as a mystery novelist. One can only wonder if this is what she intended" ("Mystery Woman," 43).

68. Diane E. Lewis, "Whodunit," par. 15.

69. This desire, as writ large in the Blanche series, also helps explain the books' popular appeal, along with their relative lack of academic appeal.

70. Neely, *Blanche Passes Go,* 318; further citations will be parenthetical in the text as *BPG*.

71. See Joy James, *Transcending the Talented Tenth,* and Gaines, *Uplifting the Race,* for first-rate history and analysis of the term and concept the "Talented Tenth."

72. Neely, *Blanche on the Lam,* 89.

73. Lubiano, "Standing in for the State," 159.

74. Baker, "Caliban's Triple Play," 387.

75. For example, Easy Rawlins stops short of thoroughgoing feminism—but so, too, I would argue, does Blanche. Blanche claims to value and to seek connection with African American women above all others. But at no point in the series as a whole does she form any lasting positive connection with any woman other than her longtime best girlfriend. Neely has referred to Blanche as a "behavioral [rather than an academic] feminist" (Collette, "Damn, She Done It," par. 9), and Blanche undeniably discounts the academic feminism of Mattie; but Mattie's written works have had a profound and empowering effect on Tina, the only other potential heroine of the novel. More important, Mattie offers a compelling alternative to bourgeois, male-centered models of racial uplift (such as Du Bois's) by advancing an academic theory of political and social change accomplished via women's "power and ascendancy" and predicated on unrestricted female sexuality (*BATT* 119, 188–90). By valuing academic as well as "behavioral" feminism, by remembering the progressivism as well as the elitism in modern African American cultural and philosophical paradigms, Blanche may well have found herself getting closer, faster to the solution of the mystery of who killed Faith.

Conclusion

1. I thank an anonymous reader for University of Minnesota Press for bringing this book to my attention.

2. Barthold, *Black Time,* 197; further citations will be parenthetical in the text.

3. Warren, "Appeals for (Mis)Recognition," 393; further citations will be parenthetical in the text.

4. Du Bois, "Talented Tenth"; Hughes, *Big Sea,* 228.

5. Bakhtin, *Dialogic Imagination,* 84.

6. Hopkins, *Winona,* 371.

7. Benedict Anderson, *Imagined Communities,* 61.

8. I have argued just that regarding *Jazz,* suggesting that Morrison's 1992 novel cautions against overly optimistic imaginings both of the Harlem Renaissance and of the period in which the book was published; see English, "Selecting the Harlem Renaissance," 818–21. Similarly, in a brilliant essay on *Beloved,* James Berger argues for that 1987 novel's critical engagement with its 1873 setting and with post-

World War II and Reagan-era social-racial policies; see James Berger, "Ghosts of Liberalism."

9. Parks, *365 Days,* 401; further citations will be parenthetical in the text.

10. Parks, "From Elements of Style," 8–9.

11. Olney, introduction to *Behind the Scenes,* xxxiii.

12. Keckley, *Behind the Scenes,* 17–18; further citations will be parenthetical in the text.

13. Mosley, *Little Scarlet,* 48.

14. Parks, "From Elements of Style," 10.

Bibliography

"African Americans Returning South." *NBC Nightly News*, May 24, 2004.

Alabama Planter. "On the Management of Slaves." *De Bow's Review: Agricultural, Commercial, and Industrial Progress and Resources* 13 (August 1852): 192–96.

Alger, Horatio. *Ragged Dick, or Street Life in New York.* 1890. In *Ragged Dick and Struggling Upward,* edited by Carl Bode, 1–132. New York: Penguin Books, 1985.

———. *Struggling Upward, or Luke Larkin's Luck.* 1890. In *Ragged Dick and Struggling Upward,* edited by Carl Bode, 133–280. New York: Penguin Books, 1985.

Ali, Bilal Sunni. "Western Sunrise." Recording. *Midnight Band: The First Minute of a New Day.* 1975. Reissue, New York: Rumai-Gia Records, 1998.

Anderson, Benedict. *Imagined Communities: Reflections on the Origins and Spread of Nationalism.* London: Verso, 1991.

Anderson, Sam, Chris Bonanos, John Homans, Jared Hohlt, Boris Kachka, Hugo Lindgren, and Ben Williams. "What to Read." *New York Magazine,* May 7, 2007, http://nymag.com/arts/books/features/31522/index1.html.

Andrews, William L. *To Tell a Free Story: The First Century of Afro-American Autobiography, 1760–1865.* Urbana: University of Illinois Press, 1988.

Andrews, William L., and Mitch Kachun. "Editors' Introduction: The Emergence of Julia C. Collins." In Julia C. Collins, *The Curse of Caste; or The Slave Bride, a Rediscovered African American Novel,* edited by William L. Andrews and Mitch Kachum, xi–liii. New York: Oxford University Press, 2006.

Arax, Max. "In a Reverse Migration, Blacks Head to New South." *Los Angeles Times,* May 24, 2004, A1.

Armstrong, Nancy. *How Novels Think: The Limits of Individualism from 1719–1900.* New York: Columbia University Press, 2005.

Aubert, Alvin. "Ernest J. Gaines's Truly Tragic Mulatto." *Callaloo* 3 (May 1978): 68–75.

Babb, Valerie. "'The Joyous Circle': The Vernacular Presence in Frederick Douglass's Narratives." *College English* 67 (March 2005): 365–77.

Babener, Liahna K. "Raymond Chandler's City of Lies." In *Los Angeles in Fiction: A Collection of Essays,* edited by David Fine, 127–49. Albuquerque: University of New Mexico Press, 1995.

Bailey, Frankie Y. *Out of the Woodpile: Black Characters in Crime and Detective Fiction.* Westport, Conn.: Greenwood Press, 1991.

Baker, Houston. "Caliban's Triple Play." In *"Race," Writing, and Difference,* edited by Henry Louis Gates Jr., 381–95. Chicago: University of Chicago Press, 1986.

Bakhtin, M. M. *The Dialogic Imagination: Four Essays by M. M. Bakhtin.* Edited by Michael Holquist. Translated by Caryl Emerson and Michael Holquist. Austin: University of Texas Press, 1981.

Baraka, Amiri (LeRoi Jones). "Afrikan Revolution." 1973. In *The LeRoi Jones/Amiri Baraka Reader,* edited by William J. Harris, 243–47. New York: Thunder's Mouth Press, 1999.

———. "Apple Cores #4." 1966. In *Black Music,* 152–56. 1967. New York: Akashic Books, 2010.

———. *Black Music.* 1967. New York: Akashic Books, 2010.

———. "The Changing Same." 1966. In *Black Music,* 205–41. 1967. New York: Akashic Books, 2010.

———. "Four for Trane." 1965. In *Black Music,* 179–84. 1967. New York: Akashic Books, 2010.

———. *It's Nation Time.* Chicago: Third World Press, 1970.

———. "The Jazz Avant-Garde." 1961. In *Black Music,* 81–93. 1967. New York: Akashic Books, 2010.

———. "New Black Music: A Concert in Benefit of the Black Arts/Repertory Theatre/School Live." 1965. In *Black Music,* 196–201. 1967. New York: Akashic Books, 2010.

———. "Peter Brötzmann, *Nipples,* and Joe McPhee, *Nation Time.*" In *Digging: The Afro-American Soul of American Classical Music,* 399–400. Berkeley: University of California Press, 2009.

———. "Three Ways to Play the Saxophone." 1963. In *Black Music,* 43–50. 1967. New York: Akashic Books, 2010.

Barthold, Bonnie J. *Black Time: Fiction of Africa, the Caribbean, and the United States.* New Haven: Yale University Press, 1981.

Bartky, Ian R. *One Time Fits All: The Campaigns for Global Uniformity.* Stanford: Stanford University Press, 2007.

———. *Selling the True Time: Nineteenth-Century Timekeeping in America.* Stanford: Stanford University Press, 2000.

Beam, Dorri Rabung. "The Flower of Black Female Sexuality in Pauline Hopkins's *Winona.*" In *Recovering the Black Female Body: Self-Representations by African American Women,* edited by Michael Bennett and Vanessa Dickerson, 71–96. New Brunswick, N.J.: Rutgers University Press, 2001.

Berger, James. "Ghosts of Liberalism: Morrison's *Beloved* and the Moynihan Report." *PMLA* 111 (May 1996): 408–20.

Berger, Roger A. "'The Black Dick': Race, Sexuality, and Discourse in the L.A. Novels of Walter Mosley." *African American Review* 31 (Summer 1997): 281–95.

Bergman, Jill. "'Everything We Hoped She'd Be': Contending Forces in Hopkins Scholarship." *African American Review* 38 (Summer 2004): 181–99.

Bergson, Henri. *Time and Free Will: An Essay on the Immediate Data of Consciousness.* 1913. Translated by F. L. Pogson. Mineola, N.Y.: Dover, 2001.

The Black Panther Intercommunal News Service, 1967–1980. Original title: Black Community News Service (changed in early 1971).

"BLATANT NAZIISM AND COVERT COMMUNISM." Headline. *Chicago Daily Tribune*, March 3, 1939, 14.

"Blaxploitation." *Black Panther Intercommunal News Service,* October 7, 1972. In *The Black Panther Intercommunal News Service, 1967–1980,* edited by David Hilliard, 85–86. New York: Atria Books, 2007.

Brady, Owen E., and Derek C. Maus. *Finding a Way Home: A Critical Assessment of Walter Mosley's Fiction.* Jackson: University Press of Mississippi, 2008.

"Breakfast for School Children." January 4, 1969. In *The Black Panther Intercommunal News Service, 1967–1980,* edited by David Hilliard, 7. New York: Atria Books, 2007.

Brown, Elaine, and the Black Panther Party. *Seize the Time.* Album, 1969. CD, Warner Brothers, 2006.

———. "The Significance of the Newspaper of the Black Panther Party." In *The Black Panther Intercommunal News Service, 1967–1980,* edited by David Hilliard, ix. New York: Atria Books, 2007.

Brown, Stephanie, and Keith Clark. "Melodramas of Beset Black Manhood? Meditations on African-American Masculinity as Scholarly Topos and Social Menace: An Introduction." *Callaloo* 26 (Summer 2003): 732–37.

Brown v. Board of Education. 347 U.S. 483 (1954).

Broyard, Anatole. "Poet and the Anthropologist." Book review. *New York Times,* May 12, 1971, 37.

Bruce, Dickson D., Jr. *The Origins of African American Literature, 1680–1865.* Charlottesville: University Press of Virginia, 2001.

The Butchers' Benevolent Association of New Orleans v. the Crescent City Live-Stock Landing and Slaughter-House Company. 83 U.S. 36 (1872).

Byerman, Keith E. *Fingering the Jagged Grain: Tradition and Form in Recent Black Fiction.* Athens: University of Georgia Press. 1985.

Carby, Hazel V. Introduction to *The Magazine Novels of Pauline Hopkins, xxix–l.* New York: Oxford University Press, 1988.

———. *Reconstructing Womanhood: The Emergence of the Afro-American Woman Novelist.* New York: Oxford University Press, 1987.

Carmichael, Stokely, and Charles V. Hamilton. *Black Power: The Politics of Liberation in America*. New York: Vintage Books, 1967.

Cary, Alice. "Grandma Just Liked to Boogie." *Boston Globe*, May 9, 2004, http://nl.newsbank.com.

Chesnutt, Charles. "The Future American: What Race is Likely to Become in the Process of Time." 1900. In *Charles Chesnutt: Essays and Speeches*, edited by Joseph R. McElrath Jr., Robert C. Leitz III, and Jesse S. Crisler, 121–25. Stanford: Stanford University Press, 1999.

———. *The House behind the Cedars*. 1900. New York: Penguin, 1993.

———. "Literature in Its Relation to Life." 1899. In *Charles Chesnutt: Essays and Speeches*, edited by Joseph R. McElrath Jr., Robert C. Leitz III, and Jesse S. Crisler, 109–16. Stanford: Stanford University Press, 1999.

———. *The Marrow of Tradition*. 1901. Edited by Nancy Bentley and Sandra Gunning. Boston: Bedford/St. Martin's, 2002.

———. "Remarks of Charles Wadell Chesnutt, of Cleveland, in Accepting the Spingarn Medal at Los Angeles." 1928. In *Charles Chesnutt: Essays and Speeches*, edited by Joseph R. McElrath Jr., Robert C. Leitz III, and Jesse S. Crisler, 510–15. Stanford: Stanford University Press, 1999.

Cleaver, Eldridge. *Soul on Ice*. New York: McGraw-Hill, 1968.

Clinton/Gore Presidential Campaign. *The Man from Hope*, directed by Jeffrey Tuchman. 1992.

Cohen, Lizabeth. *Making a New Deal: Industrial Workers in Chicago, 1919–1939*. 1990. Cambridge: Cambridge University Press, 2008.

Cohn, Dorritt. "Optics and Power in the Novel." *New Literary History* 26 (Winter 1995): 3–20.

Collette, Ann. "Damn, She Done It: Barbara Neely's Fictional Detective Fights More than Crime." *Ms. Magazine Online*, June/July 2000, http://www.msmagazine.com/jun2k/books.html.

Crane, Gregg D. *Race, Citizenship, and Law in American Literature*. Cambridge: Cambridge University Press, 2002.

Crooks, Robert. "From the Far Side of the Urban Frontier: The Detective Fiction of Chester Himes and Walter Mosley." *College Literature* 22 (October 1995): 68–81.

De Bow's Review: Agricultural, Commercial, and Industrial Progress and Resources. 1846–70.

DeLegall, Walter. "Psalm for Sonny Rollins." In Walter DeLegall, Alfred Fraser, Oswald Govan, Lance Jeffers, Percy Johnston, Nathan Richards, LeRoy Stone, and Joseph White, *Burning Spear: An Anthology of Afro-Saxon Poetry*, 8–9. Washington, D.C.: Jupiter Hammon Press, 1963.

DeLegall, Walter, Alfred Fraser, Oswald Govan, Lance Jeffers, Percy Johnston, Nathan Richards, LeRoy Stone, and Joseph White. *Burning Spear: An Anthology of Afro-Saxon Poetry*. Washington, D.C.: Jupiter Hammon Press, 1963.

Deleuze, Gilles. *Cinema 2: The Time-Image*. 1985. Translated by Hugh Tomlinson and Robert Galeta. Minneapolis: University of Minnesota Press, 2007.

———. *Difference and Repetition*. 1968. Translated by Paul Patton. New York: Columbia University Press, 1994.

———. "Lecture Course on Chapter Three of Bergson's *Creative Evolution*." 1960. Translated by Bryn Loban. *SubStance* 36.3 (2007): 72–90.

DeLombard, Jeannine. "'Eye-Witness to the Cruelty': Southern Violence and Northern Testimony in Frederick Douglass's 1845 Narrative." *American Literature* 73 (June 2001): 245–75.

Derrida, Jacques. *The Gift of Death*. 1992. Translated by David Wills. Chicago: University of Chicago Press, 1995.

Dimock, Wai Chee. *Residues of Justice: Literature, Law, Philosophy*. Berkeley: University of California Press, 1996.

———. *Through Other Continents: American Literature across Deep Time*. Princeton, N.J.: Princeton University Press, 2006.

Dohrn-van Rossum, Gerhard. *History of the Hour: Clocks and Modern Temporal Orders*. 1992. Translated by Thomas Dunlap. Chicago: University of Chicago Press, 1996.

Douglass, Frederick. *The Heroic Slave*. 1853. In *The Oxford Frederick Douglass Reader*, edited by William A. Andrews, 133–63. New York: Oxford University Press, 1996.

———. *Life and Times of Frederick Douglass*. 1881. In *Frederick Douglass: Autobiographies*, 453–1045. New York: Library of America, 1996.

———. *My Bondage and My Freedom*. 1855. In *Frederick Douglass: Autobiographies*, 103–452. New York: Library of America, 1996.

———. *Narrative of the Life of Frederick Douglass, an American Slave, Written by Himself*. 1845. New York: Signet, 1968.

———. "Santo Domingo." Box 28, folder 1 of 5. Frederick Douglass Papers, Manuscript Division, Library of Congress, Washington, D.C.

———. "What to the Slave Is the Fourth of July?" In *The Oxford Frederick Douglass Reader*, edited by William A. Andrews, 108–30. New York: Oxford University Press, 1996.

Dred Scott v. John F. A. Sandford. 60 U.S. 393 (1857).

Dubey, Madhu. *Signs and Cities: Black Literary Postmodernism*. Chicago: University of Chicago Press, 2003.

Du Bois, W. E. B. *The Souls of Black Folk*. Edited by Henry Louis Gates Jr. and Terri Hume Oliver. 1903. New York: Norton, 1999.

———. "The Talented Tenth." 1897. In *Writings by W. E. B. Du Bois in Non-Periodical Literature Edited by Others*, compiled and edited by Herbert Aptheker, 17–29. New York: Kraus-Thomson, 1982.

———. "A Winter Pilgrimage." *Crisis* 1 (June 1911): 15.

Dunbar, Paul Laurence. *The Sport of the Gods*. 1902. New York: Signet, 1999.

Edwards, Brent Hayes. *The Practice of Diaspora: Literature, Translation, and the Rise of Black Internationalism.* Cambridge, Mass.: Harvard University Press, 2003.

"Eight Negro Rapists Given Death Penalty." Headline. *Chicago Daily Tribune,* April 10, 1931, 19.

Ellis, Trey. *Platitudes.* New York: Vintage, 1988.

Ellison, Ralph. *Invisible Man.* 1952. New York: Random House, 1981.

English, Daylanne K. "Selecting the Harlem Renaissance." *Critical Inquiry* 25 (Summer 1999): 807–21.

———. *Unnatural Selections: Eugenics in American Modernism and the Harlem Renaissance.* Chapel Hill: University of North Carolina Press, 2004.

Equiano, Olaudah. *The Interesting Narrative of the Life of Olaudah Equiano or Gustavus Vassa, the African, Written by Himself.* 1794. In *The Interesting Narrative and Other Writings,* edited by Vincent Carretta, 1–236. New York: Penguin, 1995.

Fabian, Johannes. *Time and the Other: How Anthropology Makes Its Object.* 1983. New York: Columbia University Press, 2002.

Felgar, Robert. "The Cultural Work of Time in Native Son." *Notes on Mississippi Writers* 24 (1992): 99–103.

Fields, Barbara J. "Ideology and Race in American History." In *Region, Race, and Reconstruction: Essays in Honor of C. Vann Woodward,* edited by J. Morgan Kousser and James M. McPherson, 143–77. New York: Oxford University Press, 1982.

Fischer-Hornung, Dorothea, and Monika Mueller, eds. *Sleuthing Ethnicity: The Detective in Multiethnic Crime Fiction.* Cranbury, N.J.: Farleigh Dickinson University Press, 2004.

Fisher, Rudolph. *The Conjure Man Dies: A Mystery Tale of Dark Harlem.* 1933. Ann Arbor: University of Michigan Press, 1992.

Fong Yue Ting v. United States. 149 U.S. 698 (1893).

Foreman, P. Gabrielle, and Reginald H. Pitts. Introduction to *Our Nig, Or Sketches from the Life of a Free Black,* by Harriet E. Wilson, xxiii–l. New York: Penguin, 2005.

Foster, Frances Smith. Introduction to Frances E. W. Harper, *Minnie's Sacrifice, Sowing and Reaping, Trial and Triumph: Three Rediscovered Novels,* edited by Frances Smith Foster, xi–xxxvii. Boston: Beacon Press, 1994.

Frisby, Michael. "Clinton Vows to Go Beyond 'Trickle-Down.'" *Boston Globe,* September 18, 1992, 27. Boston Globe Archives, http://nl.newsbank.com.

———. "Soul-Baring on the Campaign Trail." *Boston Globe,* August 6, 1992. Boston Globe Archives, http://nl.newsbank.com.

Gaines, Ernest J. *A Lesson before Dying.* New York: Vintage, 1994.

———. "Miss Jane and I." 1978. *Callaloo* 24 (Spring 2001): 608–19.

Gaines, Kevin. *Uplifting the Race: Black Leadership, Politics, and Culture in the Twentieth Century.* Chapel Hill: University of North Carolina Press, 1996.

Garner, Bryan A., ed. *Black's Law Dictionary,* 3rd ed. St. Paul, MN: Thomson/West, 2006.

Gates, Henry Louis, Jr, *Figures in Black: Words, Signs, and the "Racial" Self.* New York: Oxford University Press, 1987.

———. *The Signifying Monkey: A Theory of African-American Literary Criticism.* New York: Oxford University Press, 1988.

Gates, Henry Louis, Jr., and Nellie Y. McKay. Preface to *The Norton Anthology of African American Literature,* edited by Henry Louis Gates Jr., Nellie Y. McKay, William A. Andrews, Houston A. Baker Jr., Barbara T. Christian, Frances Smith Foster, Deborah E. McDowell, Robert G. O'Meally, Arnold Rampersad, Hortense Spillers, and Cheryl A. Wall, xxix–xxiii. New York: Norton, 2003.

Gaudet, Marcia. "Miss Jane and Personal Experience Narrative: Ernest Gaines' *The Autobiography of Miss Jane Pittman.*" *Western Folklore* 51 (January 1992): 23–32.

Gayle, Addison, Jr. "From *The Black Aesthetic.*" In *The Norton Anthology of African American Literature,* edited by Henry Louis Gates Jr., Nellie Y. McKay, William A. Andrews, Houston A. Baker Jr., Barbara T. Christian, Frances Smith Foster, Deborah E. McDowell, Robert G. O'Meally, Arnold Rampersad, Hortense Spillers, and Cheryl A. Wall, 1912–918. New York: Norton, 2003.

Genette, Gérard. *Narrative Discourse: An Essay in Method.* Translated by Jane E. Lewin. Ithaca, N.Y.: Cornell University Press, 1980.

———. *Narrative Discourse Revisited.* 1983. Translated by Jane E. Lewin. Ithaca, N.Y.: Cornell University Press, 1988.

Gerhardt, Michael J. "The Role of Precedent in Constitutional Decisionmaking and Theory." *George Washington Law Review* 60 (1991): 68–147.

Gibbs, Jewelle Taylor Gibbs, ed. *Young, Black, and Male in America: An Endangered Species.* Westport, Conn.: Auburn House, 1988.

Giddins, Gary. *Riding on a Blue Note: Jazz and American Pop.* New York: Oxford University Press, 1981.

Gikandi, Simon. *Slavery and the Culture of Taste.* Princeton, N.J.: Princeton University Press, 2011.

Gilroy, Paul. *The Black Atlantic: Modernity and Double Consciousness.* Cambridge, Mass.: Harvard University Press, 1993.

Glaude, Eddie S., Jr. Introduction to *Is It Nation Time? Contemporary Essays on Black Power and Black Nationalism,* edited by Eddie S. Glaude Jr., 1–21. Chicago: University of Chicago Press, 2002.

Goldstein, David S., and Audrey Thacker, eds. *Complicating Constructions: Race, Ethnicity, and Hybridity in American Texts.* Seattle: University of Washington Press, 2007.

Gosselin, Adrienne Johnson, ed. *Multicultural Detective Fiction: Murder from the "Other" Side*. New York: Garland Publishing, 1999.

Govan, Oswald. "The Lynching." In Walter DeLegall, Alfred Fraser, Oswald Govan, Lance Jeffers, Percy Johnston, Nathan Richards, LeRoy Stone, and Joseph White, *Burning Spear: An Anthology of Afro-Saxon Poetry*, 17–18. Washington, D.C.: Jupiter Hammon Press, 1963.

"Governor Jeff Davis." Editorial. *Macon Telegraph*, May 16, 1902, 4.

"Gov. Jefferson Davis, the Arkansas Gentleman, Answered for Sending an Ex-Convict to Massachusetts for Reformation." Editorial. *The Topeka Plaindealer*, May 16, 1902, 1.

Griffin, Farah Jasmine. "Conflict and Chorus: Reconsidering Toni Cade's *The Black Woman: An Anthology*." In *Is It Nation Time? Contemporary Essays on Black Power and Black Nationalism*, edited by Eddie S. Glaude Jr., 113–29. Chicago: University of Chicago Press, 2002.

——. *"Who Set You Flowin'?" The African-American Migration Narrative*. New York: Oxford University Press, 1995.

Griggs, Sutton E. *The Hindered Hand, or, the Reign of the Impressionist*. 1905. New York: AMS Press, 1969.

——. *Imperium in Imperio*. 1899. New York: Modern Library, 2003.

Grimké, Angelina Weld. *Rachel*. 1916. In *Strange Fruit: Plays on Lynching by American Women*, edited by Kathy A. Perkins and Judith L. Stephens, 27–91. Bloomington: Indiana University Press, 1998.

Gronniosaw, James Albert Ukawsaw. *A narrative of the most remarkable particulars in the life of James Albert Ukawsaw Gronniosaw, an African prince, written by himself*. 1770. Electronic ed. http://docsouth.unc.edu/neh/gronniosaw /gronnios.html.

Grosz, Elizabeth. "Thinking the New: Of Futures Yet Unthought." *Symploke* 6.1 (1998): 38–55.

——. *Time Travels: Feminism, Nature, Power*. Durham, N.C.: Duke University Press, 2005.

Gyory, Andrew. *Closing the Gate: Race, Politics, and the Chinese Exclusion Act*. Chapel Hill: University of North Carolina Press, 1998.

Halloran, Vivian Nun. "Performative Mourning: Remembering Derrida Through (Re)reading." *Postmodern Culture* 15 (May 2005). http://pmc.iath.virginia.edu /text-only/issue.505/15.3halloran.txt.

Harper, Frances. *Iola Leroy, or, Shadows Uplifted*. 1892. Boston: Beacon Press, 1987.

Harper, Phillip Brian. "Nationalism and Social Division in Black Arts Poetry of the 1960s." In *Is It Nation Time? Contemporary Essays on Black Power and Black Nationalism*, edited by Eddie S. Glaude Jr., 165–88. Chicago: University of Chicago Press, 2002.

Harris, Marla. "Not Black and/or White: Reading Racial Difference in Heliodorus's *Ethiopica* and Pauline Hopkins's *Of One Blood.*" *African American Review* 35 (Fall 2001): 75–90.

Hartman, Saidiya V. *Scenes of Subjection: Terror, Slavery, and Self-Making in Nineteenth-Century America.* New York: Oxford University Press, 1997.

Hegel, Georg Wilhelm Friedrich. *The Philosophy of History.* 1899. Translated by John Sibree. New York: Cosimo, 2007.

Heidegger, Martin. *History of the Concept of Time: Prolegomena.* 1979. Translated by Theodore Kisiel. Bloomington: Indiana University Press, 1992.

Heise, Ursula K. *Chronoschisms: Time, Narrative, and Postmodernism.* Cambridge: Cambridge University Press, 1997.

Hill, Patricia Liggins, Bernard W. Bell, Trudier Harris, William J. Harris, R. Baxter Miller, and Sondra A. O'Neale. Preface to *Call and Response: The Riverside Anthology of the African American Literary Tradition,* edited by Patricia Liggins Hill, Bernard W. Bell, Trudier Harris, William J. Harris, R. Baxter Miller, and Sondra A. O'Neale, xxxiii–xxxviii. New York: Houghton Mifflin, 1998.

Hilliard, David, dir. *The Black Panther.* DVD. Oakland, Calif.: Dr. Huey P. Newton Foundation, 2007.

Himes, Chester. "His Last Day." 1933. In *Spooks, Spies, and Private Eyes: Black Mystery, Crime, and Suspense Fiction of the 20th Century,* edited by Paula L. Woods, 48–63. New York: Doubleday, 1995.

———. *My Life of Absurdity: The Later Years.* 1976. New York: Paragon House, 1990.

Holmes, Oliver Wendell, Jr. *The Common Law.* 1881. Mineola, N.Y.: Dover, 1991.

———. *The Common Law.* 1881. In *The Essential Holmes: Selections from Letters, Speeches, Judicial Opinions, and Other Writings of Oliver Wendell Holmes, Jr.,* edited by Richard A. Posner, 237–53. Chicago: University of Chicago Press, 1992.

———. "Lecture III. Torts—Trespass and Negligence," in *The Common Law,* 77–129. Mineola, N.Y.: Dover, 1991.

———. "The Path of the Law." 1897. In *The Essential Holmes: Selections from Letters, Speeches, Judicial Opinions, and Other Writings of Oliver Wendell Holmes, Jr.,* edited by Richard A. Posner, 160–77. Chicago: University of Chicago Press, 1992.

———. "Privilege, Malice, and Intent." *Harvard Law Review* 8 (April 25, 1894): 1–14.

Honan, William H. "Books, Books, and More Books: Clinton an Omnivorous Reader." *New York Times,* December 10, 1992, C15.

hooks, bell. *We Real Cool: Black Men and Masculinity.* New York: Routledge, 2004.

Hopkins, Pauline. *Contending Forces.* 1900. New York: Oxford University Press, 1988.

———. *Hagar's Daughter.* 1900–1901. In *The Magazine Novels of Pauline Hopkins,* 1–284. New York: Oxford University Press, 1988.

——. *Of One Blood*. 1902–3. In *The Magazine Novels of Pauline Hopkins*, 439–621. New York: Oxford University Press, 1988.

——. "Talma Gordon." 1900. In *Spooks, Spies, and Private Eyes: Black Mystery Crime, and Suspense Fiction of the 20th Century*, edited by Paula L. Woods, 4–18. New York: Doubleday, 1995.

——. *Winona*. 1902. In *The Magazine Novels of Pauline Hopkins*, 285–437. New York: Oxford University Press, 1988.

Houser, Nathan, and Christian Kloesel. Foreword to *The Essential Peirce: Selected Philosophical Writings, vol. 1: 1867–1893*, edited by Nathan Houser and Christian Kloesel, xi–xvii. Bloomington: Indiana University Press, 1992.

Hughes, Langston. *The Big Sea*. 1940. New York: Hill and Wang, 1993.

——. "The Negro Artist and the Racial Mountain." 1926. In *The Norton Anthology of African American Literature*, edited by Henry Louis Gates Jr., Nellie Y. McKay, William A. Andrews, Houston A. Baker Jr., Barbara T. Christian, Frances Smith Foster, Deborah E. McDowell, Robert G. O'Meally, Arnold Rampersad, Hortense Spillers, and Cheryl A. Wall, 1311–314. New York: Norton, 2003.

——. "Song for a Dark Girl." In *The Collected Poems of Langston Hughes*, edited by Arnold Rampersad and David Roessel, 104. New York: Vintage Books, 1994.

Hurston, Zora Neale. "How It Feels to Be Colored Me." 1928. In *The Norton Anthology of African American Literature*, edited by Henry Louis Gates Jr., Nellie Y. McKay, William A. Andrews, Houston A. Baker Jr., Barbara T. Christian, Frances Smith Foster, Deborah E. McDowell, Robert G. O'Meally, Arnold Rampersad, Hortense Spillers, and Cheryl A. Wall, 1030–33. New York: Norton, 2003.

Ignatiev, Noel. *How the Irish Became White*. New York: Routledge, 1995.

Innes, Catherine Lynette. *The Devil's Own Mirror: The Irishman and the African in Modern Literature*. Washington, D.C.: Three Continents Press, 1990.

"It's About Time." Website of Black Panther Party Legacy and Alumni. http://www.itsabouttimebpp.com/home/home.html.

Jacobs, Harriet. *Incidents in the Life of a Slave Girl*. 1861. Edited by Jean Fagan Yellin. Cambridge, Mass.: Harvard University Press, 2000.

James, C. L. R. *The Black Jacobins: Toussaint L'Ouverture and the San Domingo Revolution*. 1963. New York: Random House, 1989.

James, William. "What Pragmatism Means." In *The Writings of William James: A Comprehensive Edition*, edited by John J. McDermott, 376–90. Chicago: University of Chicago Press, 1977.

——. "The Will to Believe." 1896. In *The Writings of William James: A Comprehensive Edition*, edited by John J. McDermott, 717–35. Chicago: University of Chicago Press, 1977.

Jefferson, Thomas. *Notes on the State of Virginia*. 1791. In *Thomas Jefferson: Writings*, 123–325. New York: Library of America, 1984.

Johnson, Barbara. "The Re(a)d and the Black." In *Modern Critical Interpretations: Richard Wright's* Native Son, edited by Harold Bloom, 115–23. New York: Chelsea House Publishers, 1988.

Johnson, James Weldon. *The Autobiography of an Ex-Colored Man.* 1912. New York: Penguin, 1990.

———. "Preface to the First Edition." 1921. In *The Book of American Negro Poetry,* edited by James Weldon Johnson, 9–48. San Diego: Harcourt Brace, 1969.

———. "Preface to the Revised Edition." 1931. In *The Book of American Negro Poetry,* edited by James Weldon Johnson, 3–8. San Diego: Harcourt Brace, 1969.

Joyce, Joyce Anne. "The Figurative Web of *Native Son.*" In *Richard Wright: Critical Perspectives Past and Present,* edited by Henry Louis Gates Jr. and K. A. Appiah, 171–87. New York: Amistad Press, 1993.

Kaczorowski, Robert J. "Revolutionary Constitutionalism in the Era of the Civil War and Reconstruction." *New York University Law Review* (November 1986): 863–940.

Karenga, Maulana. "Black Art: Mute Matter Given Force and Function." 1968. In *The Norton Anthology of African American Literature,* edited by Henry Louis Gates Jr., Nellie Y. McKay, William A. Andrews, Houston A. Baker Jr., Barbara T. Christian, Frances Smith Foster, Deborah E. McDowell, Robert G. O'Meally, Arnold Rampersad, Hortense Spillers, and Cheryl A. Wall, 2086–90. New York: Norton, 2003.

Keckley, Elizabeth. *Behind the Scenes, Or, Thirty Years a Slave, and Four Years in the White House.* 1868. New York: Oxford University Press, 1988.

Kelley, Robin D. G. "Stormy Weather: Reconstructing Black (Inter)Nationalism in the Cold War Era." In *Is It Nation Time? Contemporary Essays on Black Power and Black Nationalism,* edited by Eddie S. Glaude Jr., 67–90. Chicago: University of Chicago Press, 2002.

Kennedy, Liam. "Black Noir: Race and Urban Space in Walter Mosley's Detective Fiction." In *Diversity and Detective Fiction,* edited by Kathleen Gregory Klein, 224–39. Bowling Green, Ky.: Bowling Green State University Popular Press, 1999.

Kern, Stephen. *The Culture of Time and Space, 1880–1918.* Cambridge, Mass.: Harvard University Press, 2003.

Ketner, Kenneth Laine. *Peirce and Contemporary Thought: Philosophical Inquiries.* New York: Fordham University Press, 1995.

King, Nicole. "'You Think Like You White': Questioning Race and Racial Community through the Lens of Middle-Class Desire(s)." *Novel: A Forum on Fiction* 35 (Spring–Summer 2002): 211–31.

Klein, Kathleen Gregory. *Diversity and Detective Fiction.* Bowling Green, Ky.: Bowling Green State University Popular Press, 1999.

Kunjufu, Jawanza. *State of Emergency: We Must Save African American Males.* 2001. Chicago: African American Images, 2009.

Lampe, Gregory P. *Frederick Douglass: Freedom's Voice, 1818–1845.* East Lansing: Michigan State University Press, 1998.

"Lawyer Expose Spurs Red Quiz into New Deal." Headline. *Chicago Daily Tribune,* February 25, 1939, 12.

Lee, Erika. *At America's Gates: Chinese Immigration During the Exclusion Era.* Chapel Hill: University of North Carolina Press, 2003.

Lee, Felicia R. "Black Men: Are They Imperiled?" *New York Times,* June 26, 1990, B3.

Le Poidevin, Robin, and Murray MacBeath. Introduction to *The Philosophy of Time,* edited by Robin Le Poidevin and Murray MacBeath, 1–20. Oxford: Oxford University Press, 1993.

Levine, Robert S. *Dislocating Race and Nation: Episodes in Nineteenth-Century American Literary Nationalism.* Chapel Hill: University of North Carolina Press, 2008.

Lewis, Diane E. "Whodunit? Not the Maid." *Boston Globe,* March 26, 1995, 24. Lexis-Nexis. Macalester College Library, http://0-web.lexis-nexis.com.

Lewis, Leslie W. "Towards a New 'Colored' Consciousness: Biracial Identity in Pauline Hopkins's Fiction." In *Women's Experience of Modernity, 1875–1945,* edited by Ann L. Ardis and Leslie W. Lewis, 31–46. Baltimore: Johns Hopkins University Press, 2002.

Lewis, Raymond. "1969: The Year of the Panther." January 4, 1969. In *The Black Panther Intercommunal News Service, 1967–1980,* edited by David Hilliard, 11. New York: Atria Books, 2007.

Lock, Helen. *A Case of Mis-Taken Identity: Detective Undercurrents in Recent African American Fiction.* New York: Peter Lang, 1994.

———. "Invisible Detection: The Case of Walter Mosley." *MELUS* 26 (Spring 2001): 77–89.

Locke, Alain. "Enter the New Negro." *Survey Graphic* 6 (March 1925): 631–34.

———. Foreword. 1925. In *The New Negro,* edited by Alain Locke, xxv–xxvii. New York: MacMillan Publishing Company, 1992.

———. "The New Negro." 1925. In *The New Negro,* edited by Alain Locke, 3–16. New York: MacMillan, 1992.

———. "Youth Speaks." *Survey Graphic* 6 (March 1925): 659–60.

Logan, Rayford. *The Negro in American Life and Thought: The Nadir, 1877–1901.* New York: Dial Press, 1954.

Lott, Eric. *Love and Theft: Blackface Minstrelsy and the American Working Class.* New York: Oxford University Press, 1993.

Lubiano, Wahneema. "Standing in for the State: Black Nationalism and 'Writing' the Black Subject." In *Is It Nation Time? Contemporary Essays on Black Power and Black Nationalism,* edited by Eddie S. Glaude Jr., 156–64. Chicago: University of Chicago Press, 2002.

"Lucy Terry." Headnote in *The Norton Anthology of African American Literature*, edited by Henry Louis Gates Jr., Nellie Y. McKay, William A. Andrews, Houston A. Baker Jr., Barbara T. Christian, Frances Smith Foster, Deborah E. McDowell, Robert G. O'Meally, Arnold Rampersad, Hortense Spillers, and Cheryl A. Wall, 186. New York: Norton, 2003.

Macon Telegraph. 1860–1922.

Manchester, William. *Portrait of a President: John Kennedy in Profile*. Boston: Little, Brown, 1962.

Mason, Theodore O. "Walter Mosley's Easy Rawlins: The Detective and Afro-American Fiction." *Kenyon Review* 14 (Autumn 1992): 173–83.

Matthews, Stan, dir. *Black Men: An Endangered Species*. KERA-TV, Dallas, 1988.

McCallum, E. L. "The Timezone Endgame." *CR: The New Centennial Review* 1 (Spring 2001): 141–73.

McCann, Sean. *Gumshoe America: Hard-Boiled Crime Fiction and the Rise and Fall of New Deal Liberalism*. Durham, N.C.: Duke University Press, 2000.

McCoy, Beth. "Rumors of Grace: White Masculinity in Pauline Hopkins's *Contending Forces*." *African American Review* 37 (Winter 2003): 569–81.

McCrossen, Alexis. "By the Clock." *Reviews in American History* 28 (December 2000): 553–59.

McKay, Claude. "If We Must Die." 1919. In *The Black Panther Intercommunal News Service, 1967–1980*, edited by David Hilliard, 11. New York: Atria Books, 2007.

McKay, Nellie Y. Introduction to *The Unruly Voice: Rediscovering Pauline Hopkins*, edited by John Cullen Gruesser, 1–20. Urbana: University of Illinois Press, 1996.

McPhee, Joe. *Nation Time*. Recording. JoMac-BMI, 1971. Reissue, New York: CjR Record Productions, 1999.

McWhorter, Diane. "Strom's Skeleton: The Late Segregationist's Black Daughter." *Slate* (July 2003), http://slate.msn.com/id/2085087/.

Mead, Margaret, and James Baldwin. *A Rap on Race*. Philadelphia: Lippincott, 1971.

"Membership Has Its Privileges and Immunities: Congressional Power to Define and Enforce the Rights of National Citizenship." *Harvard Law Review* 102 (June 1989): 1925.

Menand, Louis. *The Metaphysical Club: A Story of Ideas in America*. New York: Farrar, Straus, and Giroux, 2001.

Meyler, Bernadette. "The Gestation of Birthright Citizenship, 1868–1898: States' Rights, the Law of Nations, and Mutual Consent." *Georgetown Immigration Law Journal* (Spring 2001): 519–62.

Miller, D. A. *The Novel and the Police*. Berkeley: University of California Press, 1988.

Mitgang, Herbert. "Anatole Broyard, 70, Book Critic And Editor at The Times, Is Dead." Obituary. *New York Times*, October 12, 1990.

Molesworth, Jesse M. "Equiano's 'Loud Voice': Witnessing the Performance of *The Interesting Narrative.*" *Texas Studies in Literature and Language* 48 (Summer 2006): 123–44.

Morrison, Toni. "Comment: Talk of the Town." *New Yorker,* October 5, 1998, 31–32.

———. *A Mercy.* New York: Knopf, 2008.

Mosley, Walter. *Bad Boy Brawly Brown.* New York: Warner Books, 2002.

———. *Black Betty.* New York: Washington Square Press, 1994.

———. *Blonde Faith.* New York: Little, Brown, 2007.

———. *Cinnamon Kiss.* New York: Little, Brown, 2005.

———. *Devil in a Blue Dress.* New York: Pocket Books, 1990.

———. *Life Out of Context, Which Includes a Proposal for the Non-violent Takeover of the House of Representatives.* New York: Nation Books, 2006.

———. *Little Scarlet.* New York: Little, Brown, 2004.

Mott, James "Ricky Vincent and James Mott, The Lumpen Pt. 2." Interview, July 1, 2009, http://www.itsabouttimebpp.com/Our_Stories/the_lumpen_index.html.

Moyers, Bill. "Now: Interview with Walter Mosley." September 9, 2003. http://www.pbs.org/now/arts/mosley.html.

Mudge, Alden. "New Crime Fiction with a Twist from Noir Master Walter Mosley." BookPage. June 2001. http://www.bookpage.com/0106bp/walter_mosley.html.

Muller, Gilbert H. "Double Agent: The Los Angeles Crime Cycle of Walter Mosley." In *Los Angeles in Fiction: A Collection of Essays,* edited by David Fine, 287–301. Albuquerque: University of New Mexico Press, 1995.

Mumford, Lewis. *Technics and Civilization.* 1934. New York: Harcourt, Brace and World, 1963.

Napier, Winston. "The Howard Poets." In *Washington and Washington Writing,* edited by David McAleavey, 57–67. Washington, D.C.: Center of Washington Area Studies, 1986.

Neal, Larry. "The Black Arts Movement." 1968. In *The Norton Anthology of African American Literature,* edited by Henry Louis Gates Jr., Nellie Y. McKay, William A. Andrews, Houston A. Baker Jr., Barbara T. Christian, Frances Smith Foster, Deborah E. McDowell, Robert G. O'Meally, Arnold Rampersad, Hortense Spillers, and Cheryl A. Wall, 2039–50. New York: Norton, 2003.

Neely, Barbara. *Blanche among the Talented Tenth.* New York: Penguin Books, 1994.

———. *Blanche on the Lam.* New York: Penguin Books, 1992.

———. *Blanche Passes Go.* New York: Penguin Books, 2000.

Nerad, Julie Cary. " 'So Strangely Interwoven': The Property of Inheritance, Race, and Sexual Morality in Pauline E. Hopkins's *Contending Forces.*" *African American Review* (Autumn 2001): 357–73.

Newton, Huey P. "Let Us Hold High the Banner of Intercommunalism and the Invincible Thoughts of Huey P. Newton, Minister of Defense and Supreme

Commander of the Black Panther Party." January 23, 1971. In *The Black Panther Intercommunal News Service, 1967–1980,* edited by David Hilliard, 54. New York: Atria Books, 2007.

———. "Quotations from Huey." February 17, 1969. In *The Black Panther Intercommunal News Service, 1967–1980,* edited by David Hilliard, 13. New York: Atria Books, 2007.

Nielsen, Aldon Lynn. *Black Chant: Languages of African-American Postmodernism.* Cambridge: Cambridge University Press, 1997.

Niswonger, Richard L. "A Study in Southern Demagoguery: Jeff Davis of Arkansas." *Arkansas Historical Quarterly* 39 (Summer 1980): 114–24.

Olivas, Michael A. "The Chronicles, My Grandfather's Stories, and Immigration Law: The Slave Traders Chronicle as Racial History." In *Critical Race Theory: The Cutting Edge,* edited by Richard Delgado and Jean Stefancic, 9–20. Philadelphia: Temple University Press, 2001.

Olney, James. Introduction to Elizabeth Keckley, *Behind the Scenes, Or, Thirty Years a Slave, and Four Years in the White House,* xxvii–xxxvi. New York: Oxford University Press, 1988.

O'Malley, Michael. *Keeping Watch: A History of American Time.* Washington, D.C.: Smithsonian Institution Press, 1990.

Parks, Suzan-Lori. *The Death of the Last Black Man in the Whole Entire World.* 1989–1992. In *The America Play and Other Works,* 99–131. New York: Theatre Communications Group, 1995.

———. "From Elements of Style." 1994. In *The America Play and Other Works,* 6–18. New York: Theatre Communications Group, 1995.

———. "Possession." 1994. In *The America Play and Other Works,* 1–5. New York: Theatre Communications Group, 1995.

———. *365 Days/365 Plays.* New York: Theatre Communications Group, 2006.

Peirce, Charles Sanders. *Collected Papers of Charles Sanders Peirce,* vols. 1 and 2: *Principles of Philosophy* and *Elements of Logic.* Edited by Charles Hartshorne, Paul Weiss, and Arthur Burks. Cambridge, Mass.: Harvard University Press, 1932.

———. "The Doctrine of Chances." 1878. In *The Essential Peirce: Selected Philosophical Writings,* vol. 1: *1867–1893,* edited by Nathan Houser and Christian Kloesel, 142–54. Bloomington: Indiana University Press, 1992.

———. "How to Make Our Ideas Clear." 1878. In *The Essential Peirce: Selected Philosophical Writings,* vol. 1: *1867–1893,* edited by Nathan Houser and Christian Kloesel, 124–41. Bloomington: Indiana University Press, 1992.

———. "Of Reasoning in General." 1895. In *The Essential Peirce: Selected Philosophical Writings,* vol. 2: *1893–1913,* edited by the Peirce Edition Project, Nathan Houser, Jonathan R. Eller, Albert C. Lewis, André De Tienne, Cathy L. Clark, and D. Bront Davis, 11–26. Bloomington: Indiana University Press, 1998.

————. "Philosophy and the Conduct of Life." 1898. In *The Essential Peirce: Selected Philosophical Writings*, vol. 2: *1893–1913*, edited by the Peirce Edition Project, Nathan Houser et al., 27–41. Bloomington: Indiana University Press, 1998.

Phillips, Kathy. "Mystery Woman." *Women's Review of Books* 17 (July 2000): 42–43.

Pitre, Merline. "Frederick Douglass and the Annexation of Santo Domingo." *Journal of Negro History* 62 (October 1977): 390–400.

Plaindealer (Topeka, Kansas). 1899–1931.

Plessy v. Ferguson. 163 U.S. 537 (1896).

Pratt, Lloyd. *Archives of American Time: Literature and Modernity in the Nineteenth Century*. Philadelphia: University of Pennsylvania Press, 2010.

————. "Progress, Labor, Revolution: The Modern Times of Antebellum African American Life Writing." *Novel: A Forum on Fiction* 35 (Fall 2000): 56–76.

"Preface." In *Phillis Wheatley, Complete Writings*, edited by Vincent Carretta, 5. New York: Penguin, 2001.

Purcell, Edward A., Jr. "On the Complexity of 'Ideas in America': Origins and Achievements of the Classical Age of Pragmatism." *Law and Social Inquiry* 27 (Autumn 2002): 967–99.

Putzi, Jennifer. "'Raising the Stigma': Black Womanhood and the Marked Body in Pauline Hopkins's *Contending Forces*." *College Literature* 31 (Spring 2004): 1–21.

"Quotations from Huey." February 17, 1969. In *The Black Panther Intercommunal News Service, 1967–1980*, edited by David Hilliard, 13. New York: Atria Books, 2007.

"Railroad Police Slay Negro Robbing Box Car." Headline. *Chicago Daily Tribune*, March 12, 1939, 14.

Rampersad, Arnold. Introduction to *Native Son*, ix–xxii. New York: HarperCollins, 2005.

Reddy, Maureen T. *Traces, Codes, and Clues: Reading Race in Crime Fiction*. New Brunswick, N.J.: Rutgers University Press, 2003.

Redmond, Eugene B. *Drumvoices: The Mission of Afro-American Poetry, a Critical History*. New York: Doubleday, 1976.

Reed, Adolph L., Jr. "Black Particularity Reconsidered." 1979. In *Is It Nation Time? Contemporary Essays on Black Power and Black Nationalism*, edited by Eddie S. Glaude Jr., 39–66. Chicago: University of Chicago Press, 2002.

Reitz, Caroline. "Do We Need Another Hero?" In *Multicultural Detective Fiction: Murder from the "Other" Side*, edited by Adrienne Johnson Gosselin, 213–33. New York: Garland, 1999.

Rhodes, Jane. *Framing the Black Panthers: The Spectacular Rise of a Black Power Icon*. New York: The New Press, 2007.

Rosenblatt, Roger. "Bigger's Infernal Assumption." In *Modern Critical Interpretations: Richard Wright's Native Son*, edited by Harold Bloom, 23–37. New York: Chelsea House, 1988.

Roth, Laurence. *Inspecting Jews: American Jewish Detective Stories*. New Brunswick, N.J.: Rutgers University Press, 2004.

"Rules of the Black Panther Party." May 4, 1969. In *The Black Panther Intercommunal News Service, 1967–1980*, edited by David Hilliard, 25. New York: Atria Books, 2007.

Russell, Bertrand. *Power: A New Social Analysis*. 1938. New York: Routledge, 1996.

———. "Pragmatism." 1909. In *Philosophical Essays*, 79–111. New York: Simon and Schuster, 1966.

Sabol, William J., and Heather Couture. "Prison Inmates at Midyear 2007." *Bureau of Justice Statistics Bulletin* (June 2008): 1–11.

Salyer, Lucy E. *Laws Harsh as Tigers: Chinese Immigrants and the Shaping of Modern Immigration Law*. Chapel Hill: University of North Carolina Press, 1995.

Sanchez, Sonia. "Summer Words of a Sistuh Addict." In *The Norton Anthology of African American Literature*, edited by Henry Louis Gates Jr., Nellie Y. McKay, William A. Andrews, Houston A. Baker Jr., Barbara T. Christian, Frances Smith Foster, Deborah E. McDowell, Robert G. O'Meally, Arnold Rampersad, Hortense Spillers, and Cheryl A. Wall, 1966. New York: Norton, 2003.

———. "Summer Words of a Sistuh Addict." Recording. *A Sun Lady for All Seasons Reads Her Poetry*. 1971. Reissue, Washington, D.C.: Smithsonian Folkways Recordings, 2004.

"Scan Cold Trail for Three Negro Rapist Slayers." Headline. *Chicago Daily Tribune*, August 2, 1937, 5.

Scott-Heron, Gil. "Winter in America." Recording. *Midnight Band: The First Minute of a New Day*. 1975. Reissue, New York: Rumai-Gia Records, 1998.

Scott-Heron, Gil, and Brian Jackson. "Pardon Our Analysis (We Beg Your Pardon)." Recording. *Midnight Band: The First Minute of a New Day*. 1975. Reissue, New York: Rumai-Gia Records, 1998.

Seale, Bobby. *Seize the Time: The Story of the Black Panther Party and Huey P. Newton*. 1970. Baltimore: Black Classic Press, 1991.

Sebeok, Thomas A., and Jean Umiker Sebeok. *"You Know My Method": A Juxtaposition of Charles S. Peirce and Sherlock Holmes*. Bloomington, Ind.: Gaslight, 1980.

"Shot Plucks a Clew from Fleeing Thief, Leads to His Arrest." Headline. *Chicago Daily Tribune*, February 17, 1939, 22.

Siddiqi, Yumna. "Police and Postcolonial Rationality in Amitav Ghosh's *The Circle of Reason*." *Cultural Critique* 50 (Winter 2002): 175–211.

Skenazy, Paul. "Behind the Territory Ahead." In *Los Angeles in Fiction: A Collection of Essays*, edited by David Fine, 103–25. Albuquerque: University of New Mexico Press, 1995.

Smethurst, James. *The Black Arts Movement: Literary Nationalism in the 1960s and 1970s*. Chapel Hill: University of North Carolina Press, 2005.

———. "Invented by Horror: The Gothic and African American Literary Ideology in *Native Son*." *African American Review* 35 (Spring 2001): 29–40.

Smith, Mark M. *Mastered by the Clock: Time, Slavery, and Freedom in the American South*. Chapel Hill: University of North Carolina Press, 1997.

Smith, Rochelle and Sharon L. Jones. Preface to *The Prentice Hall Anthology of African American Literature*, edited by Rochelle Smith and Sharon L. Jones, xvii–xx. Upper Saddle River, N.J.: Prentice Hall, 2000.

Smith, Suzanne E. *Dancing in the Street: Motown and the Cultural Politics of Detroit*. Cambridge, Mass.: Harvard University Press, 1999.

Soitos, Stephen F. *The Blues Detective: A Study of African American Detective Fiction*. Amherst: University of Massachusetts Press, 1996.

Sollors, Werner. *Ethnic Modernism*. Cambridge, Mass.: Harvard University Press, 2008.

———. *Neither Black nor White Yet Both: Thematic Explorations of Interracial Literature*. New York: Oxford University Press, 1997.

Somerville, Siobhan B. "'The Prettiest Specimen of Boyhood': Cross-Gender and Racial Disguise in Pauline E. Hopkins's *Winona*." In *Skin Deep, Spirit Strong: The Black Female Body*, edited by Kimberly Wallace-Sanders, 201–17. Ann Arbor: University of Michigan Press, 2002.

"Spirituals." Headnote in *The Norton Anthology of African American Literature*, edited by Henry Louis Gates Jr., Nellie Y. McKay, William A. Andrews, Houston A. Baker Jr., Barbara T. Christian, Frances Smith Foster, Deborah E. McDowell, Robert G. O'Meally, Arnold Rampersad, Hortense Spillers, and Cheryl A. Wall, 8–10. New York: Norton, 2003.

Stein, Gertrude. "Composition as Explanation." 1926. In *Selected Writings of Gertrude Stein*, edited by Carl Van Vechten, 453–61. New York: Random House, 1946.

———. *Mexico*. 1916. In *Geography and Plays*, 304–30. Madison: University of Wisconsin Press, 1993.

Stevenson, Pascha A. "Of One Blood, of One Race: Pauline E. Hopkins' Engagement of Racialized Science." *CLA Journal* 45 (June 2002): 422–43.

Stone, LeRoy. "Flamenco Sketches (To Miles Davis)." In Walter DeLegall, Alfred Fraser, Oswald Govan, Lance Jeffers, Percy Johnston, Nathan Richards, LeRoy Stone, and Joseph White, *Burning Spear: An Anthology of Afro-Saxon Poetry*, 53–54. Washington, D.C.: Jupiter Hammon Press, 1963.

Sundquist, Eric J. *To Wake the Nations: Race in the Making of American Literature*. Cambridge, Mass.: Belknap Press of Harvard University Press, 1993.

Swindle, Michael. "Louisiana Justice." *Los Angeles Times*, May 30, 1993, BR11.

"3 Negro Rapists Draw Death as Mob Threatens." Headline. *Chicago Daily Tribune*, February 13, 1934, 15.

Todorov, Tzvetan. *The Poetics of Prose*. Ithaca, N.Y.: Cornell University Press, 1977.

"Topics of the Times." Editorial. *New York Times*, May 19, 1902, 8.

Torok, John Hayakawa. "Reconstruction and Racial Nativism: Chinese Immigrants and the Debates on the Thirteenth, Fourteenth, and Fifteenth Amendments and Civil Rights Laws." *Asian Law Journal* 3 (1996): 55–103.

Torrance, Michael. "KPFA, The Roots of Funk and The Lumpen." Interview with Rickey Vincent. October 2006. Website. *It's About Time—Black Panther Party Legacy and Alumni*. http://www.itsabouttimebpp.com/Our_Stories/The_Lumpen /sound/KPFA_Roots_of_Funk_THE_LUMPEN.wma.

Truth, Sojourner. *Narrative of Sojourner Truth, a Northern Slave*. 1850. In *Classic African American Women's Narratives*, edited by William L. Andrews, 39–126. New York: Oxford University Press, 2003.

United States v. Wong Kim Ark. 169 U.S. 649 (1898).

U.S. Bureau of the Census. "South Attracts More People Than It Loses." October 30, 2003. http://www.census.gov/Press-Release/www/releases/archives/census _2000/001505.html.

Vandevelde, Kenneth J. "The Modern Prima Facie Tort Doctrine." *Kentucky Law Journal* 79 (1991): 519–55.

Vargas Llosa, Mario. *A Writer's Reality*. Edited by Myron I. Lichtblau. New York: Houghton Mifflin, 1991.

Vaughan, Michael. "Introduction: Henri Bergson's *Creative Evolution*." *SubStance* 36.3 (2007): 7–24.

Walcott, Derek. *White Egrets*. New York: Farrar, Straus, and Giroux, 2010.

Ward, Brian. *Just My Soul Responding: Rhythm and Blues, Black Consciousness, and Race Relations*. Berkeley: University of California Press, 1998.

Warren, Kenneth W. "Appeals for (Mis)Recognition: Theorizing the Diaspora." In *Cultures of United States Imperialism*, edited by Amy Kaplan and Donald E. Pease, 392–406. Durham, N.C.: Duke University Press, 1993.

Waterbury Watch. Advertisement. 1882. The Waterbury Watch Museum, http:// www.geocities.org/waterburywatch/home.html.

Watkins, Patricia D. "Rape, Lynching, Law, and *Contending Forces*: Pauline Hopkins— Forerunner of Critical Race Theory." *CLA Journal* 46 (June 2003): 521–42.

Watkins, S. Craig. "'Black Is Back, and It's Bound to Sell!' Nationalist Desire and the Production of Black Culture." In *Is It Nation Time? Contemporary Essays on Black Power and Black Nationalism*, edited by Eddie S. Glaude Jr., 189–214. Chicago: University of Chicago Press, 2002.

Watt, Ian. *The Rise of the Novel: Studies in Defoe, Richardson, and Fielding*. 1957. Berkeley: University of California Press, 2001.

Webb, Frank J. *The Garies and Their Friends*. 1857. Baltimore: Johns Hopkins University Press, 1997.

Weheliye, Alexander G. *Phonographies: Grooves in Sonic Afro-Modernity.* Durham, N.C.: Duke University Press, 2005.

Wheatley, Phillis. "To the University of Cambridge, in New England." In *Phillis Wheatley, Complete Writings,* edited by Vincent Carretta, 11–12. New York: Penguin, 2001.

White, E. Frances. "Africa on My Mind: Gender, Counter Discourse, and African American Nationalism." In *Is It Nation Time? Contemporary Essays on Black Power and Black Nationalism,* edited by Eddie S. Glaude Jr., 130–55. Chicago: University of Chicago Press, 2002.

White, Jack E. "Endangered Species." *Time Magazine,* March 1, 1999, http://www .time.com/time/magazine/article/0,9171,990357,00.html.

"Why Was Denzil Dowell Killed." *The Black Panther: Black Community News Service,* April 25, 1967. In *The Black Panther Intercommunal News Service, 1967– 1980,* edited by David Hilliard, 3. New York: Atria Books, 2007.

Wideman, John Edgar. "Dead Black Men and Other Fallout from the American Dream." *Esquire* (September 1992): 149–56.

———. *The Lynchers.* 1973. In *Identities: Three Novels by John Edgar Wideman,* 377– 642. New York: Henry Holt, 1994.

Williams, John A. "My Man Himes: An Interview with Chester Himes." In *Conversations with Chester Himes,* edited by Michael Fabre and Robert E. Skinner, 29–82. Jackson: University Press of Mississippi, 1995.

———. "The Use of Communications Media in Four Novels by Richard Wright." *Callaloo* 28 (Summer 1986): 529–39.

Wilson, Harriet E. Preface to *Our Nig.* 1859. In *Our Nig, Or Sketches from the Life of a Free Black,* edited by Gabrielle P. Foreman and Reginald H. Pitts, 3. New York: Penguin, 2005.

Wilson, Matthew. Introduction to Charles W. Chesnutt, *Paul Marchand, F.M.C.,* vii–xxxv. Jackson: University Press of Mississippi, 1998.

"Witnesses Bare New Deal Books' Red Propaganda." Headline. *Chicago Daily Tribune,* February 18, 1939, 18.

Witt, Doris. "Detecting Bodies: BarbaraNeely's Domestic Sleuth and the Trope of the (In)visible Woman." In *Recovering the Black Female Body: Self-Representations by African American Women,* edited by Michael Bennett and Vanessa D. Dickerson, 165–94. New Brunswick, N.J.: Rutgers University Press, 2001.

Wong, Edlie L. *Neither Fugitive nor Free: Atlantic Slavery, Freedom Suits, and the Legal Culture of Travel.* New York: New York University Press, 2009.

Woods, Paula L., ed. Introduction to *Spooks, Spies, and Private Eyes: Black Mystery Crime, and Suspense Fiction,* xiii–xviii. New York: Doubleday, 1995.

Wright, Michelle M. *Becoming Black: Creating Identity in the Black Diaspora.* Durham, N.C.: Duke University Press, 2004.

Wright, Richard. "Blueprint for Negro Writing." 1937. In *The New Negro: Readings on Race, Representation, and African American Culture,* edited by Henry Louis Gates Jr. and Gene Andrew Jarrett, 268–74. Princeton, N.J.: Princeton University Press, 2007.

———. *Native Son.* 1940. New York: HarperCollins, 2005.

Yancy, George. "Geneva Smitherman: The Social Ontology of African-American Language, the Power of Nommo, and the Dynamics of Resistance and Identity through Language." *Journal of Speculative Philosophy* 18.4 (2004): 273–99.

Yick Wo v. Hopkins, Sheriff; Wo Lee v. Hopkins, Sheriff. 118 U.S. 356 (1886).

Zox-Weaver, Annalisa. *Women Modernists and Fascism.* Cambridge: Cambridge University Press, 2011.

Index

Africa: and Black Arts Movement, 108–9, 110–11; and diaspora, 159, 190n10; and Gronniosaw, 35–36; and Hegel, 7, 26; literary representation of, 77, 84–85, 152; and oral culture, 32; and racial identity, 61–62; as source for African American literature, 25, 27–28, 31–32, 166; and time, 120, 158

Alger, Horatio, 86–87, 89; *Ragged Dick*, 87, 89; *Struggling Upward*, 87

anachronism. *See* strategic anachronism

Anderson, Benedict: challenges to, 2, 5; and Douglass, 28; and personhood, 28, 43; and print culture, 161; and simultaneity, 1–2, 104, 119–20

Andrews, William L., 47, 175n3

anthologies, 25, 103, 113–14

antilynching drama: and Bergson, 20, 21, 86; and *A Lesson before Dying*, 96; and modernist art and drama, 15–19; and mortality, 99–100; and *Native Son*, 82, 91; and racially differential time, 11–12; staging of, 14–15; and strategic anachronism, 19, 81–82, 104, 122, 130, 160. *See also* genre; lynching

Armstrong, Nancy, 50–51

Autobiography of an Ex-Colored Man, The (Johnson), 59, 63

Autobiography of Miss Jane Pittman, The (Gaines), 96–97

Ayler, Albert, 115–16, 187n40

Baldwin, James, 95, 107, 125–27

Baraka, Amiri, 105, 111–17, 124–26, 156, 187n40. *See also* Baraka, Amiri, works of

Baraka, Amiri, works of: *Black Music*, 105; "The Changing Same," 105, 115; *It's Nation Time* (book), 105, 125; "It's Nation Time" (poem), 105, 111–12, 113; review of Albert Ayler albums, 115–16; review of Joe McPhee's *Nation Time*, 124–25, 126; "SOS," 123–24

Barthold, Bonnie J., *Black Time*, 158

Bartky, Ian, 29, 30, 98

being there. *See* Dasein

Bergson, Henri: and antilynching drama, 16, 20, 21; and élan vital, 12, 18, 135; and open future, 12, 18, 86, 135, 149

Birth of a Nation, 122

Black Arts Movement: and Africa, 111, 159–60; and aural/oral culture, 20–21, 105–8, 115–16, 124–25; and Dasein poets, 105; and diaspora, 159–60; and failure, 123–29, 154; and Harlem Renaissance, 118–24; historical contexts of, 123; and internationalism, 119–20;

Harlem Renaissance, 107; and aural/
oral culture, 32, 117–18, 120, 122; and
Black Arts Movement, 117–25; and
diaspora, 158, 159–60, and failure,
91, 116, 123, 187n46, 194n8; historical
contexts of, 121–22; internationalism
in, 119–20, 159–60; literature of, 78,
81; pessimism in, 188n60; and
strategic presentism, 11, 19–20,
80–81, 120, 160, 165. See also New
Negro/New Negro Movement
Harper, Frances, 46, 48–49, 50, 56; Iola
Leroy, 50, 78
Harper, Philip Brian, 116–17, 118,
123–24
Hegel, Georg Wilhelm Friedrich: on
Africa, 6–7, 26–27; The Philosophy
of History, 25–27; in relation to
Douglass, 27–28, 39–40, 41–43, 56,
142; on slavery, 25, 81; on time, 7, 23
Heidegger, Martin, 20–23, 103–4, 130,
142, 144. See also Dasein
Hilliard, David, 109
Himes, Chester, 132–33, 140, 142; "His
Last Day," 81; If He Hollers Let Him
Go, 82
Holiday, Billie, 115
Holmes, Oliver Wendell: and African
American literature, 9, 62, 65, 71,
75; "The Common Law," 62, 71; as
founder of pragmatism, 9; as
justice, 54; and legal pragmatism, 9,
48, 54; "Privilege, Malice, and
Intent," 73–74; and race, 55–56; and
temporal damage, 73–74. See also
pragmatism
Hopkins, Pauline, 11, 78, 80, 161, 165;
and challenge to pragmatism, 9, 56,
61, 71, 74–75; and citizenship,
literary representation of, 58–59,
66–67, 68, 73–74; and journalism,

50, 53, 160, 175n13; and novel form,
46, 49, 53, 76–77, 160, 178n61; and
race, 63–64, 66–68, 76, 177n54,
178n63, 180n75; and slave time, 9;
and strategic anachronism, 1, 51–52,
73, 104, 161. See also Contending
Forces (Hopkins); Hopkins, Pauline,
works of
Hopkins, Pauline, works of, 178n63,
179n68; Hagar's Daughter, 9, 67,
171n22; Of One Blood, 67, 77;
"Talma Gordon," 142; Winona, 9,
52–53, 74–76, 77. See also
Contending Forces (Hopkins)
House behind the Cedars, The
(Chesnutt), 9–10, 61–62, 77, 78,
177n54
Howard University, 17, 20, 103
Hughes, Langston, 79, 91, 107, 117–18,
122, 160
humor, 76, 100–101, 164, 168
Hurston, Zora Neale, 80–81, 117, 148;
"How It Feels to Be Colored Me,"
80–81

Ibsen, Henrik, A Doll's House, 16
"If We Must Die" (McKay), 81, 92, 93,
183n7
immigrants, representation of, 48, 66,
68, 76, 159, 180n75. See also
Chinese; Irish
Imperium in Imperio (Griggs), 49, 77,
78, 107, 117
incarceration rates, 95–96
Incidents in the Life of a Slave Girl
(Jacobs), 8, 31, 38–39, 117
Indians, American, 4, 33–34, 70, 74, 76,
123
Interesting Narrative of the Life of
Olaudah Equiano, The (Equiano),
36–37, 106, 173n24

37–38, 60, 82–87, 183n9; women, representation of, 89–90, 96, 149. *See also* Wright, Richard

naturalism/naturalist, 19, 82, 91, 101, 104

Neal, Larry, 114; "The Black Arts Movement," 105, 111, 117, 123; on Harlem Renaissance, 116, 123

Neely, Barbara, 21, 129–31, 149, 150, 151, 194n75; Blanche White character, 130–31, 149, 156–57, 189n8, 191n32, 194n75. *See also* Neely, Barbara, works of

Neely, Barbara, works of: *Blanche among the Talented Tenth*, 142, 150, 151–57, 194n75; *Blanche Cleans Up*, 189n8; *Blanche on the Lam*, 142, 155; *Blanche Passes Go*, 149, 150, 154. *See also* detective fiction, African American

New Negro/New Negro Movement, 11, 107, 121, 123; and Black Arts Movement, 116–19; historical contexts of, 121–22; internationalism of, 159; and simultaneity, 11; sources of, 10, 49, 78. *See also* Harlem Renaissance

newspapers. *See* journalism

Newton, Huey, 108–10

New York Armory Show, 15

Nielsen, Aldon, 32, 103, 105, 118, 185n1, 185n3

Norris, Frank, 19, 104

Norton Anthology of African American Literature, The, 25

novels, African American: as challenge to *Plessy v. Ferguson*, 48–49, 53–54, 63–68; as challenge to pragmatism, 57–63; as political form, 9, 46–53, 141, 160, 191n24; and representation of future, 77–78; and representation

of time, 37, 147; as sources for slave narratives, 31. *See also* genre

observatories, 29–30

O'Malley, Michael, *Keeping Watch*, 84, 86, 87, 101

oral culture, 166; in Black Arts Movement, 106–8, 112–13, 118, 121; in Harlem Renaissance, 118, 121; in slave narratives, 27–28, 31–33, 117

Page, Thomas Nelson, 51–52

Parks, Suzan-Lori, 1, 3, 20, 22, 161, 163–168; *The Death of the Last Black Man in the Whole Entire World*, 19, 82, 97–102; *Rep & Rev*, 99–101, 163–64, 166; *365 Days/365 Plays*, 161–69

Peirce, Charles, 57, 68; and African American literature, 56, 64–65; as founder of pragmatism, 9, 54; "How to Make Our Ideas Clear," 54, 58–59; and pragmatist maxim, 54; and race, 55–56, 58–61, 64, 179n67; and religion, 72; and watch incident, 59–61, 87. *See also* pragmatism

Petry, Ann, 79, 91, 104, 130, 149; *The Street*, 79

Pitre, Merline, 43

Plessy v. Ferguson, 76, 87, 122; and African American citizenship, 69, 71, 72, 73, 180n73; and African American novels, 9, 47–49, 63–67, 73; and time, 4, 58, 72

police, 109, 136, 180n73, 183n24; in Blanche White novels, 155; in Easy Rawlins novels, 132, 134, 137–38, 140–43, 192n41; in *Native Son*, 90; in *365 Days/365 Plays*, 167–68